ADVANCE PRAISE FOR *MONUMENTAL*

"Visually compelling, deeply researched, and original in its account of Reconstruction in Louisiana, *Monumental* reminds us of the remarkable career of Oscar Dunn and of the unfinished agenda of Reconstruction. At a time of a renewed struggle for racial justice, it speaks to our moment as well as that of post–Civil War America." —**ERIC FONER**, Pulitzer Prize winner and author of *Reconstruction: America's Unfinished Revolution, 1863–1877*

"Oscar Dunn's incredibly heroic and staunch support of freedom and equality is powerfully realized in this collaboration by Mitchell and Edwards. Filled with insightful research and searing graphic imagery, *Monumental* is quite an apt title for this work." —**JOHN JENNINGS**, Eisner Award–winning and No. 1 *New York Times*–bestselling editor and artist

"*Monumental* presents an important figure from the past in a format engaging in the present. With deep research, brisk storytelling, and energetic graphics, this book evokes a turbulent time and a brave leader for a new generation." —**EDWARD L. AYERS**, National Humanities Medal winner and author of Pulitzer Prize finalist *The Promise of the New South: Life After Reconstruction*

"Brian Mitchell treats us to one of the most original and important contributions to the most vital, urgent aspects of Southern and Louisiana history. Through his thorough, tireless, original research, he establishes the great impact of the uncompromising integrity of Oscar Dunn, a previously almost invisible figure, on the most positive aspects of Radical Reconstruction in Louisiana." —**GWENDOLYN MIDLO HALL**, creator of the Louisiana Slave Database and author of *Africans in Colonial Louisiana: The Development of Afro-Creole Culture in the Eighteenth Century*

"Edwards's expressive and engaging art helps shape Mitchell's incredible story of Oscar Dunn, an uncelebrated narrative of an American patriot whom history has tried to ignore." —**JOEL CHRISTIAN GILL**, cartoonist, historian, and author of *Strange Fruit: Uncelebrated Narratives from Black History*

"Oscar J. Dunn was one of the most important African American men of the nineteenth century. With the publication of this work he will no longer be forgotten in the pages of history." —**JAMES R. MORGAN III**, author of *The Lost Empire: Black Freemasonry in the Old West (1867–1906)*

"When we think about how to share new public histories of Reconstruction, we now have *Monumental* as both tool and model. In order to shift the narrative away from post–Civil War, white supremacist fictions and toward real, often silenced struggles and strides for racial democracy and equality, we must give young people powerful stories like this one." —**MARY NIALL MITCHELL**, director of the Midlo Center for New Orleans Studies at the University of New Orleans

"*Monumental* is well researched, powerfully written, and much needed during these times. It belongs in the hands of every student as Dunn deserves his rightful place in our collective memory. This book gives justice to Dunn's legacy."—**CHRIS DIER**, 2020 Louisiana Teacher of the Year and author of *The 1868 St. Bernard Parish Massacre: Blood in the Cane Fields*

"If you do not know about Oscar Dunn, this book is the place to start. It captures the incredible drama of his life and times. Once I started reading, I could not put it down."
—**BRYAN WAGNER**, author of *Disturbing the Peace: Black Culture and the Police Power after Slavery*

"Mitchell's narrative, whispered in his ear by his ancestor Oscar Dunn, reveals important historical truths about men of African descent who empowered themselves despite racial and societal obstacles designed to devalue our people. *Monumental* belongs in school curriculums, and is a must-read for anyone interested in the Civil War and Reconstruction."
—**MADAME BARBARA TREVIGNE**, artist, author, and historian of Afro-Creole culture

"Mitchell's graphic history of Oscar Dunn provides an important corrective to the historical record. But it is more. Much like Dunn's own lifelong fight, it is an act of resistance to white supremacist violence in the archive and on the street. *Monumental* demonstrates the ways in which we find ourselves through history, as well as the meanings and ramifications of the past in the present." —**TREVOR R. GETZ**, author of *Abina and the Important Men: A Graphic History*

"Finally, an accessible and riveting study of Reconstruction Louisiana! *Monumental* is an imaginatively daring combination of authoritative history, luminous artistry, and a compelling personal story. Mitchell's revelatory findings surrounding Dunn's political career and his suspicious death are especially important for future studies of Louisiana Reconstruction." —**CARYN COSSÉ BELL**, author of *Revolution, Romanticism, and the Afro-Creole Protest Tradition in Louisiana, 1718–1868*

"For too long, we have either forgotten or purposefully failed to tell the story of our whole history, especially of the achievements of Black Southerners during Reconstruction. While the four-year aberration that was the Confederacy is celebrated with its Lost Cause idolatry, nostalgia, and rewriting of history, the story of Reconstruction remains obscured. This important work on Oscar Dunn helps to correct that historical malfeasance. It should be mandatory reading for every history student in Louisiana." —**MITCH LANDRIEU**, former New Orleans mayor and author of *In the Shadow of Statues: A White Southerner Confronts History*

"This biography of Oscar Dunn is a sublime act of recovery in both senses of that word. Not only does it recover from obscurity the life of a remarkable man, but it also provides a guide for us Americans to recover from the scourge of white supremacy. We need to share stories like these—stories of ordinary people in adverse circumstances who, through both their cunning and compassion, show us a way forward." —**GUY LANCASTER**, coauthor of *Blood in Their Eyes: The Elaine Massacre of 1919* (revised edition)

MONUMENTAL

MONUMENTAL

OSCAR DUNN AND HIS RADICAL FIGHT IN RECONSTRUCTION LOUISIANA

BRIAN K. MITCHELL / BARRINGTON S. EDWARDS / NICK WELDON

THE HISTORIC NEW ORLEANS COLLECTION 2021

The Historic New Orleans Collection is a museum, research center, and publisher dedicated to the study and preservation of the history and culture of New Orleans, the lower Mississippi valley, and the Gulf South region. The Collection is operated by the Kemper and Leila Williams Foundation, a Louisiana nonprofit corporation.

533 Royal Street
New Orleans, Louisiana 70130
www.hnoc.org

Project editor: Nick Weldon
Director of publications: Jessica Dorman
President and CEO: Daniel Hammer
Design and lettering: Tana Coman Design

First edition.

Printed in Canada by Friesens.

25 24 23 22 21 1 2 3 4 5

ISBN: 978-0-917860-83-6

Library of Congress Cataloging-in-Publication Data
Names: Mitchell, Brian K., author. | Edwards, Barrington S., artist. | Weldon, Nick, 1987- editor.
Title: Monumental : Oscar Dunn and his radical fight in Reconstruction Louisiana / Brian K. Mitchell, Barrington S. Edwards, Nick Weldon.
Description: First edition. | New Orleans : The Historic New Orleans Collection, 2021. | Includes bibliographical references and index.
Identifiers: LCCN 2020039133 | ISBN 9780917860836 (paperback)
Subjects: LCSH: Dunn, Oscar, 1822-1871—Comic books, strips, etc. | Lieutenant governors—Louisiana—Biography—Comic books, strips, etc. | African American men—Louisiana—New Orleans—Biography—Comic books, strips, etc. | Louisiana--Politics and government—1865-1950—Comic books, strips, etc. | New Orleans (La.)—History—19th century—Comic books, strips, etc. | LCGFT: Biographical comics.
Classification: LCC F375 .M59 2021 | DDC 976.3/05092 [B]—dc23
LC record available at https://lccn.loc.gov/2020039133

THIS BOOK IS DEDICATED TO OUR ANCESTORS WHO BORE YOKES OF OPPRESSION BUT NEVER STOPPED FIGHTING, WORKING, AND PRAYING THAT THEIR PROGENY WOULD LIVE BETTER LIVES THAN THEIR OWN. THIS BOOK IS DEDICATED TO OUR HEROES WHO RODE THE BUSES, MARCHED COUNTLESS MILES, PROTESTED THROUGHOUT OUR NATION, AND DEFIANTLY KNELT SO THAT OTHERS MIGHT STAND PROUDLY. THIS BOOK IS DEDICATED TO EVERY CHILD, BORN OF MEAGER MEANS, THAT DREAMS OF CHANGING THE WORLD—KNOW THAT YOU, TOO, ARE AMERICA!

—Brian K. Mitchell

CONTENTS

INTRODUCTION

OSCAR DUNN, FORGOTTEN HERO

WHO KNOWS WHETHER THE BEST OF MEN BE KNOWN, OR WHETHER THERE BE NOT MORE REMARKABLE PERSONS FORGOT, THAN ANY THAT STAND REMEMBERED IN THE KNOWN ACCOUNT OF TIME?

—Sir Thomas Browne, *Hydriotaphia* (1658)

THE STUDY OF African American leaders from the Reconstruction era has presented a variety of unique challenges for modern historians. This important work has been complicated by scant primary source data about their lives before the Civil War, the post-Reconstruction destruction of essential documents, and the disparagement and dismissal of these figures by early historians. This book begins the work of illuminating the life of one of Louisiana's foremost leaders from this era: Oscar James Dunn, the first African American lieutenant governor and acting governor in US history.

I have a personal stake in telling this story: Dunn is my ancestor. I didn't learn about him until I was eight—and not in a classroom, but through my family's own oral history. It was 1976, and after spending my early childhood in Chicago, I had just come back to my native New Orleans to live with relatives and begin second grade. The city was quite foreign to me when I arrived; I recall wondering why it was so hot and people spoke so funny. My great-grandmother Mattie Dunn, "Grandmaw" to me, would say, "It will take you a minute to get your New Orleans legs back, but it is in your blood."

OSCAR J. DUNN, LIEUT. GOVR. OF LOUISIANA; between 1868 and 1871; lithograph by Currier and Ives; *THNOC, The L. Kemper and Leila Moore Williams Founders Collection, 1949.24*

PUBLISHED BY CURRIER & IVES, 152 NASSAU ST. N.Y.

OSCAR J. DUNN,

LIEUT. GOVR. OF LOUISIANA

That year I attended Paul Laurence Dunbar Elementary. After school I would walk to Grandmaw's house, just a few blocks away. I marveled at her residence because she kept chickens in the city, in a coop behind her house. I was afraid of them, and no other kids dared come to her yard. She didn't have a television and, after a week or two, I had read through her stack of old magazines. One day I asked her to help me find something to do, and she sat me down on her couch. She went to her room and returned with several dusty old photo albums and scrapbooks. I was mesmerized. She sat next to me and carefully opened the fragile books. She showed me a picture that looked more like a drawing than a photograph. It was of a family: a mother and father and six children, including a baby girl, all well-dressed in old-fashioned clothing. I asked her who they were, and she replied that it was her family. Correcting herself, she added, "They are your family, too." I asked her where she was, and her wrinkled finger pointed to the baby. She told me about her three sisters, who all died during a flu epidemic. I learned about her father and the family plantation in East Feliciana Parish.

Every day after that, I rushed to her house from school and asked her to pull out a picture or artifact from one of her books and to tell me its story. During one of these sessions, she showed me a few tattered old newspaper clippings. She asked me to read them while she made glasses of water for us to drink. On the top of one were the words, "Lt. Governor Dunn Dead."

THIS BOOK CORRECTS THE RECORD ON A SIGNIFICANT HISTORICAL DISTINCTION: DUNN WAS THE FIRST BLACK GOVERNOR IN US HISTORY, NOT P. B. S. PINCHBACK.

"Wow, Grandmaw! He's got your last name." She sat next to me and recounted stories her late husband, my great-grandfather Emanuel Dunn, had told her about Oscar. Our family's oral history, it turned out, held that the Dunn line descended from Charles Dunn, Oscar's adopted son through his marriage to the widow Ellen Boyd Marshall.

"He was quite a big deal!" she said.

"Did he do something important?" I replied.

"That he did," she said. "He was one of our nation's first Black leaders. He was lieutenant governor of this state, you know." I listened intently as she described his achievements.

Dunn had lived a remarkable life. As a youngster, he was an avid reader, just like me. He learned to play the guitar—quite well, in fact—and a trade, in plastering, that led him to Freemasonry, where he developed a sense of civic responsibility. After the Civil War, he married Ellen and adopted her three children. He emerged as a champion of freedmen, first by helping them negotiate fair pay, and later in the political arena as a fierce advocate for universal male suffrage, civil rights, and integrated public schools. He was elected as the first Black lieutenant governor in US history in 1868. During a violent and corrupt era, friends and enemies alike admired his integrity.

Some of these facts I learned that day sitting on my Grandmaw's couch, and others I filled in over the years as I came to learn more about my trailblazing ancestor. But there was a lot more

HENRY C. WARMOTH; between 1870 and 1880; *courtesy of the Brady-Handy photograph collection, Library of Congress, Prints and Photographs Division, LC-DIG-cwpbh-03725*
P. B. S. PINCHBACK; between 1870 and 1880; *courtesy of the Brady-Handy photograph collection, Library of Congress, Prints and Photographs Division, LC-DIG-cwpbh-03857*

I didn't know—not until over three decades later, when I wrote my doctoral dissertation on Dunn. That research, which forms the foundation of this book, made use of an array of sources, including overlooked letters and speeches, Masonic records, Senate journals, newspaper articles, and government documents, to clarify vital details about Dunn's life. One of the most significant discoveries was a conveyance record for Dunn, his sister, and his mother, that confirmed that he had been enslaved, a fact that had been uncertain. I also uncovered a record showing that Dunn was emancipated by his stepfather when he was ten. This book also corrects the record on a significant distinction: Dunn was the first Black governor in US history, not P. B. S. Pinchback, a political rival and his successor as lieutenant governor. Pinchback is popularly credited as the first for serving as acting governor of Louisiana for thirty-six days beginning in December 1872, but Dunn served in the same capacity for about thirty-nine days eighteen months earlier (see page 232 for more).

Dunn died under mysterious circumstances at the height of a feud with Governor Henry Clay Warmoth, and his death registered as a horrific tragedy, especially in the Black community. One newspaper estimated that more people attended his funeral procession than any other in the history of New Orleans—noteworthy considering the city's reputation for its funerary traditions. "When a future historian shall record the transition of the colored race from bondage to freedom," one of his eulogists predicted, "Lieutenant-Governor Dunn will not be lost in the multitude, but will appear high above his fellows, in himself a type of that very transition." I discovered, however, one lofty commemoration of Dunn that had been lost, and it inspired the title of this book: Act 57, passed by the Louisiana state legislature and approved by Gov. William Pitt Kellogg in 1873. The act established a committee and appropriated funds for the purpose of erecting a monument in honor of Dunn. For unknown reasons, it was never built.

Four years later, Reconstruction ended as the last federal troops protecting the hard-won rights of African Americans were withdrawn from the South. Soon, Jim Crow laws nullified much of the progress made by Dunn and his fellow Radical Republicans. All the while a very different history was being written. So-called Redeemers, bent on restoring white supremacy, reclaimed the South, and a generation of like-minded historians dismissed Reconstruction as an era rife with corruption and incompetence, ignoring the accomplishments and agency of its Black leaders. Statues dedicated to Confederate leaders and an obelisk commemorating a white supremacist uprising went up in New Orleans, all erected years after the Dunn monument was approved.

In the century that passed between Dunn's death and when my great-grandmother first introduced me to his story, a lot had been forgotten, I'd soon learn. Weeks after Grandmaw showed me those timeworn newspaper clippings, my teacher at Dunbar Elementary led a discussion about state and local government. She asked the class if anyone could name a governor or lieutenant governor, and I enthusiastically proclaimed that Oscar Dunn was one of my ancestors and that he had been lieutenant governor of Louisiana.

"Brian, I think you're mistaken," my teacher said. "There have been no Black governors or lieutenant governors." The class erupted in laughter.

"I know it's true because my Grandmaw showed it to me in an old newspaper," I replied. My classmates teased me about it the whole day. I ran to my great-grandmother's house after the last bell rang. With tears in my eyes I told her what had happened; that no one believed me.

"Why don't they know about him, Grandmaw?"

She sighed and sat me down. She went to her kitchen, poured two glasses of water, and peeled an orange, dividing the wedges onto two saucers. She placed one saucer and my glass of water on the table in front of me. "They'd like to forget," she said.

"Forget what?" I replied.

"They'd like to forget how good of a man he was and how he tried to change America," she said. "But we won't forget, right baby?"

I've chosen to share Oscar Dunn's story as a graphic history to make sure that people, especially younger readers, won't forget. Decades after my own teacher denied the story of this critical person in not only my family's history, but America's, I still feel the sting. Oscar and his wife, Ellen, a schoolteacher, both valued education, and Oscar fought to expand its reach to all children. In that spirit, it's my hope that the images and words in this book help amplify their story—and the many other moments from Reconstruction history represented here—for generations to come.

—Brian K. Mitchell

THE ONLY KNOWN IMAGE OF DUNN WITH HIS FAMILY, AFTER A FLOOD (ELLEN ON BALCONY); wood engraving by Alfred Rudolph Waud; from *Every Saturday*, July 8, 1871; *THNOC, 1974.25.11.49 ii*

PART ONE

ORIGINS

BUT--

HOW COULD SHE NOT KNOW?

NEW ORLEANS, 1822

LITTLE IS KNOWN ABOUT MARIA, A WOMAN ENSLAVED BY A MAN NAMED GEORGE P. BOWERS. SHE MIGHT HAVE BEEN LIVING IN A BUILDING BEHIND HIS FRENCH QUARTER TOWNHOUSE WHEN SHE WENT INTO LABOR.
HERE, IN THE HISTORIC CORE OF NEW ORLEANS, MARIA GAVE BIRTH TO A BABY BOY.

SHE NAMED HIM OSCAR.

NEW ORLEANS HAD BEEN ESTABLISHED BY THE FRENCH IN 1718, WAS RULED BY SPAIN FOR A PERIOD, AND MAINTAINED DEEP AFRICAN ROOTS, WITH LARGE POPULATIONS OF ENSLAVED AND FREE PEOPLE OF COLOR.
AFTER THE UNITED STATES ACQUIRED THE CITY AS PART OF THE LOUISIANA PURCHASE OF 1803, AMERICANS CAME TO TOWN IN DROVES. ONE OF THEM, JAMES CALDWELL, ESTABLISHED THE CITY'S FIRST ENGLISH-LANGUAGE THEATER IN THE EARLY 1820S.

CALDWELL HAD COME TO NEW ORLEANS FROM VIRGINIA, BRINGING ALONG HIS STAGE CARPENTER, A FREE MAN OF COLOR NAMED JAMES DUNN.

AT SOME POINT, MARIA--STILL ENSLAVED AND NOW A MOTHER OF TWO--MET DUNN, AND THE TWO BEGAN A RELATIONSHIP.

THEIR RELATIONSHIP WAS NOT UNCOMMON IN ANTEBELLUM NEW ORLEANS, WHICH, UNLIKE MOST PLACES, HAD ABOUT AS MANY FREE PEOPLE OF COLOR AS ENSLAVED PEOPLE OF COLOR.

BUT THEY YEARNED FOR A BETTER LIFE. IN 1831, THEY TOOK THEIR FIRST STEPS IN THAT DIRECTION WHEN DUNN MET BOWERS AT A NEW ORLEANS NOTARY'S OFFICE.

DUNN HAD SAVED UP $800 TO PURCHASE MARIA AND HER CHILDREN, OSCAR AND JANE, FROM BOWERS.
Maria (35)
Oscar (9)
Jane (6)
$800

HE THEN HAD TO PETITION A POLICE JURY FOR THEIR FREEDOM.

ON DECEMBER 8, 1832, TWO MONTHS AFTER DUNN FIRST WENT BEFORE THE POLICE JURY, HIS PETITION WAS APPROVED. MARIA, OSCAR, AND JANE WERE FREE.

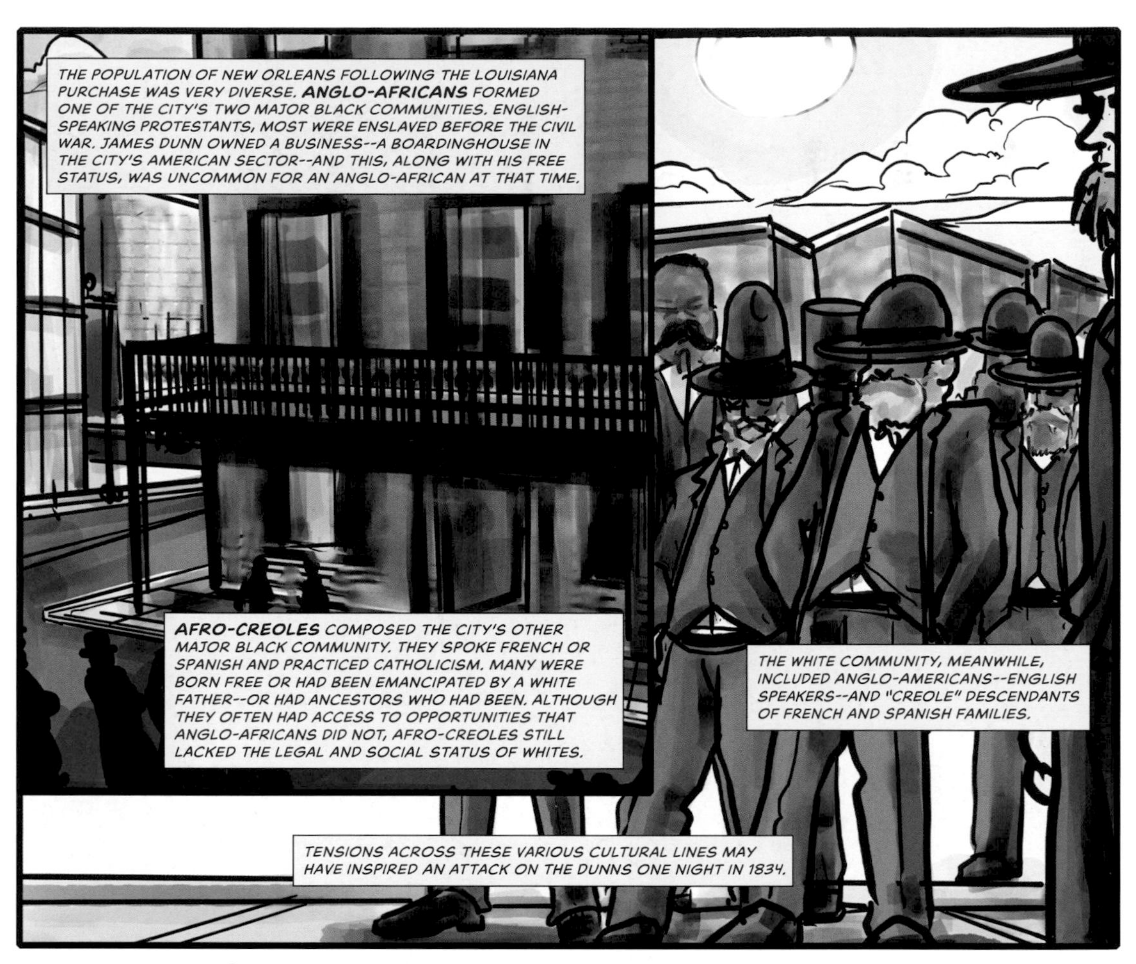
THE POPULATION OF NEW ORLEANS FOLLOWING THE LOUISIANA PURCHASE WAS VERY DIVERSE. **ANGLO-AFRICANS** FORMED ONE OF THE CITY'S TWO MAJOR BLACK COMMUNITIES. ENGLISH-SPEAKING PROTESTANTS, MOST WERE ENSLAVED BEFORE THE CIVIL WAR. JAMES DUNN OWNED A BUSINESS--A BOARDINGHOUSE IN THE CITY'S AMERICAN SECTOR--AND THIS, ALONG WITH HIS FREE STATUS, WAS UNCOMMON FOR AN ANGLO-AFRICAN AT THAT TIME.
AFRO-CREOLES COMPOSED THE CITY'S OTHER MAJOR BLACK COMMUNITY. THEY SPOKE FRENCH OR SPANISH AND PRACTICED CATHOLICISM. MANY WERE BORN FREE OR HAD BEEN EMANCIPATED BY A WHITE FATHER--OR HAD ANCESTORS WHO HAD BEEN. ALTHOUGH THEY OFTEN HAD ACCESS TO OPPORTUNITIES THAT ANGLO-AFRICANS DID NOT, AFRO-CREOLES STILL LACKED THE LEGAL AND SOCIAL STATUS OF WHITES.
THE WHITE COMMUNITY, MEANWHILE, INCLUDED ANGLO-AMERICANS--ENGLISH SPEAKERS--AND "CREOLE" DESCENDANTS OF FRENCH AND SPANISH FAMILIES.
TENSIONS ACROSS THESE VARIOUS CULTURAL LINES MAY HAVE INSPIRED AN ATTACK ON THE DUNNS ONE NIGHT IN 1834.

A MOB OF 14 MEN, ALL LOCAL BUSINESSMEN AND CRAFTSMEN, BROKE INTO THE BOARDINGHOUSE.
BASED ON THE REPORTED NAMES OF THE ATTACKERS, THE MOB APPEARED TO INCLUDE MEN FROM VARIOUS ETHNIC BACKGROUNDS, INCLUDING TWO FREE MEN OF COLOR WHO MIGHT HAVE BEEN AFRO-CREOLE.

THE MOB SAVAGELY ATTACKED THE DUNNS . . .

. . . AND JAMES SUFFERED SERIOUS INJURIES.
SEVEN MONTHS LATER, THE ATTACKERS WERE FINALLY ARRESTED.

A YEAR LATER HUNDREDS OF WHITE LABORERS AND ARTISANS GATHERED TO VOICE THEIR VIOLENT DISAPPROVAL OF THE EMPLOYMENT OF BLACK PEOPLE IN THEIR TRADES. THE NEAR-RIOT, AND THE ASSAULT ON THE DUNNS, PORTENDED VIOLENCE YET TO COME.
SEND THEM BACK TO VIRGINIA AND CHARLESTON!
WE WILL NOT BE REPLACED!

OSCAR DUNN RECEIVED WHAT A FRIEND DESCRIBED AS AN "ORDINARY ENGLISH EDUCATION."
AaBbCcDdEeFfGgHhIiJjKkLlMmNnOoPpQqRrSsTtUuVvWwXxYyZz
DUNN WAS AN AMBITIOUS LEARNER . . .
. . . AND AN AVID READER.

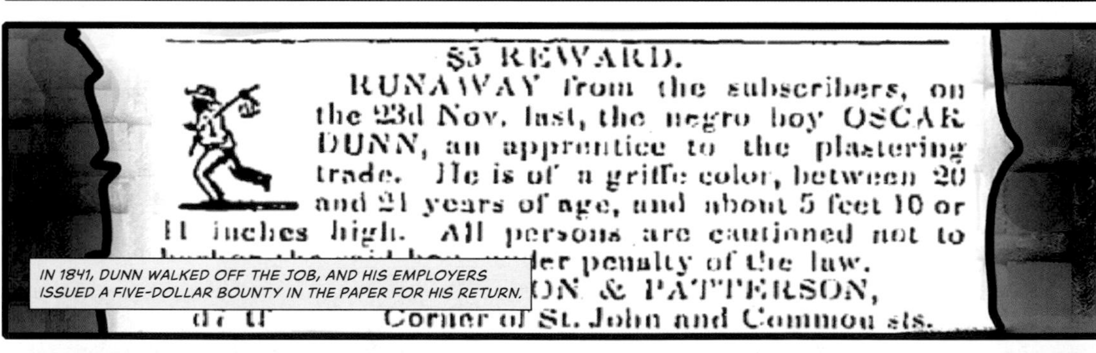
$5 REWARD.

RUNAWAY from the subscribers, on the 23d Nov. last, the negro boy OSCAR DUNN, an apprentice to the plastering trade. He is of a griffe color, between 20 and 21 years of age, and about 5 feet 10 or 11 inches high. All persons are cautioned not to ... under penalty of the law.

...ON & PATTERSON,

d7 ... Corner of St. John and Common sts.

AS A YOUNG ADULT,
HE BEGAN LEARNING THE
GUITAR UNDER AN ITALIAN
INSTRUCTOR NAMED TORNA.

HE WAS A QUICK STUDY ON
THE GUITAR AND SOON BEGAN
TAKING ON PUPILS OF HIS OWN.

IN 1848, NOW IN HIS MID-20S, DUNN BEGAN BOARDING WITH PETER MARSHALL AND ELLEN BOYD MARSHALL, FREE PEOPLE OF COLOR LIVING IN THE AMERICAN SECTOR.

THE LIVING CONDITIONS WERE NOT IDEAL.

DUNN MADE NEW CONNECTIONS WHEN HIS FRIEND JOHN PARSONS INTRODUCED HIM TO **FREEMASONRY,** A CENTURIES-OLD FRATERNAL SECRET SOCIETY THAT HAS MEMBER LODGES ALL OVER THE WORLD.
G

ON NOVEMBER 3, 1852, DUNN WAS APPRENTICED AS A MASON IN RICHMOND LODGE NO. 4, THE CITY'S FIRST BLACK LODGE.

THE SECRET SOCIETY BROUGHT TOGETHER CIVIC-MINDED LEADERS IN THE CITY'S BLACK COMMUNITY WHO WERE SHUT OUT FROM THE WELL-ESTABLISHED WHITE LODGES.

ANOTHER ACQUAINTANCE OF DUNN'S WAS THOMAS J. MARTIN, A FREE PERSON OF COLOR AND ONE OF THE PREMIER MUSICIANS AND COMPOSERS IN THE CITY.

MARTIN'S EXPERTISE AS A PIANO INSTRUCTOR WAS IN HIGH DEMAND AMONG WEALTHY WHITE NEW ORLEANIANS--UNTIL JUNE 1860.

MARTIN AND ONE OF HIS STUDENTS, FANNY THAYER, HAD REPORTEDLY BEEN ROMANTICALLY INVOLVED FOR THREE YEARS.
SCANDAL ERUPTED WHEN WORD GOT OUT THAT THEY'D HAD A CHILD TOGETHER AND THAT THAYER HAD MOVED OUT OF HER MOTHER'S HOME TO LIVE WITH MARTIN.

HER MOTHER, THE RETIRED ACTRESS ANN SEVERS, CONFRONTED MARTIN.
YOU SEDUCED MY DAUGHTER! I'M GOING TO MAKE SURE YOU NEVER TEACH OR PERFORM IN THIS CITY **EVER AGAIN**!
IF YOU EVER SPEAK OF THIS, I'LL **BURN DOWN YOUR HOME**!

MARTIN WAS ARRESTED FOR THREATENING ARSON. WHITE NEWSPAPERS STOKED FURTHER OUTRAGE BY ALLEGING THAT HE'D HAD AFFAIRS WITH AS MANY AS 30 WOMEN, MOSTLY THE DAUGHTERS OF WEALTHY WHITE FAMILIES.

MARTIN WAS DUBBED THE "COFFEE-COLORED LOTHARIO." RUMORS THAT HE HAD "ACCOMPLICES" LED TO A MANHUNT, WHICH REACHED A FEVER PITCH WHEN A 2,000-PERSON MOB GATHERED IN LAFAYETTE SQUARE.
WE'LL TAR AND FEATHER THEM!

MARTIN NEVER STOOD TRIAL, BUT SEEMS TO HAVE LEFT HIS CAREER AND THE CITY BEHIND.

THE SCANDAL CREATED A TOXIC CLIMATE FOR BLACK MUSIC TEACHERS, AND DUNN, RELUCTANTLY, ABANDONED MUSIC AND RETURNED TO PLASTERING FULL-TIME.

PART TWO

WAR AND EMANCIPATION

IN A FOUR-WAY CONTEST, ABRAHAM LINCOLN WAS ELECTED PRESIDENT ON NOVEMBER 6, 1860. HE WAS THE CANDIDATE OF THE REPUBLICAN PARTY, NEWLY FORMED TO OPPOSE THE EXPANSION OF SLAVERY IN THE U.S.
HIS ELECTION ELICITED CONDEMNATIONS THROUGHOUT THE SOUTH, INCLUDING AT FIRST PRESBYTERIAN CHURCH IN NEW ORLEANS.
IN DETERMINING OUR DUTY IN THIS EMERGENCY, IT IS NECESSARY THAT WE SHOULD FIRST ASCERTAIN THE NATURE OF THE TRUST PROVIDENTIALLY COMMITTED TO US.
I ANSWER, THAT IT IS TO CONSERVE AND PERPETUATE THE INSTITUTION OF DOMESTIC SLAVERY AS NOW EXISTING.
THERE, THE INFLUENTIAL REV. BENJAMIN PALMER RAILED AGAINST THE THREAT OF LINCOLN IN A THANKSGIVING DAY SPEECH THAT WAS QUICKLY PRINTED AND DISTRIBUTED WIDELY.

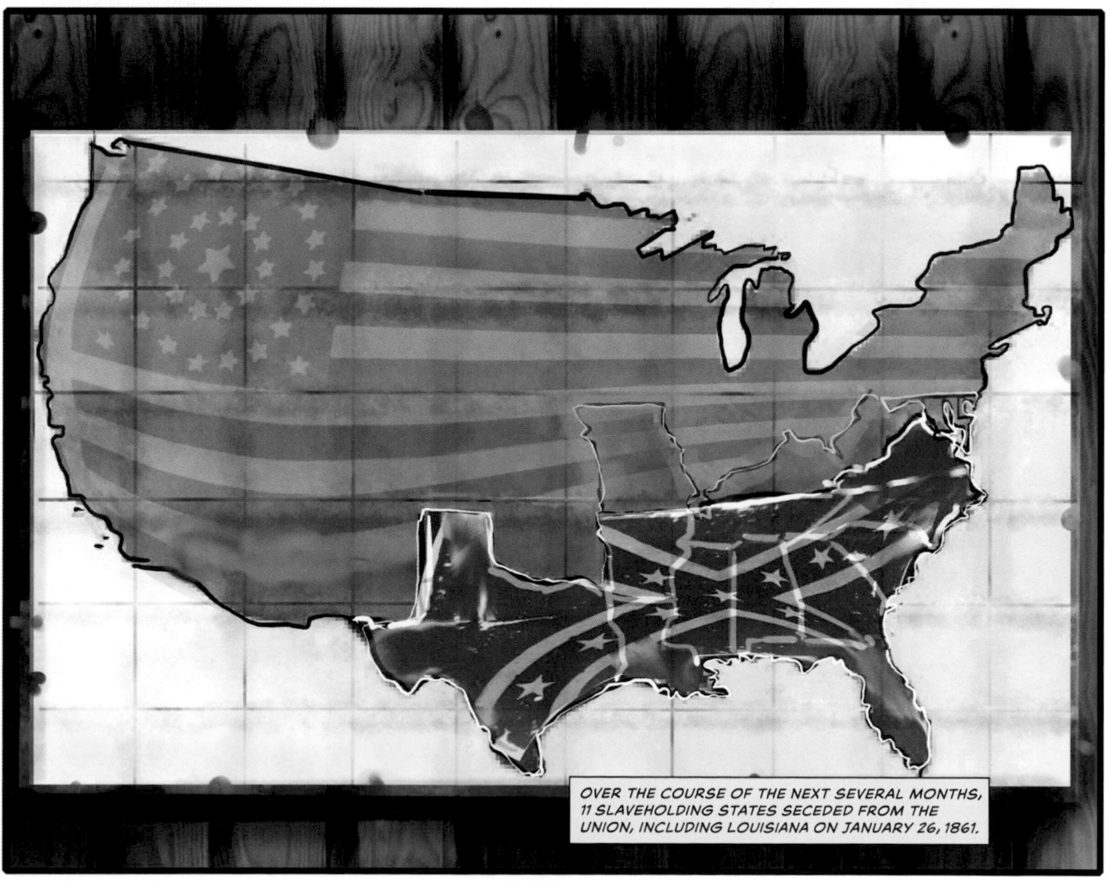
OVER THE COURSE OF THE NEXT SEVERAL MONTHS, 11 SLAVEHOLDING STATES SECEDED FROM THE UNION, INCLUDING LOUISIANA ON JANUARY 26, 1861.

LINCOLN WAS INAUGURATED ON MARCH 4, 1861 . . .
. . . AND WAR BROKE OUT ON APRIL 12, WHEN CONFEDERATE TROOPS ATTACKED THE U.S. ARMY AT FORT SUMTER IN CHARLESTON, SOUTH CAROLINA.
THE ATTACK WAS ORDERED BY BRIG. GEN. P. G. T. BEAUREGARD, A LOUISIANA NATIVE.

NEW ORLEANS, THE SOUTH'S BIGGEST CITY AND A MAJOR PORT NEAR THE MOUTH OF THE MISSISSIPPI RIVER, BECAME A KEY UNION TARGET.
THE U.S. NAVY ATTACKED RIVER FORTS PROTECTING NEW ORLEANS IN APRIL 1862, AND CONFEDERATE TROOPS EVACUATED THE CITY WITHOUT A FIGHT.

BARELY A YEAR AFTER THE WAR STARTED, NEW ORLEANS FELL UNDER UNION CONTROL, AND GEN. BENJAMIN BUTLER TOOK OVER AS MILITARY GOVERNOR. BLACK NEW ORLEANIANS CELEBRATED THE ARRIVAL OF UNION FORCES, BUT MUCH OF THE WHITE POPULATION LOATHED THEIR PRESENCE.
IN LOUISIANA, THIS ARGUABLY MARKED THE DAWN OF **RECONSTRUCTION**--THE REVOLUTIONARY, TUMULTUOUS ERA OF U.S. HISTORY THAT IN MOST PLACES BEGAN AFTER THE WAR CONCLUDED.

SOON, UNION TROOPS ARRIVED AT PLANTATIONS IN LOUISIANA'S SUGAR COUNTRY, EMPOWERING MANY ENSLAVED PEOPLE TO DEFY THEIR OWNERS AND QUIT WORKING, EVEN THOUGH THEY WERE NOT YET LEGALLY EMANCIPATED.

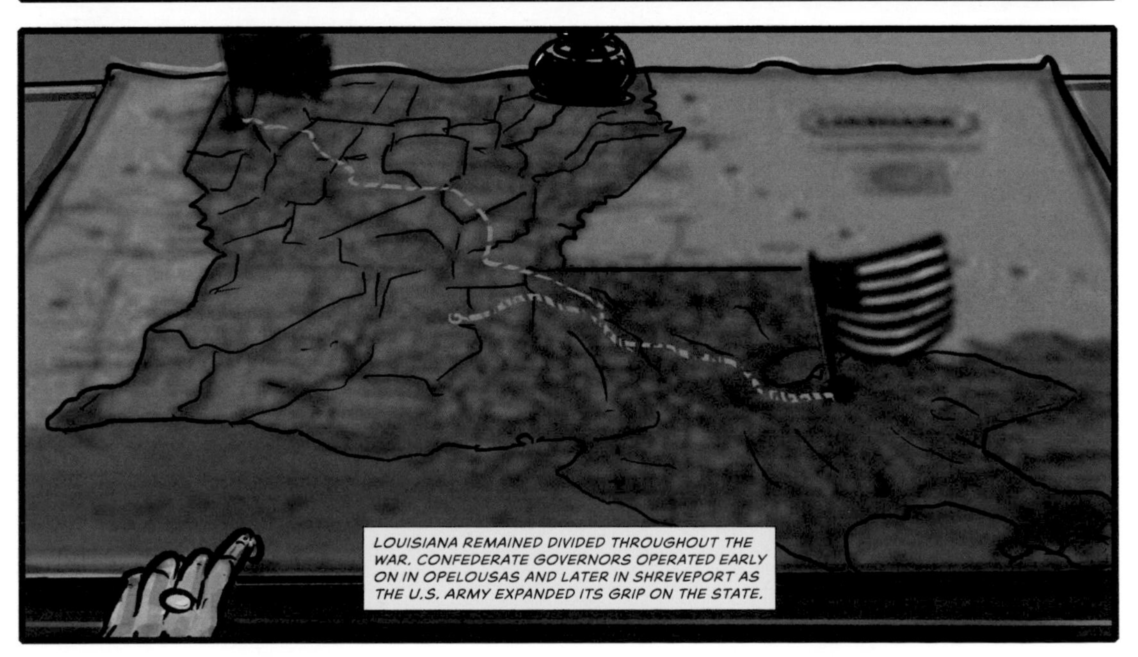
LOUISIANA REMAINED DIVIDED THROUGHOUT THE WAR. CONFEDERATE GOVERNORS OPERATED EARLY ON IN OPELOUSAS AND LATER IN SHREVEPORT AS THE U.S. ARMY EXPANDED ITS GRIP ON THE STATE.

MEANWHILE, DUNN, NO LONGER TEACHING MUSIC, CONTINUED HIS PLASTERING WORK.
HE HAD BIGGER DREAMS, THOUGH, AND WAS FRUSTRATED THAT PLASTERING LIMITED HIS HOURS OF STUDY TO THE EVENING.
HE CONTINUED TO GROW HIS PERSONAL NETWORK BY ATTENDING ST. JAMES AFRICAN METHODIST EPISCOPAL CHURCH, A CORNERSTONE OF THE ANGLO-AFRICAN COMMUNITY. THE CHURCH HAD CLOSE TIES TO DUNN'S MASONIC LODGE, WHICH HAD BEEN FOUNDED BY CHURCH MEMBERS IN 1849.

DUNN'S STATURE WITHIN THE LODGE AND THE MASONIC FRATERNITY GREW DURING THE WAR.
IN 1863 HE PASSED ITS FIRST THREE DEGREES--STAGES OF MORAL INSTRUCTION THAT INITIATE ONE INTO FREEMASONRY.

HE HELD LEADERSHIP POSTS AND HELPED WRITE THE CONSTITUTION FOR THE NEW EUREKA GRAND LODGE, WHICH WOULD OVERSEE THE GROWING BLACK MASONIC COMMUNITY IN LOUISIANA.

ON DECEMBER 26, 1864, DUNN WAS INSTALLED AS THE MOST WORSHIPFUL GRAND MASTER OF THE EUREKA GRAND LODGE, THE HIGHEST OFFICE AMONG BLACK MASONS IN LOUISIANA.
DUNN'S ALLIANCES AND FRIENDSHIPS IN THE CHURCH AND MASONIC COMMUNITY WOULD FORM THE BEDROCK OF HIS POLITICAL CAREER.

DUNN'S CAREER PATH CAME INTO CLEARER FOCUS AFTER PRESIDENT LINCOLN SIGNED THE EMANCIPATION PROCLAMATION, WHICH FORMALLY FREED MORE THAN 3 MILLION ENSLAVED PEOPLE LIVING IN REBEL TERRITORY ON JANUARY 1, 1863.

WITH AN ALREADY WELL-ESTABLISHED FREE BLACK COMMUNITY, NEW ORLEANS BECAME A HOTBED FOR DEBATE ON ALLOWING FREE AFRICAN AMERICANS TO VOTE. DUNN JOINED OTHER LOCAL LEADERS IN SENDING A PETITION FOR BLACK SUFFRAGE TO LINCOLN.

THE GROUP SENT TWO EDUCATED, LIGHTER-SKINNED AFRO-CREOLE MEN, HOPING THEY STOOD A BETTER CHANCE OF CONVINCING LINCOLN.

LINCOLN RESPONDED BY ASKING LOUISIANA GOVERNOR MICHAEL HAHN, JUST ELECTED IN THE UNION-CONTROLLED PART OF THE STATE, TO CONSIDER LIMITED BLACK SUFFRAGE AT THE STATE'S 1864 CONSTITUTIONAL CONVENTION.
LINCOLN HAD ORDERED THE CONVENTION WITH HOPES OF SETTING AN EXAMPLE FOR THE REST OF THE SOUTH. DELEGATES ABOLISHED SLAVERY IN LOUISIANA, BUT IGNORED THE TOPIC OF BLACK SUFFRAGE.

WITH THE WAR WINDING DOWN IN MARCH 1865, CONGRESS ESTABLISHED THE FREEDMEN'S BUREAU TO ASSIST THE MILLIONS OF RECENTLY EMANCIPATED AFRICAN AMERICANS.
INTELLIGENCE OFFICE
DUNN BECAME ONE OF THE FIRST IN NEW ORLEANS TO OPEN AN EMPLOYMENT OFFICE TO HELP **FREEDMEN** FIND FAIR WORK.

DUNN SERVED AS AN INTERMEDIARY BETWEEN FREEDMEN AND PLANTERS DESPERATE FOR LABOR.
HE HELPED WORKERS EARN MONTHLY PAY RATES--TYPICALLY $15 FOR MEN AND $10 FOR WOMEN--THAT WERE WELL ABOVE GOVERNMENT-ESTABLISHED MINIMUM WAGES.

THE WAR EFFECTIVELY ENDED WITH GEN. ROBERT E. LEE'S SURRENDER TO U.S. ARMY GEN. ULYSSES S. GRANT. IT WAS HARDLY THE END OF THE BLOODSHED.
APPOMATTOX, VIRGINIA, APRIL 9, 1865

WASHINGTON, D.C., APRIL 14, 1865
FIVE DAYS LATER, PRESIDENT LINCOLN WAS SHOT BY AN ASSASSIN. HE DIED THE NEXT DAY.

LINCOLN WAS SUCCEEDED BY ANDREW JOHNSON, HIS CONSERVATIVE VICE PRESIDENT.
JOHNSON PARDONED MOST EX-CONFEDERATES AND IMPLEMENTED "PRESIDENTIAL RECONSTRUCTION," A HANDS-OFF APPROACH THAT PERMITTED SOUTHERN GOVERNMENTS TO REBUILD THEMSELVES, WITHOUT REQUIRING THEM TO ENFRANCHISE FREEDMEN.

ALTHOUGH THERE WERE CONFEDERATE SYMPATHIZERS IN NEW ORLEANS WHO CELEBRATED LINCOLN'S DEATH, MANY IN THE CITY GRIEVED IN THE FOLLOWING DAYS.

THREE DAYS AFTER LINCOLN'S DEATH, A CROWD OF 25,000 PEOPLE GATHERED IN LAFAYETTE SQUARE IN A SHOW OF MOURNING.

MEANWHILE, THE SUFFRAGE FIGHT CONTINUED.
New Orleans Tribune,
Published Daily, Mondays Excepted.
ON JUNE 16, 1865, THE NEW ORLEANS TRIBUNE, THE FIRST BLACK-OWNED DAILY NEWSPAPER IN THE COUNTRY, RAN AN ADVERTISEMENT IN FRENCH AND ENGLISH FOR A MEETING OF A NEW ORGANIZATION CALLED THE **FRIENDS OF UNIVERSAL SUFFRAGE** AT 49 UNION STREET.

AT THE MEETING, DUNN JOINED THE CENTRAL EXECUTIVE COMMITTEE.
THOMAS J. DURANT, A PENNSYLVANIA NATIVE AND THE PRESIDENT OF THE ORGANIZATION, ADDRESSED THE ASSEMBLY.
THE WAR IS OVER AND THE TIME HAS COME FOR STATESMANSHIP. UNIVERSAL SUFFRAGE IS THE ONLY WAY TO SECURE ALL THE FRUITS OF OUR VICTORIES. . . .
WE SHOULD DIRECT OUR EFFORTS TOWARD THE VOLUNTARY REGISTRATION OF AMERICAN CITIZENS WHO ARE NOT RECOGNIZED AS VOTERS.

DUNN JOINED A COMMITTEE FORMED TO "SET FORTH THE TRUE SPIRIT AND PRINCIPLES OF THIS LAUDABLE ORGANIZATION," WHICH WOULD CHAMPION RADICAL POSITIONS ON EXPANDING BLACK RIGHTS.
MEMBERS INCLUDED LOCAL BLACK LEADERS AND TWO OTHER GROUPS DERIDED BY EX-REBELS: SCALAWAGS, OR SOUTHERN WHITES WHO ALIGNED WITH NORTHERN REPUBLICANS, AND CARPETBAGGERS, NORTHERNERS WHO RELOCATED SOUTH AND--ACCORDING TO THEIR CRITICS--GOT INTO POLITICS FOR PERSONAL PROFIT.

SOON AFTER, DUNN WAS INVITED TO MEET WITH HENRY CLAY WARMOTH, A PRECOCIOUS 23-YEAR-OLD LAWYER FROM ILLINOIS. WARMOTH HAD BEEN A LIEUTENANT COLONEL IN THE UNION ARMY BEFORE SETTLING IN NEW ORLEANS.

DUNN WENT TO WARMOTH'S OFFICE. THEY CHATTED FOR A WHILE ABOUT THE NEWS OF THE DAY AND POLITICS BEFORE DUNN MADE A FATEFUL SUGGESTION.
YOU SHOULD ATTEND THE NEXT MEETING OF THE FRIENDS OF UNIVERSAL SUFFRAGE.
IT WOULD BE MY HONOR.

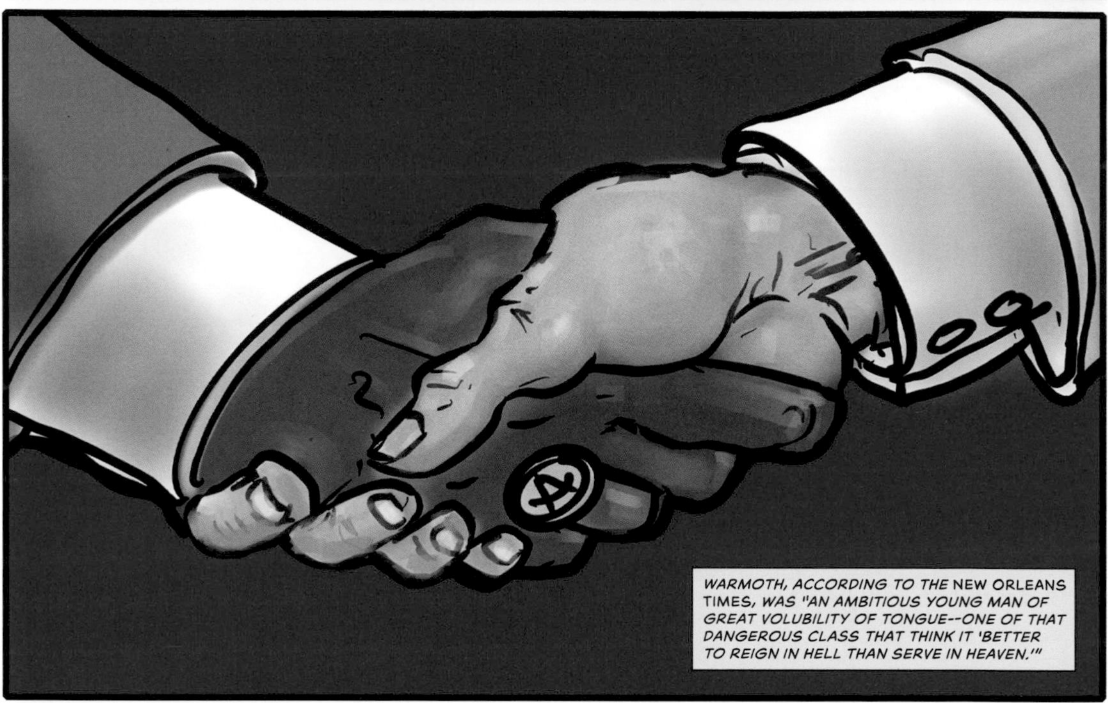
WARMOTH, ACCORDING TO THE NEW ORLEANS TIMES, WAS "AN AMBITIOUS YOUNG MAN OF GREAT VOLUBILITY OF TONGUE--ONE OF THAT DANGEROUS CLASS THAT THINK IT 'BETTER TO REIGN IN HELL THAN SERVE IN HEAVEN.'"

AT THE NEXT MEETING, DUNN WOULD PRESENT WARMOTH TO THE GROUP. ON DUNN'S RECOMMENDATION, WARMOTH BECAME A MEMBER.
DUNN LATER SAID THAT THIS WAS THE SINGLE ACTION WHICH HE COULD "NEVER FORGIVE HIMSELF FOR."

THE GROUP HAD A NEW GOVERNOR TO CONTEND WITH: JAMES MADISON WELLS, WHO HAD BEEN A LOYAL UNIONIST BUT WAS ALSO A WEALTHY PLANTER AND FORMER SLAVEHOLDER.
DUNN AND OTHER FRIENDS OF UNIVERSAL SUFFRAGE LEADERS WROTE TO GOVERNOR WELLS ON THE ISSUE OF BLACK SUFFRAGE.

From my Knowledge of the negro character, nine out of ten of the late entire Slave Population would Support their former masters
WELLS RESPONDED THAT SUFFRAGE WOULDN'T BE NECESSARY BECAUSE FREEDMEN WOULD JUST SUPPORT THEIR FORMER ENSLAVERS.

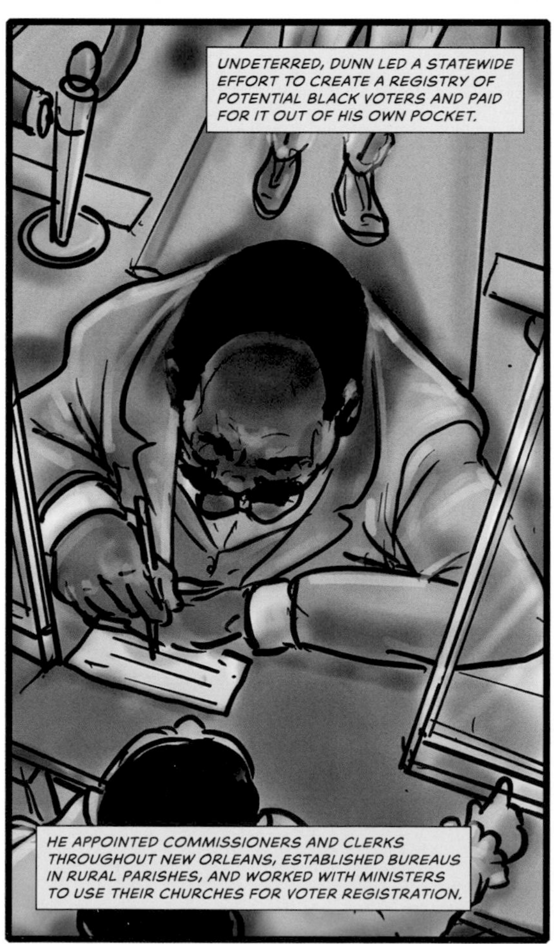
UNDETERRED, DUNN LED A STATEWIDE EFFORT TO CREATE A REGISTRY OF POTENTIAL BLACK VOTERS AND PAID FOR IT OUT OF HIS OWN POCKET.
HE APPOINTED COMMISSIONERS AND CLERKS THROUGHOUT NEW ORLEANS, ESTABLISHED BUREAUS IN RURAL PARISHES, AND WORKED WITH MINISTERS TO USE THEIR CHURCHES FOR VOTER REGISTRATION.

REGISTER TO VOTE HERE
THE PLAN WAS TO REGISTER A "NUMERICAL FORCE" OF BLACK VOTERS LOYAL TO THE REPUBLICAN CAUSE IN ORDER TO CONVINCE THE REPUBLICAN-MAJORITY CONGRESS TO SUPPORT UNIVERSAL MALE SUFFRAGE.

AFTER THE REGISTRATION CAMPAIGN, THE FRIENDS OF UNIVERSAL SUFFRAGE HELD A CONVENTION IN NEW ORLEANS, WITH DELEGATES TRAVELING FROM ALL OVER THE STATE.

IF LIFE, LIBERTY, AND THE PURSUIT OF HAPPINESS ARE RIGHTS WHICH BELONG TO ALL MEN, LET ***ALL*** MEN ENJOY THEM.
LIFE IS INSECURE WHEN THE PROSCRIBED RACE HAS NO VOICE IN THE LEGISLATIVE HALL, AND NO FRIEND IN THE JURY BOX.
LIBERTY IS BUT A WORD AS LONG AS TAXATION, ELECTIONS, AND THE WHOLE POLITICAL MACHINERY ARE CONFINED IN THE HANDS OF AN INIMICAL RACE.
HAPPINESS ITSELF . . . CANNOT BE ATTAINED WITHOUT ADEQUATE PROTECTION AND JUSTICE TO THE INDIVIDUAL.
THEREFORE, LET OUR REPUBLICAN GOVERNMENT BE UPHELD BY ALL CITIZENS AND DERIVE ITS JUST POWER FROM THE EXPRESSED CONSENT OF ***ALL*** GOVERNED!

DELEGATES DEBATED ALIGNING WITH THE NATIONAL REPUBLICAN PARTY. THE MOST RADICAL MEMBERS ARGUED THAT IT WASN'T SUFFICIENTLY SUPPORTIVE OF BLACK RIGHTS.

WARMOTH MADE THE CASE FOR NATIONAL ALIGNMENT.
THE NATIONAL REPUBLICAN PARTY HAD COMMITTED THEMSELVES IN FAVOR OF UNIVERSAL SUFFRAGE . . . THE VERY REFORM THE CONVENTION WISHES TO NOW FOLLOW.
ALIGNMENT WON OUT, AND THE REPUBLICAN PARTY OF LOUISIANA WAS BORN.

WARMOTH PASSIONATELY ADVOCATED FOR REDRAFTING THE STATE CONSTITUTION AND WAS MET WITH DEAFENING APPLAUSE.
THE PARTY AGREED THAT DURING STATE ELECTIONS THAT FALL--STILL LIMITED TO WHITE MEN LOYAL TO THE UNION--THEY WOULD SOLICIT VOLUNTARY BALLOTS FROM BLACK VOTERS, HOPING TO DEMONSTRATE THEIR POTENTIAL ELECTORAL IMPACT IF GRANTED SUFFRAGE.

WARMOTH EMERGED AS A LEADER IN THE PARTY AND WAS CHOSEN TO TAKE THEIR CASE FOR BLACK SUFFRAGE TO PRESIDENT JOHNSON LATER IN THE YEAR.

DESPITE REPORTS OF SOME WHITE EMPLOYERS REFUSING TO LET BLACK WORKERS VOTE, DUNN'S REGISTRATION EFFORTS PAID OFF.
WARMOTH WENT TO WASHINGTON WITH DOCUMENTS SHOWING THAT MORE THAN 16,000 BLACK VOTERS PARTICIPATED--REPRESENTING WHAT WOULD HAVE BEEN 87 PERCENT OF THE STATE'S REPUBLICAN ELECTORATE IF THEY HAD COUNTED.

THE STATE'S OFFICIAL, WHITES-ONLY ELECTION PUT GOVERNOR WELLS BACK INTO OFFICE. HE WON WITH SUPPORT FROM CONSERVATIVES, INCLUDING THE STATE'S DEMOCRATIC PARTY, WHICH COUNTED MANY EX-CONFEDERATES AMONG ITS MEMBERS.
THE DEMOCRATS' PLATFORM STATED THAT LOUISIANA SHOULD HAVE **"A GOVERNMENT OF WHITE PEOPLE, MADE AND TO BE PERPETUATED FOR THE EXCLUSIVE BENEFIT OF THE WHITE RACE."**

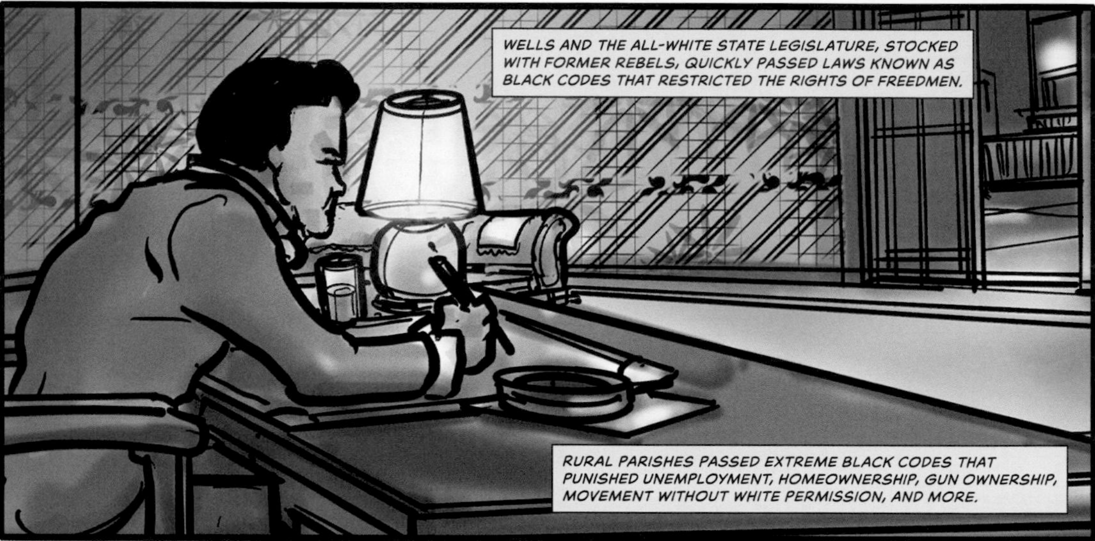
WELLS AND THE ALL-WHITE STATE LEGISLATURE, STOCKED WITH FORMER REBELS, QUICKLY PASSED LAWS KNOWN AS BLACK CODES THAT RESTRICTED THE RIGHTS OF FREEDMEN.
RURAL PARISHES PASSED EXTREME BLACK CODES THAT PUNISHED UNEMPLOYMENT, HOMEOWNERSHIP, GUN OWNERSHIP, MOVEMENT WITHOUT WHITE PERMISSION, AND MORE.

IN NEW ORLEANS, THE MAYOR AUTHORIZED POLICE TO ARREST FREEDMEN IN THE STREET WHO DIDN'T HAVE WRITTEN PROOF OF EMPLOYMENT FROM THEIR FORMER OWNERS OR OTHER WHITE CITIZENS.

AROUND THIS TIME, DUNN RECONNECTED WITH ELLEN BOYD MARSHALL, THE WIDOW OF PETER MARSHALL, DUNN'S FORMER LANDLORD.

ELLEN HAD GROWN UP IN CINCINNATI AND WAS THE DAUGHTER OF HENRY BOYD, WHO HAD ESCAPED SLAVERY AND BECOME A SUCCESSFUL CARPENTER AND BUSINESSMAN.

SHE HAD MARRIED PETER AROUND THE AGE OF 17 AND LEFT WITH HIM FOR NEW ORLEANS IN 1842.

IN ADDITION TO HELPING PETER RUN THE BOARDINGHOUSE, ELLEN WAS A TEACHER.

WHEN PETER DIED, HE LEFT BEHIND ELLEN AND THEIR THREE CHILDREN, FANNY, EMMA, AND CHARLES.

OVER THE COURSE OF 1865, ELLEN'S RELATIONSHIP WITH DUNN BLOSSOMED.

DUNN CONTINUED TO EXPAND HIS COMMUNITY OUTREACH, JOINING THE BOARD OF THE LOUISIANA ASSOCIATION FOR THE BENEFIT OF COLORED ORPHANS.
THERE, HE RUBBED ELBOWS WITH PROMINENT AFRO-CREOLES, INCLUDING DR. LOUIS C. ROUDANEZ, A PHYSICIAN AND THE PUBLISHER OF THE NEW ORLEANS TRIBUNE.

BLACK ORPHANS WERE VULNERABLE TO BEING PLACED IN VIRTUAL SLAVERY IF GIVEN OVER TO PLANTATION OWNERS DESPERATE FOR DOCILE LABOR.
AMONG OTHER THINGS, THE ASSOCIATION INTERVENED TO MAKE SURE THAT BLACK ORPHANS OLD ENOUGH TO WORK COULD ONLY BE INDENTURED TO PEOPLE OF COLOR.

PEOPLE'S BAKERY
DUNN WAS ALSO THE PRESIDENT OF THE PEOPLE'S BAKERY, AN INITIATIVE MODELED OFF OF EUROPEAN CO-OPS THAT SOUGHT TO EMPOWER BLACK WORKERS THROUGH THE POOLING OF RESOURCES.

THE BAKERY STARTED WITH A SIMPLE STAPLE: BREAD.
EVERY WEEK, MEMBERS CONTRIBUTED MODEST SUMS THAT THE CO-OP USED TO BUY SUPPLIES AT WHOLESALE RATES. THE SAVINGS WERE PASSED ON TO MEMBERS.

DUNN AND HIS FELLOW FOUNDERS HOPED THAT BY REINVESTING THE BAKERY'S PROFITS THEY COULD EXPAND THE CO-OP TO OTHER TRADES, LIKE BLACKSMITHING AND CONSTRUCTION.

THREE HUNDRED FREEDMEN JOINED THE BAKERY, BUT THE ORGANIZATION STRUGGLED WITH FUNDING AND DISTRUST BETWEEN ANGLO-AFRICAN FREEDMEN AND THE AFRO-CREOLES WHO DOMINATED ITS MEMBERSHIP.
STILL, IT REPRESENTED A HISTORIC EFFORT BY BLACK PEOPLE IN NEW ORLEANS TO ENGINEER THEIR OWN ECONOMIC EMPOWERMENT.

DUNN'S REPUTATION AS AN ADVOCATE FOR FREEDMEN CONTINUED TO GROW, ESPECIALLY AFTER CONTRACTS BETWEEN PLANTERS AND LABORERS BECAME MANDATORY.
"NO ONE IS MORE COMPETENT THAN MR. DUNN," WROTE THE TRIBUNE, NOR BETTER POSITIONED TO EXPRESS THE "SPIRIT OF BOTH EMPLOYERS AND LABORERS" DUE TO HIS "CLOSE AND CONSTANT CONTACT WITH BOTH."

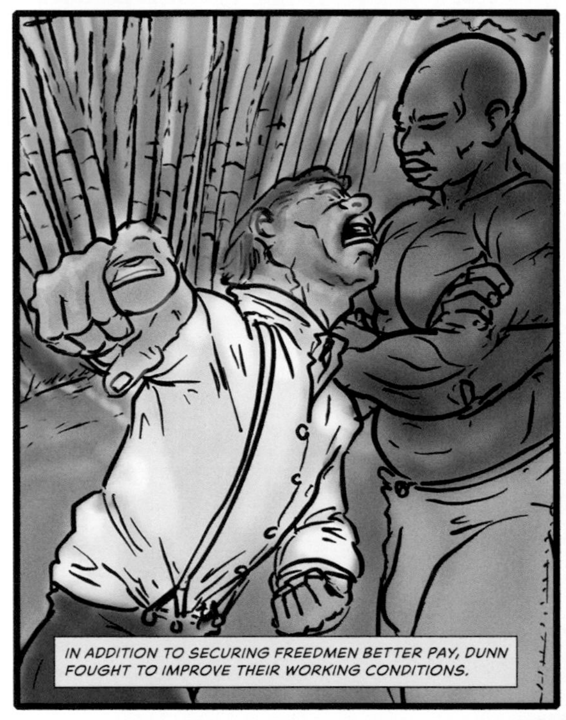
IN ADDITION TO SECURING FREEDMEN BETTER PAY, DUNN FOUGHT TO IMPROVE THEIR WORKING CONDITIONS.

THE NEGROES WILL NOT WORK NOW THAT THEY ARE FREE!
IF WE ARE FORCED TO HIRE WHITE FIELD HANDS, I CAN PROMISE WE'LL **NEVER** GO BACK TO HIRING NEGROES.

THEY WILL WORK WHEN THEY ARE TREATED **JUSTLY**.
I WOULD BE PLEASED TO SEE YOU EMPLOY WHITE LABORERS FOR YOUR PLANTATIONS, FOR THEN YOU WOULD PROPERLY APPRECIATE THE POOR NEGRO.

NEW ORLEANS, MAY 1866
AT ECONOMY HALL, A CENTER FOR BLACK ACTIVISM IN THE TREMÉ NEIGHBORHOOD OF NEW ORLEANS, A NEW BENEVOLENT GROUP NAMED THE FREEDMEN'S AID ASSOCIATION MET FOR THE FIRST TIME.

DUNN WAS ELECTED PRESIDENT OF THE GROUP.
A CIVIL RIGHTS BILL HAS BEEN SIGNED INTO LAW BY CONGRESS!
AT THE SAME MEETING, THOMAS J. DURANT, ONE OF THE LEADERS OF THE SUFFRAGE MOVEMENT, DELIVERED MAJOR NEWS.

WASHINGTON, D.C.
OVER PRESIDENT JOHNSON'S VETO, CONGRESS PASSED A CIVIL RIGHTS ACT THAT DEFINED CITIZENSHIP AND AFFIRMED THAT ALL CITIZENS WERE EQUALLY PROTECTED UNDER THE LAW--A REBUKE OF BLACK CODES IN THE SOUTH.
ITS PASSAGE FOLLOWED THE RATIFICATION OF THE **THIRTEENTH AMENDMENT** TO THE CONSTITUTION, WHICH HAD OFFICIALLY ABOLISHED SLAVERY, EXCEPT AS PUNISHMENT FOR A CRIME.

CIVIL RIGHTS CAN ONLY BE OBTAINED WHEN COUPLED WITH ***POLITICAL*** RIGHTS!
THE NEWS ENCOURAGED LOUISIANA RADICALS--THE REPUBLICAN FACTION MOST CONCERNED WITH EXPANDING BLACK RIGHTS.
BUT GOVERNOR WELLS'S ADMINISTRATION REMAINED HOSTILE. A BITTER, BLOODY FIGHT FOR SUFFRAGE LAY AHEAD.

PART THREE

THE RIOT AND THE RADICALS

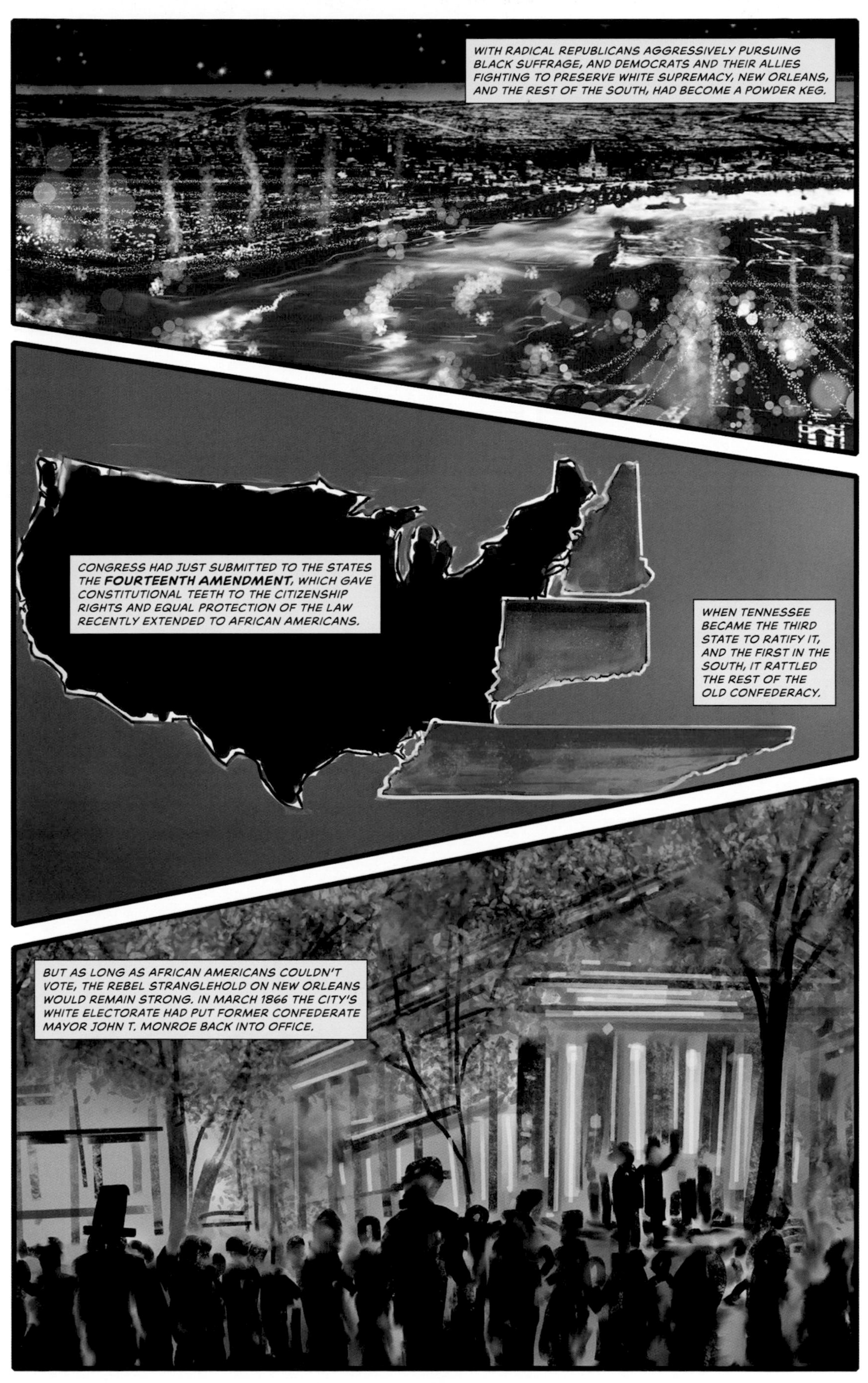
WITH RADICAL REPUBLICANS AGGRESSIVELY PURSUING BLACK SUFFRAGE, AND DEMOCRATS AND THEIR ALLIES FIGHTING TO PRESERVE WHITE SUPREMACY, NEW ORLEANS, AND THE REST OF THE SOUTH, HAD BECOME A POWDER KEG.
CONGRESS HAD JUST SUBMITTED TO THE STATES THE **FOURTEENTH AMENDMENT**, WHICH GAVE CONSTITUTIONAL TEETH TO THE CITIZENSHIP RIGHTS AND EQUAL PROTECTION OF THE LAW RECENTLY EXTENDED TO AFRICAN AMERICANS.
WHEN TENNESSEE BECAME THE THIRD STATE TO RATIFY IT, AND THE FIRST IN THE SOUTH, IT RATTLED THE REST OF THE OLD CONFEDERACY.
BUT AS LONG AS AFRICAN AMERICANS COULDN'T VOTE, THE REBEL STRANGLEHOLD ON NEW ORLEANS WOULD REMAIN STRONG. IN MARCH 1866 THE CITY'S WHITE ELECTORATE HAD PUT FORMER CONFEDERATE MAYOR JOHN T. MONROE BACK INTO OFFICE.

GOVERNOR WELLS HAD LOST CONTROL OF THE CONSERVATIVE FORCES THAT HAD HELPED HIM WIN RE-ELECTION. VIOLENCE SPIKED, AS EX-REBELS FOUGHT TO RESTORE THE ANTEBELLUM ORDER.
TO COUNTER THIS REGRESSION, SOME MEMBERS FROM THE 1864 CONSTITUTIONAL CONVENTION SOUGHT TO RECONVENE AND CONSIDER THE ENFRANCHISEMENT OF AFRICAN AMERICANS, THE DISENFRANCHISEMENT OF EX-CONFEDERATES, AND A NEW STATE GOVERNMENT.

THEY CHOSE TO HOLD A CONVENTION IN NEW ORLEANS AT THE NEW STATE CAPITOL BUILDING, THE MECHANICS' INSTITUTE, ON JULY 30, 1866.

A NUMBER OF REPUBLICAN LEADERS WERE WARNED AGAINST ATTENDING.
GOOD AFTERNOON, MR. DUNN.
TO WHAT DO I OWE THIS VISIT?

Be advised,
There will be
Mechanics
Institute.
Stay

ON THE DAY OF THE CONVENTION, ABOUT 200 UNARMED BLACK SUPPORTERS, INCLUDING A MARCHING BAND AND CIVIL WAR VETERANS, MARCHED TO THE MECHANICS' INSTITUTE.
ON THE INSIDE, ONLY 26 DELEGATES SHOWED UP, BUT THEY WERE JOINED BY MORE SUPPORTERS.
THE BLACK PARADERS WERE SOON MET BY A WHITE MOB, LARGELY COMPOSED OF POLICE OFFICERS AND FIREMEN, SENT BY MAYOR MONROE TO BREAK UP THE CONVENTION.

THE MOB BEGAN RUTHLESSLY ATTACKING PARADERS ON THE STREET.

MERCY!

SOON, THE ATTACKERS WENT INTO THE MECHANICS' INSTITUTE.

WE SURRENDER! WE SURRENDER!
PLEASE, DON'T SHOOT!

THE MERCILESS ASSAULT ONLY ABATED AFTER FEDERAL TROOPS ARRIVED, BUT BY THEN THE DAMAGE HAD LARGELY BEEN DONE. MARTIAL LAW WAS DECLARED IN THE CITY.

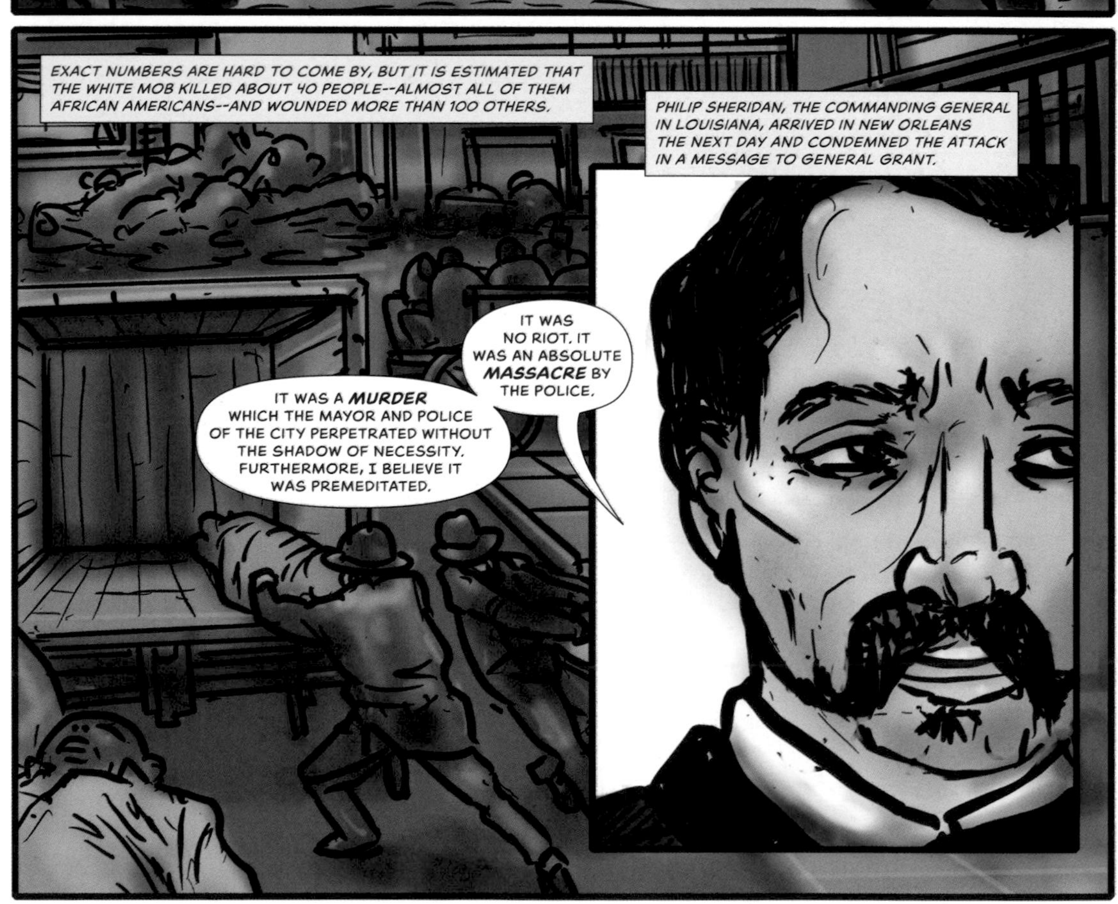
EXACT NUMBERS ARE HARD TO COME BY, BUT IT IS ESTIMATED THAT THE WHITE MOB KILLED ABOUT 40 PEOPLE--ALMOST ALL OF THEM AFRICAN AMERICANS--AND WOUNDED MORE THAN 100 OTHERS.
PHILIP SHERIDAN, THE COMMANDING GENERAL IN LOUISIANA, ARRIVED IN NEW ORLEANS THE NEXT DAY AND CONDEMNED THE ATTACK IN A MESSAGE TO GENERAL GRANT.
IT WAS NO RIOT. IT WAS AN ABSOLUTE **MASSACRE** BY THE POLICE.
IT WAS A **MURDER** WHICH THE MAYOR AND POLICE OF THE CITY PERPETRATED WITHOUT THE SHADOW OF NECESSITY. FURTHERMORE, I BELIEVE IT WAS PREMEDITATED.

MANY RADICAL LEADERS WHO WEREN'T EVEN PRESENT FOR THE ATTACK, LIKE THOMAS J. DURANT, FLED THE CITY FOR GOOD.

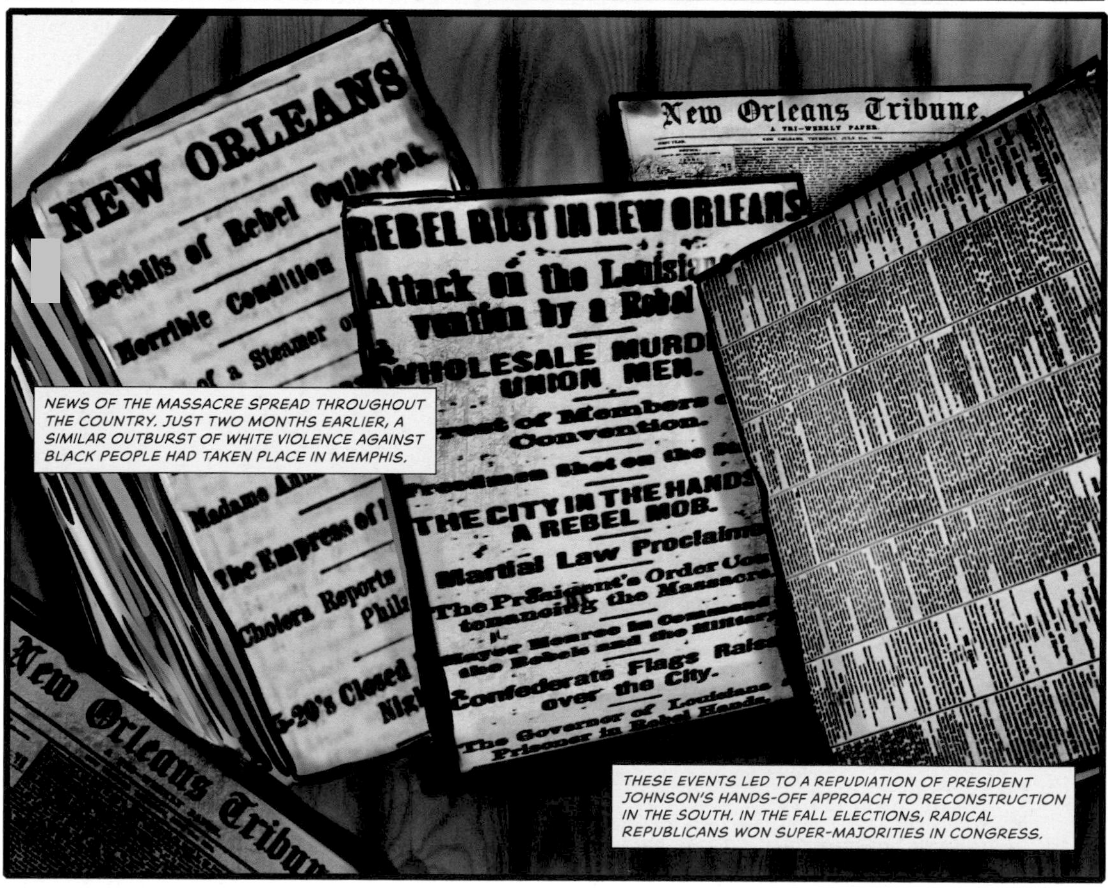
NEW ORLEANS
New Orleans Tribune
REBEL RIOT IN NEW ORLEANS
Horrible Condition
UNION MEN.
Convention.
THE CITY IN THE HANDS
A REBEL MOB.
over the City.
NEWS OF THE MASSACRE SPREAD THROUGHOUT THE COUNTRY. JUST TWO MONTHS EARLIER, A SIMILAR OUTBURST OF WHITE VIOLENCE AGAINST BLACK PEOPLE HAD TAKEN PLACE IN MEMPHIS.
THESE EVENTS LED TO A REPUDIATION OF PRESIDENT JOHNSON'S HANDS-OFF APPROACH TO RECONSTRUCTION IN THE SOUTH. IN THE FALL ELECTIONS, RADICAL REPUBLICANS WON SUPER-MAJORITIES IN CONGRESS.

A THREE-PERSON CONGRESSIONAL COMMITTEE CAME TO NEW ORLEANS TO INVESTIGATE THE RIOT, INTERVIEWING 197 PEOPLE, INCLUDING DUNN.
STATE WHETHER YOU HAVE ANY KNOWLEDGE OF THE FEELINGS AND OPINIONS OF THE COLORED CITIZENS HERE.
THE FEELING AMONG THEM IS THAT THERE IS NO SECURITY FOR THEM UNDER THE PRESENT MUNICIPAL GOVERNMENT; THAT THERE IS NO JUSTICE FOR THEM. THEY HAVE OCCASION EVERY DAY TO BE SATISFIED OF THAT FACT.

THE COMMITTEE DETERMINED THAT THE MAYOR, POLICE CHIEF, AND LIEUTENANT GOVERNOR PREARRANGED THE ATTACK.
BACK IN CONGRESS, THEY PROPOSED A BILL CALLING FOR THE DISENFRANCHISEMENT OF EX-CONFEDERATES AND A NEW GOVERNMENT ELECTED BY BLACK AND LOYAL WHITE VOTERS IN LOUISIANA.

CONGRESS PASSED A SERIES OF RECONSTRUCTION ACTS, CREATING FIVE MILITARY DISTRICTS IN THE SOUTH, WITH GENERALS DEPLOYED AS ACTING GOVERNORS.
THE ACTS CALLED FOR NEW STATE GOVERNMENTS, ENFRANCHISED BLACK MEN, AND REQUIRED STATES TO RATIFY THE FOURTEENTH AMENDMENT BEFORE BEING READMITTED INTO THE UNION.
THUS BEGAN THE ERA OF RADICAL RECONSTRUCTION.

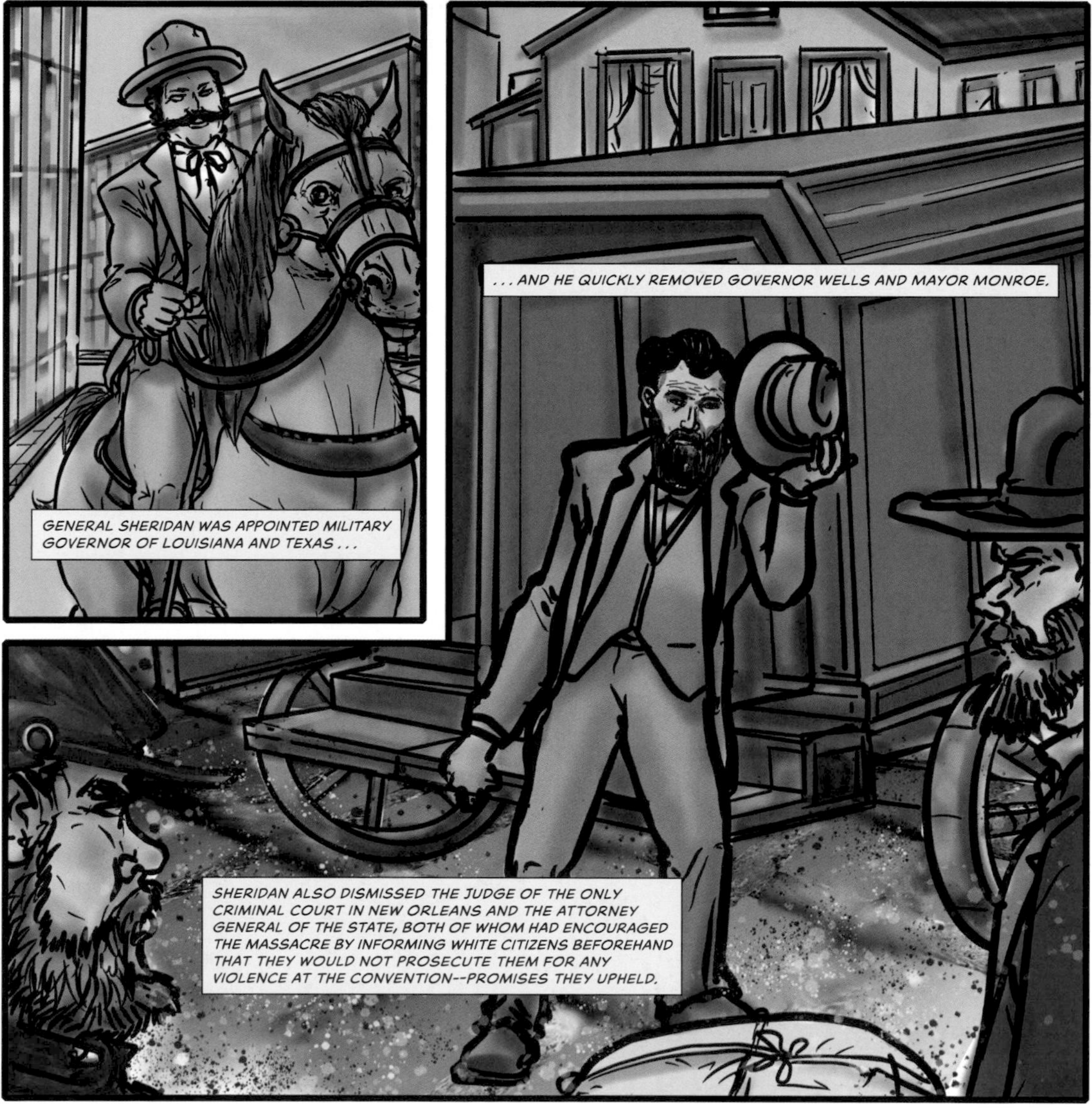
GENERAL SHERIDAN WAS APPOINTED MILITARY GOVERNOR OF LOUISIANA AND TEXAS . . .
. . . AND HE QUICKLY REMOVED GOVERNOR WELLS AND MAYOR MONROE.
SHERIDAN ALSO DISMISSED THE JUDGE OF THE ONLY CRIMINAL COURT IN NEW ORLEANS AND THE ATTORNEY GENERAL OF THE STATE, BOTH OF WHOM HAD ENCOURAGED THE MASSACRE BY INFORMING WHITE CITIZENS BEFOREHAND THAT THEY WOULD NOT PROSECUTE THEM FOR ANY VIOLENCE AT THE CONVENTION--PROMISES THEY UPHELD.

A FEW MONTHS EARLIER, ON DECEMBER 27, 1866, DUNN TOOK A MAJOR STEP IN HIS PERSONAL LIFE: HE MARRIED ELLEN.

DUNN BECAME A HUSBAND AND A FATHER--ADOPTING ELLEN'S THREE CHILDREN, WHO ALL TOOK HIS LAST NAME.

JUST AS DUNN WAS SETTLING INTO HIS NEW FAMILY LIFE, HIS RELATIONSHIPS WITH HIS MASONIC BROTHERS WERE TESTED, WHEN MEMBERS OF LOCAL WHITE LODGES INVITED BLACK MASONS--PREDOMINANTLY AFRO-CREOLES--TO FRATERNIZE WITH THEM.

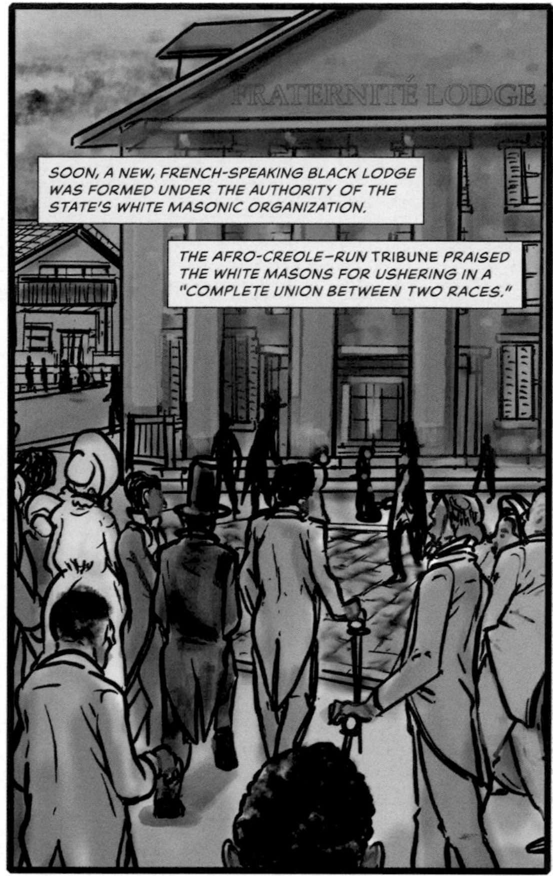
FRATERNITÉ LODGE
SOON, A NEW, FRENCH-SPEAKING BLACK LODGE WAS FORMED UNDER THE AUTHORITY OF THE STATE'S WHITE MASONIC ORGANIZATION.
THE AFRO-CREOLE–RUN TRIBUNE PRAISED THE WHITE MASONS FOR USHERING IN A "COMPLETE UNION BETWEEN TWO RACES."

DUNN DISPUTED THIS ASSERTION IN A LETTER TO THE TRIBUNE.
The statement that several colored lodges have fused, and are now working harmoniously under the supreme council of the accepted Scotch Rite for Louisiana, is a sad mistake or gross misrepresentation.

DUNN SAW THE MOVE AS AN ATTEMPT TO UNDERMINE HIS AUTHORITY AS THE LEADER OF LOUISIANA'S BLACK LODGES AND STRAIN ALREADY TENUOUS POLITICAL ALLIANCES BETWEEN AFRO-CREOLES AND ANGLO-AFRICANS.

OUR ORGANIZATION MUST ADOPT A GUARANTEE FOR THE AFRICAN RACE TO BE REPRESENTED!
DUNN HAD BEGUN TO FEAR THAT, DESPITE FEDERAL ENFORCEMENT OF RADICAL RECONSTRUCTION, WHITE REPUBLICANS WERE DRIFTING FROM THEIR BLACK ALLIES, UNDERCUTTING THE PARTY'S ORGANIZING PRINCIPLES.

WHEN REPUBLICANS BEGAN TO FORM A NEW CITY POLICE FORCE IN MAY 1867, AFRICAN AMERICANS WERE EXCLUDED FROM APPOINTMENTS.

WHEN DUNN QUESTIONED A NUMBER OF CONSERVATIVE NOMINEES FOR COMMITTEE APPOINTMENTS, WARMOTH SHUT HIM DOWN.

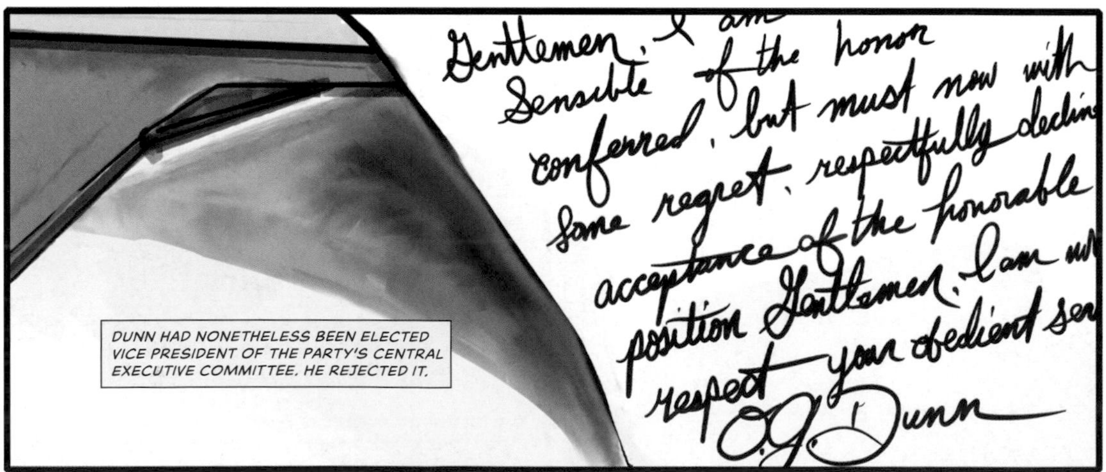
DUNN HAD NONETHELESS BEEN ELECTED VICE PRESIDENT OF THE PARTY'S CENTRAL EXECUTIVE COMMITTEE. HE REJECTED IT.
Gentlemen, I am
Sensible of the honor
conferred, but must now with
Same regret, respectfully
acceptance of the honorable
position Gentlemen. I am
respect your obedient
O.J. Dunn

SOON, THOUGH, GENERAL SHERIDAN FORCED THE ISSUE OF REPRESENTATION AND APPOINTED DUNN AND SEVERAL OTHER BLACK MEN TO THE NEW ORLEANS CITY COUNCIL.

DUNN'S FELLOW COUNCILORS ELECTED HIM ASSISTANT RECORDER OF THE SECOND DISTRICT, AN AREA INCLUDING THE FRENCH QUARTER AND TREMÉ NEIGHBORHOODS, MAKING HIM THE FIRST BLACK MAN IN LOUISIANA TO SERVE IN A JUDICIAL CAPACITY.

ON THE COUNCIL, DUNN ORIGINATED A POTENTIALLY HISTORIC SCHOOL INTEGRATION BILL . . .
THE TIME HAS COME TO INTEGRATE NEW ORLEANS PUBLIC SCHOOLS!
. . . BUT MAYOR EDWARD HEATH REJECTED IT. DUNN COULDN'T RALLY ENOUGH SUPPORT WITHIN THE COUNCIL TO OVERRIDE HIS DECISION.

SIXTEEN MONTHS AFTER THE MASSACRE THAT LED TO THEIR COMING INTO POWER, LOUISIANA'S REPUBLICANS RETURNED TO THE MECHANICS' INSTITUTE, BEING RENOVATED AT THE TIME, TO FINALLY REWRITE THE STATE'S CONSTITUTION.
MECHANICS' INSTITUTE
OVER THE COURSE OF SEVERAL MONTHS, DELEGATES DRAFTED A CONSTITUTION THAT INCLUDED . . .

. . . UNIVERSAL MALE SUFFRAGE, EXCLUDING SOME EX-CONFEDERATES . . .

. . . THE INTEGRATION OF PUBLIC SCHOOLS . . .

. . . AND THE GUARANTEE OF EQUAL RIGHTS AND ACCESS TO PUBLIC CONVEYANCES AND BUSINESSES. THE PUBLIC WOULD VOTE ON THE CONSTITUTION IN THE APRIL 1868 ELECTION.

THE PARTY ALSO NEEDED A CANDIDATE FOR GOVERNOR.
A "PURE RADICAL" FACTION AND THE TRIBUNE'S PUBLISHER, DR. ROUDANEZ, PREFERRED FRANCIS E. DUMAS, A WEALTHY AFRO-CREOLE CITY COUNCILOR AND UNION VETERAN--WHO HAD ALSO BEEN A MAJOR SLAVEHOLDER.

WHITE REPUBLICANS, HOWEVER, FAVORED WARMOTH.

ON THE FIRST BALLOT, DUMAS RECEIVED 41 VOTES TO WARMOTH'S 37, BUT WITH THREE OTHER CANDIDATES IN CONTENTION, NEITHER RECEIVED A MAJORITY OF THE 88 VOTES CAST. IN A RUNOFF BALLOT, WARMOTH EKED OUT A 45-43 VICTORY.

DUMAS REFUSED TO JOIN WARMOTH'S TICKET, INSTEAD JOINING A CURIOUS SLATE BACKED BY THE TRIBUNE AND LED BY A WHITE FORMER SLAVEHOLDER NAMED JAMES TALIAFERRO.
THIS LEFT WARMOTH'S RUNNING-MATE SPOT OPEN.

P. B. S. PINCHBACK, A BIRACIAL CARPETBAGGER FROM OHIO AND A RISING POLITICAL STAR HIMSELF, SUGGESTED A SURPRISE NAME FOR LOUISIANA'S SECOND-HIGHEST OFFICE--A NAME RESPECTED BY THE STATE'S SIZABLE FREEDMEN POPULATION.
I NOMINATE OSCAR J. DUNN FOR THE POSITION OF LIEUTENANT GOVERNOR!
DELEGATES ELECTED DUNN OVER FOUR OTHER NOMINEES.

SUDDENLY, THE MOST CONSEQUENTIAL DECISION OF DUNN'S LIFE WAS UPON HIM. SHOULD HE ACCEPT?

PART FOUR

THE BLACK LIEUTENANT GOVERNOR

DUNN NEEDED TO TAKE A WALK. A VERY LONG WALK.

HE SOUGHT THE COUNSEL OF JOHN MERCER LANGSTON, A NOTED ORATOR AND BLACK LEADER VISITING NEW ORLEANS AT THE TIME OF THE CONVENTION.

I HAVE GREAT RESERVATIONS ABOUT BEING ON THE TICKET WITH WARMOTH.
HE COULD BE USING ME TO GAIN INFLUENCE WITH THE FREEDMEN AND AT THE SAME TIME DIVIDE THE BLACK LEADERSHIP.

I FEAR THAT MY POLITICAL EXPERIENCE IS GREATLY INADEQUATE. I'M NOT SURE I'M CAPABLE OF DISCHARGING MY DUTIES IN AN ACCEPTABLE MANNER.
BUT I DON'T WANT TO ABANDON THE STATE TO MEN I DON'T TRUST.

THE TWO MEN PACED FOR HOURS, UP AND DOWN CANAL STREET IN THE CENTER OF THE CITY, AS LANGSTON PLED WITH DUNN TO ACCEPT.

YOUR PARTY NEEDS YOU--YOUR PEOPLE NEED YOU.

THEY RETURNED TO THE DUNN HOUSEHOLD AROUND 4 A.M. ELLEN MET THEM AT THE DOOR.

YOU MUST ACCEPT, IN THE NAME OF YOUR RACE, THE HIGH HONOR AND RESPONSIBILITY TENDERED TO YOU.

MY HUSBAND, YOU MUST DO YOUR DUTY.

IT'S SETTLED, THEN. I WILL ACCEPT THE NOMINATION.

I HAVE NOT SOUGHT THE NOMINATION OF LIEUTENANT GOVERNOR, BUT I WILL SERVE IN THE INTEREST OF MY PARTY.

WE MUST CHAMPION OUR NEW STATE CONSTITUTION, WHICH WILL GUARANTEE ALL MEN PRIVILEGES AND RIGHTS, CIVIL AND POLITICAL.

WITH DUMAS OPPOSING HIM AS AN INDEPENDENT, DUNN TOOK HIS CAMPAIGN TO THE RURAL PARISHES, RALLYING HIS BASE OF FREEDMEN.
THE TRIBUNE STOKED DIVISIONS WITHIN THE BLACK COMMUNITY WHEN IT PUBLISHED CONTROVERSIAL REMARKS ALLEGEDLY SPOKEN BY DUNN DURING A SPEECH IN PLAQUEMINES PARISH.

OUR CONSTITUTION MAY BE DEFEATED BY A SEGMENT WHOSE GREATEST EFFORT HERETOFORE HAS BEEN TO OBLITERATE ALL IDENTITY WITH US, BUT WHO SINCE WE HAVE BECOME A POWER IN THE LAND, RAMPANTLY PROCLAIM THEIR RELATIONSHIP, AND CAN AT TIMES CRY OUT AS LUSTILY, "WE THE NEGRO."
A SHORT TIME AGO THEY COULD USE THAT TERM WITH WHICH TO STIGMATIZE US.

THIS VAIN, CONCEITED AND POMPOUS QUADROON ELEMENT HAS BROUGHT OUT ANOTHER TICKET TO DIVIDE AND DESTROY THE REPUBLICAN PARTY!
"QUADROON" WAS USED TO DESCRIBE A PERSON CONSIDERED TO BE ONE-QUARTER BLACK--SOMETIMES AS AN EPITHET FOR AFRO-CREOLES.
DUNN WROTE TO THE TRIBUNE CLAIMING THAT HE HAD BEEN "GROSSLY MISREPRESENTED"--BUT THE PAPER REFUSED TO PUBLISH HIS REBUTTAL.

April 17-18 1868
DUNN

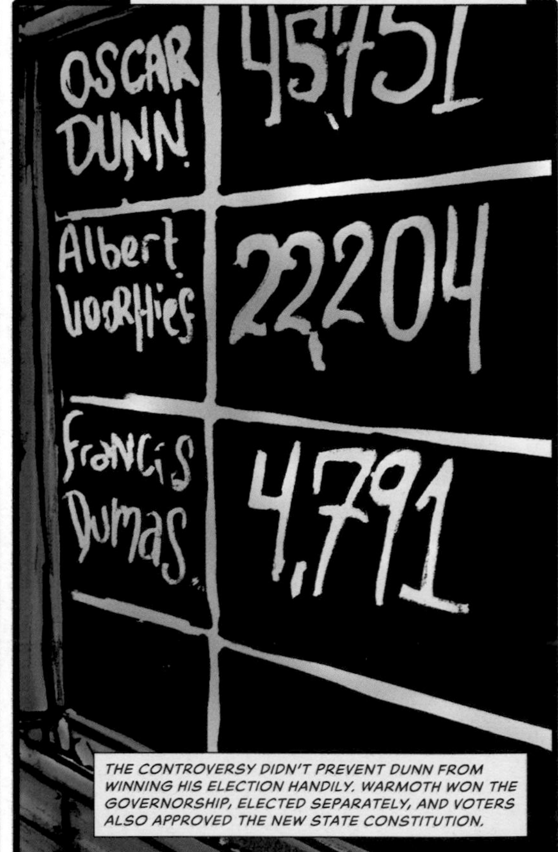
OSCAR DUNN
45,751
Albert Voorhies
22,204
Francis Dumas
4,791
THE CONTROVERSY DIDN'T PREVENT DUNN FROM WINNING HIS ELECTION HANDILY. WARMOTH WON THE GOVERNORSHIP, ELECTED SEPARATELY, AND VOTERS ALSO APPROVED THE NEW STATE CONSTITUTION.

WITH A NEW CONSTITUTION, THE NEW REPUBLICAN-MAJORITY STATE LEGISLATURE RATIFIED THE FOURTEENTH AMENDMENT, AND LOUISIANA WAS READMITTED INTO THE UNION.
ON JULY 11, 1868, DUNN TOOK THE OATH OF OFFICE, BECOMING THE FIRST BLACK LIEUTENANT GOVERNOR IN U.S. HISTORY.

IN THAT CAPACITY, DUNN WOULD ALSO SERVE AS THE PRESIDENT OF THE STATE SENATE. HE TONED DOWN HIS RHETORIC IN HIS FIRST ADDRESS TO THE LEGISLATURE.
AS TO MYSELF AND MY PEOPLE, WE ARE NOT SEEKING SOCIAL EQUALITY.
WE SIMPLY ASK TO BE ALLOWED AN EQUAL CHANCE IN THE RACE OF LIFE. AN EQUAL OPPORTUNITY OF SUPPORTING OUR FAMILIES, OF EDUCATING OUR CHILDREN AND OF BECOMING WORTHY CITIZENS OF THIS GOVERNMENT.

ACTIONS BY DUNN'S ALLIES IN THE LOUISIANA HOUSE, HOWEVER, REVEALED A MORE RADICAL AGENDA.
REP. R. H. ISABELLE, THE HOUSE CHAIRMAN, INTRODUCED A CIVIL RIGHTS BILL THAT WOULD PUNISH, WITH FINES OR IMPRISONMENT, OWNERS OF HOTELS, STEAMBOATS, RAILROADS, AND OTHER PUBLIC ENTITIES WHO DISCRIMINATED AGAINST PEOPLE BASED ON RACE OR COLOR.

THE NEW GOVERNOR, MEANWHILE, HARBORED SOME DISDAIN FOR HIS ADOPTED CITY, WHICH HE LATER ARTICULATED IN HIS MEMOIR.
NEW ORLEANS WAS A DIRTY, IMPOVERISHED, AND HOPELESS CITY, WITH A MIXED, IGNORANT, CORRUPT, AND BLOODTHIRSTY GANG IN CONTROL.
IT WAS FLOODED WITH LOTTERIES, GAMBLING DENS, AND LICENSED BROTHELS.
MANY OF THE CITY OFFICIALS, AS WELL AS THE POLICE FORCE, WERE THUGS AND MURDERERS.
VIOLENCE WAS RAMPANT, AND HARDLY A DAY PASSED THAT SOMEONE WAS NOT SHOT, OUT UNDER THE OAKS, IN DEFENSE OF HIS HONOR.

MINDFUL OF THE EVER-PRESENT SPECTER OF VIOLENCE, REPUBLICAN LEADERS INTRODUCED A METROPOLITAN POLICE BILL.
IT PLACED THE POLICE FORCES OF NEW ORLEANS AND THE SURROUNDING PARISHES IN THE HANDS OF A GOVERNOR-APPOINTED BOARD OF COMMISSIONERS, PRESIDED OVER BY THE LIEUTENANT GOVERNOR--DUNN.

THE **METROPOLITANS** INCLUDED 243 BLACK OFFICERS AND 130 WHITE OFFICERS AND REPRESENTED A SHOW OF STRENGTH FOR REPUBLICANS AS POLITICAL TENSIONS GREW.

PINCHBACK, NOW A STATE SENATOR, DELIVERED A FIERY MESSAGE TO WHITE DEMOCRATS CONSIDERING VIOLENCE AGAINST REPUBLICANS.
THE NEXT OUTRAGE . . . WILL BE THE SIGNAL FOR THE DAWN OF RETRIBUTION. . . .
FOR PATIENCE WILL THEN HAVE CEASED TO BE A VIRTUE AND **THIS CITY WILL BE REDUCED TO ASHES.**

LOUISIANA'S PARTISAN RANCOR RESEMBLED THE SITUATION IN WASHINGTON, WHERE THE HOUSE OF REPRESENTATIVES HAD RECENTLY IMPEACHED PRESIDENT JOHNSON.

JOHNSON SURVIVED HIS IMPEACHMENT TRIAL, BUT LOST THE DEMOCRATIC NOMINATION FOR PRESIDENT. THE PARTY RAN A TICKET OF HORATIO SEYMOUR AND FRANK BLAIR--THE LATTER AN UNAPOLOGETIC RACIST.

REPUBLICANS NOMINATED ULYSSES S. GRANT AND SCHUYLER COLFAX. GRANT, THE WAR HERO, INTENDED TO REVERSE JOHNSON'S HANDS-OFF COURSE ON RECONSTRUCTION. THE PROSPECT OF FEDERAL INTERVENTION UNDER GRANT LED TO VIOLENT BACKLASH IN THE SOUTH.

NEW ORLEANS REMAINED BITTERLY DIVIDED ALONG PARTY LINES, HAVING ELECTED DEMOCRATIC MAYOR JOHN R. CONWAY AT THE SAME TIME RURAL BLACK VOTERS PUT WARMOTH, DUNN, AND REPUBLICANS IN POWER AT THE STATE LEVEL.
DURING THE COURSE OF THE 1868 PRESIDENTIAL CAMPAIGN, THE PARTIES WOULD COME TO BLOWS IN NEW ORLEANS.

REMEMBER LINCOLN!!!
GRANT AND COLFAX
LET US HAVE PEACE
SEYMOUR MEANS SLAVER
NO COMPROMISE WITH THE REBELS!!!
LET US HAVE PEACE
ONE EVENING, TWO MOSTLY BLACK REPUBLICAN WARD CLUBS--SOCIAL AND POLITICAL ORGANIZATIONS THAT OFTEN PARADED IN THE STREETS--ASSEMBLED ON CANAL STREET.

A WHITE MAN TAUNTED THE PARADERS AS THEY PASSED.
SEYMOUR AND BLAIR!
THE MERE MENTION OF THE DEMOCRATIC TICKET HAD RACIST UNDERTONES. BLAIR WAS A PROUD WHITE SUPREMACIST WHO CRITICIZED REPUBLICANS FOR EMPOWERING "A SEMI-BARBAROUS RACE OF BLACKS."

DUMONTEIL'S CONFECTIONERY
WHITE AGITATORS DASHED INTO A NEARBY CONFECTIONERY.
SOME OF THE BLACK PARADERS CHASED AFTER THEM.

A BRAWL ERUPTED INSIDE THE SHOP.

BEFORE LONG, THE ENTIRE FRENCH QUARTER HAD BECOME A BATTLEFIELD AS OTHER PEOPLE JOINED THE MELEE.

Dumonteil's Confectionery

YOU WILL NEVER

MANY PEOPLE WERE INJURED, AND ONE BLACK MAN WAS KILLED.

THE UNREPENTANT VIOLENCE AGAINST BLACK PEOPLE WOULD HEIGHTEN THE DEBATE OVER CIVIL RIGHTS PROTECTIONS.

IF THIS BILL BRINGS ON A CONFLICT, LET IT COME! WE ARE **READY**!
CONSERVATIVE REPUBLICANS HAD RESISTED ISABELLE'S BILL, WHICH WOULD MAKE CIVIL RIGHTS VIOLATIONS PUNISHABLE BY A FINE OF UP TO $500 OR IMPRISONMENT OF UP TO ONE YEAR, BUT PURE RADICALS CONTINUED THEIR FIGHT.

THE BILL MADE IT ALL THE WAY TO THE DESK OF GOVERNOR WARMOTH, WHO MERE MONTHS EARLIER HAD BEEN ELECTED BY BLACK VOTERS ON A MESSAGE CHAMPIONING SUFFRAGE AND CIVIL RIGHTS.
PRESENTED WITH THE CHANCE TO ENSHRINE SOME OF THESE PROMISES, WARMOTH--ECHOING PRESIDENT JOHNSON--VETOED IT.

WARMOTH HAS VETOED THE BILL.
NO, THIS ISN'T POSSIBLE . . . HE *COULDN'T* . . .

THE MEANS PROPOSED . . . FOR ENFORCING THESE RIGHTS ARE . . . IMPRACTICABLE AND PERNICIOUS.
THE PREJUDICES UPON WHICH THESE BARRIERS ARE FOUNDED . . . WILL SURELY GIVE WAY TO THE SOFTENING INFLUENCES OF TIME.

DUNN CONSIDERED WARMOTH'S VETO OF THE CIVIL RIGHTS BILL AN UNFORGIVABLE BETRAYAL.
WARMOTH'S DECISION HELPED UNIFY THE PURE RADICAL FACTION, CREATING A COMMON CAUSE FOR OFT-DIVIDED ANGLO-AFRICAN AND AFRO-CREOLE LEADERS, ALONG WITH THEIR WHITE ALLIES.

WARMOTH'S BID TO PLACATE WHITES SHOWED FEW EARLY RETURNS.
INNOCENTS
HEAVILY ARMED DEMOCRATIC WARD CLUBS, ESPECIALLY A NOTORIOUS GROUP KNOWN AS THE INNOCENTS, ESCALATED THE STREET VIOLENCE.

THE DEMOCRATIC CLUBS RESENTED THE NEW MULTIRACIAL METROPOLITAN POLICE FORCE AND THE REPUBLICAN-LED LEGISLATURE.

THEY RANSACKED REPUBLICAN HOMES, BUSINESSES, AND CLUBROOMS, LOOTED AND DESTROYED PROPERTY, AND EVEN STOLE VOTER REGISTRATION CERTIFICATES.

THE INNOCENTS WENT A STEP FURTHER, OPENLY MURDERING BLACK BYSTANDERS IN THE STREETS OF NEW ORLEANS.
WITH ARMED DEMOCRATIC GROUPS OUTNUMBERING FEDERAL TROOPS, ANARCHY REIGNED IN THE LEAD-UP TO THE 1868 PRESIDENTIAL ELECTION. BLACK POLICE, FEARING FOR THEIR LIVES, STOPPED REPORTING TO WORK.

BLACK LOUISIANANS WERE VULNERABLE TO EXTREME VOTER SUPPRESSION AND TERROR EFFORTS BY ARMED WHITE GANGS, INCLUDING THE **KNIGHTS OF THE WHITE CAMELLIA,** AN AVOWED WHITE SUPREMACIST GROUP SIMILAR TO THE KU KLUX KLAN.

A WHITE MOB IN ST. LANDRY PARISH DESTROYED THE PRINTING PRESS OF A REPUBLICAN NEWSPAPER BEFORE WANTONLY MURDERING ROUGHLY 200 BLACK PEOPLE ON NEARBY PLANTATIONS.

WHITE MOBS MURDERED BLACK PEOPLE AND SYMPATHETIC WHITES IN ST. BERNARD PARISH, WHICH NEIGHBORS NEW ORLEANS. FEDERAL TROOPS, DISPATCHED TO PATROL ITS LEVEES, WERE FREQUENTLY SHOT AT BY THE MOBS.
GET OUT OF OUR STATE!

ONE EVENING OUTSIDE HIS HOME, DUNN WAS STARTLED BY A MAN RUNNING PAST HIM.
WHAT'S HAPPENED TO YOU, SIR?
I WAS PARADING WITH A REPUBLICAN CLUB, WHEN WHITE MEN STARTED SHOOTING AT US!
GO HOME AS SOON AS POSSIBLE, AND KEEP OUT OF DIFFICULTY.
THE REST OF THE NIGHT, DUNN'S FAMILY WAS TERRORIZED BY THE CONSTANT SOUND OF NEARBY GUNFIRE.

DAYS BEFORE THE ELECTION, A FURIOUS WHITE MOB GATHERED OUTSIDE OF CITY HALL.
DEATH TO GRANT!
DEATH TO ALL CARPETBAGGERS!
DEATH TO NIGGERS!
WE ARE GOING TO RULE!

DEMOCRATIC LEADERS MIXED DENUNCIATIONS OF RECONSTRUCTION WITH PLEAS FOR PEACE.
GO ON HOME. ALL WILL BE RIGHT WHEN SEYMOUR AND BLAIR ARE ELECTED.

MAYOR CONWAY SEEMED TO LEAVE THE DOOR OPEN FOR FUTURE CONFLICT.
PLEASE DISPERSE. WHEN I NEED YOUR HELP, I WILL CALL ON YOU.

CALL ON THEM, HE DID, WHEN MAYOR CONWAY ESTABLISHED HIS OWN ALL-WHITE POLICE FORCE TO COUNTER THE METROPOLITANS.

DUNN PRESENTED AN INJUNCTION FROM THE METROPOLITAN POLICE BOARD BARRING CONWAY FROM INTERFERING IN THE CITY'S POLICE MATTERS . . .

. . . BUT JUDGE WILLIAM COOLEY, A DEMOCRAT, RULED IN FAVOR OF CONWAY.

THE RULING ESTABLISHED RIVAL POLICE FORCES IN THE CITY, STOKING THE FLAMES FOR FUTURE CLASHES.

DESPITE REGISTERED REPUBLICANS OUTNUMBERING DEMOCRATS, SEYMOUR WON LOUISIANA IN A LANDSLIDE, TRIGGERING A STATE INVESTIGATION OF VOTER SUPPRESSION.
THOUSANDS OF BLACK VOTERS HAD AVOIDED THE POLLS, AND MANY CAST COERCED BALLOTS. DUNN HIMSELF DID NOT VOTE, FEARING VIOLENCE.

GRANT
AN OFFICIAL IN ONE PARISH SAID "NO MAN ON THAT DAY COULD HAVE VOTED ANY OTHER THAN THE DEMOCRATIC TICKET AND NOT BEEN KILLED INSIDE OF 24 HOURS."

GRANT WON THE PRESIDENCY WITHOUT LOUISIANA, THOUGH, CARRYING 26 STATES TO SEYMOUR'S 8.
IN HIS INAUGURAL ADDRESS, GRANT ENDORSED THE FIFTEENTH AMENDMENT TO THE U.S. CONSTITUTION, WHICH WOULD PROHIBIT FEDERAL OR STATE DENIAL OF VOTING RIGHTS BASED ON RACE, COLOR, OR PREVIOUS CONDITION OF SERVITUDE.

UNDER GRANT, CONGRESS WOULD PASS A SERIES OF ENFORCEMENT ACTS AND THE KU KLUX KLAN ACT, GIVING THE FEDERAL GOVERNMENT AUTHORITY TO PROSECUTE ELECTION FRAUD, BRIBERY, VOTER INTIMIDATION, AND WHITE TERRORISTS.

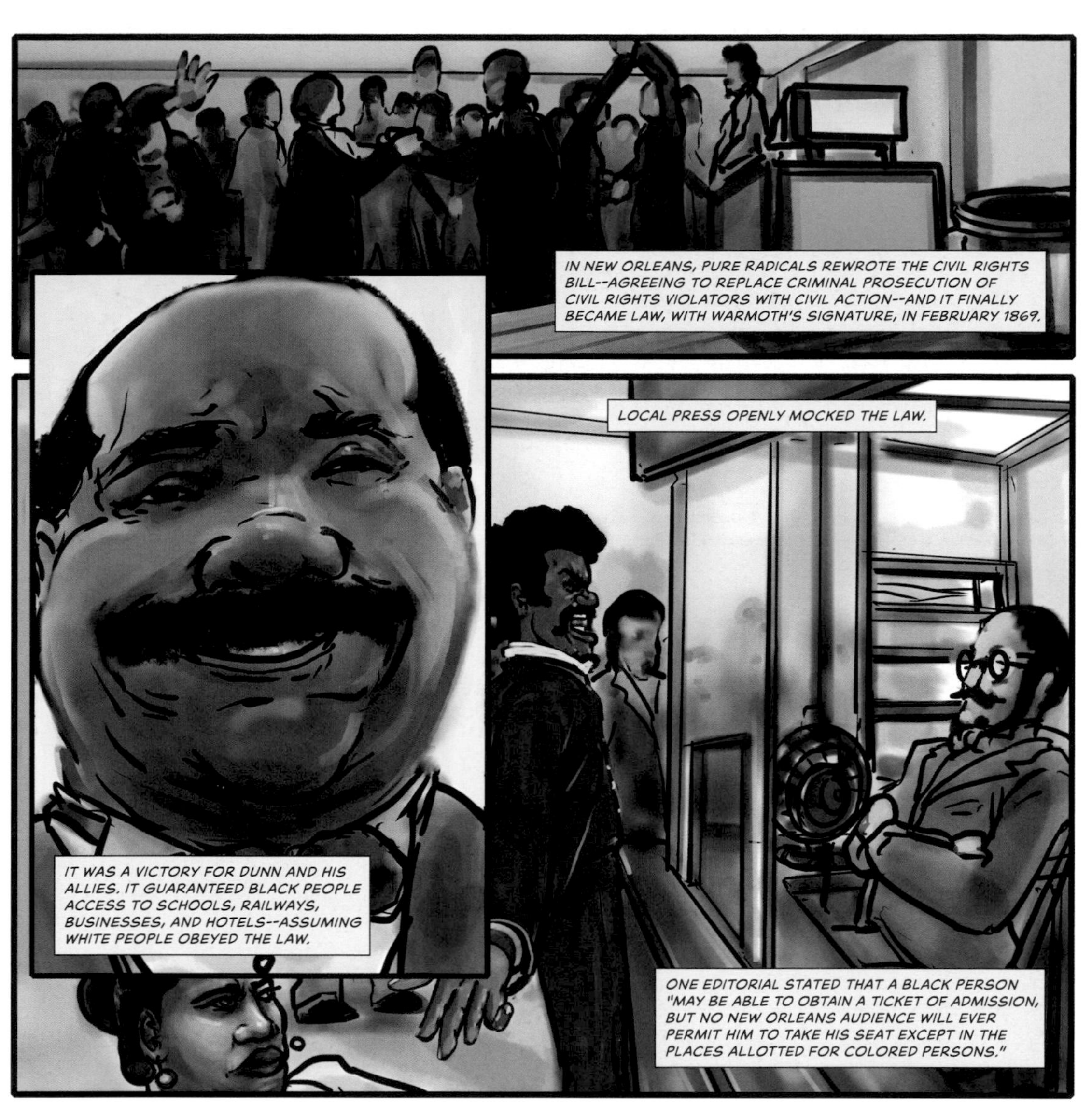
IN NEW ORLEANS, PURE RADICALS REWROTE THE CIVIL RIGHTS BILL--AGREEING TO REPLACE CRIMINAL PROSECUTION OF CIVIL RIGHTS VIOLATORS WITH CIVIL ACTION--AND IT FINALLY BECAME LAW, WITH WARMOTH'S SIGNATURE, IN FEBRUARY 1869.
IT WAS A VICTORY FOR DUNN AND HIS ALLIES. IT GUARANTEED BLACK PEOPLE ACCESS TO SCHOOLS, RAILWAYS, BUSINESSES, AND HOTELS--ASSUMING WHITE PEOPLE OBEYED THE LAW.
LOCAL PRESS OPENLY MOCKED THE LAW.
ONE EDITORIAL STATED THAT A BLACK PERSON "MAY BE ABLE TO OBTAIN A TICKET OF ADMISSION, BUT NO NEW ORLEANS AUDIENCE WILL EVER PERMIT HIM TO TAKE HIS SEAT EXCEPT IN THE PLACES ALLOTTED FOR COLORED PERSONS."

NEXT ON DUNN'S AGENDA: TO TRAVEL TO WASHINGTON, D.C., TO GO MEET THE NEW PRESIDENT.

NEW ORLEANS, MARCH 1869
DUNN FACED THE DIFFICULTY IN ENFORCING CIVIL RIGHTS HIMSELF WHEN REQUESTING A FIRST-CLASS SEAT FROM P. G. T. BEAUREGARD, THE EX-CONFEDERATE GENERAL WHO WAS NOW PRESIDENT OF THE LOCAL RAILROAD.
DUNN AND HIS TRAVELING PARTNER, A WHITE STATE SENATOR NAMED JOHN LYNCH, INTENDED TO DEPART THAT DAY, BUT BEAUREGARD MADE NO EFFORT TO HELP THEM.
MAY I EXPECT THE SAME ACCOMMODATIONS ON YOUR RAILROAD AS ARE EXTENDED TO OTHER PASSENGERS?

COLORED PEOPLE ARE NOT ALLOWED IN THE CAR OCCUPIED BY LADIES AND GENTLEMEN, OR WHITE GENTLEMEN.
I'VE PAID THE CUSTOMARY FARE, AND I HOLD A TICKET WHICH ENTITLES THE HOLDER TO THE ORDINARY ACCOMMODATIONS OF THE ROAD AND TO ADMISSION INTO THE CARS OPEN TO OTHER GENTLEMEN.

YOU CAN TAKE YOUR COMPLAINTS TO THE BOARD OF DIRECTORS, WHICH IS MEETING TONIGHT.
IF THE BOARD DOES NOT FEEL DISPOSED TO ACT TONIGHT, YOU COULD APPLY TO THE NEXT MEETING OF THE BOARD IN EIGHT TO TEN DAYS.

BEAUREGARD'S DEFIANCE OF THE NEW CIVIL RIGHTS LAW OUTRAGED DUNN AND LYNCH.

LYNCH IMMEDIATELY PENNED A LETTER TO BEAUREGARD PROTESTING DUNN'S TREATMENT.
Sir—some unknown person placed on my desk in the Senate chamber . . . a free pass for the year 1869, on the Jackson and Great Northern Railroad. I herewith return the "pass." I can be the recipient of no favors from any corporation governed by such rules as you stated today.
LYNCH JOINED DUNN IN THE POORLY KEPT "COLORED" CAR. IT LACKED SLEEPING ACCOMMODATIONS, SO THE MEN SAT UPRIGHT FOR THE DURATION OF THEIR OVERNIGHT JOURNEY.

THEY DISEMBARKED FROM THE TRAIN IN LOUISVILLE, KENTUCKY, AND TRANSFERRED TO A CROWDED, INDIANA-BOUND CARRIAGE, WHERE THE INDIGNITIES CONTINUED.

REMOVE HIM AT ONCE!
CHUCK HIM OUT THE WINDOW!

WE WILL NOT BE TREATED THIS WAY!
YOU CAN RIDE IN THE NIGGER'S CAR, ON TOP OF THE BUS.

DUNN AND LYNCH HIRED A PRIVATE CARRIAGE TO CARRY THEM AHEAD INSTEAD.

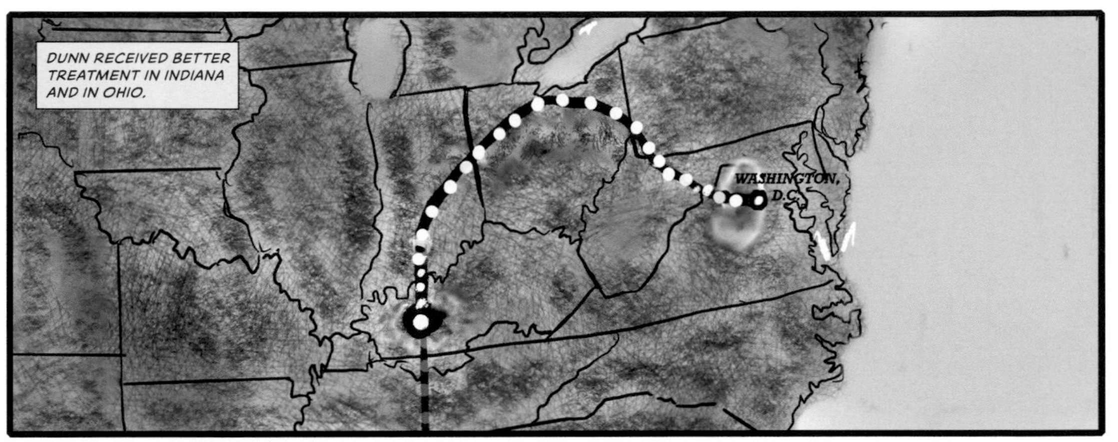
DUNN RECEIVED BETTER TREATMENT IN INDIANA AND IN OHIO.
WASHINGTON, D.C.

FROM CLEVELAND, HE ATTEMPTED TO TELEGRAPH THE WILLARD HOTEL IN WASHINGTON TO MAKE RESERVATIONS.

THE HOTEL'S PROPRIETORS DECLINED DUNN'S REQUEST, INFORMING HIM THAT IF HE SHOWED UP, THEY WOULD PROMPTLY TELL HIM THE HOTEL WAS FULL.

DUNN AND HIS PARTY FOUND ACCOMMODATIONS AT THE WASHINGTON HOUSE HOTEL INSTEAD.

WASHINGTON, D.C., APRIL 2, 1869

DUNN BECAME THE FIRST BLACK PUBLIC OFFICIAL EVER TO VISIT THE WHITE HOUSE.

GRANT AND DUNN SPOKE PRIVATELY FOR A HALF HOUR, DISCUSSING FEDERAL APPOINTMENTS IN NEW ORLEANS.
WE WOULD BE WELL SERVED TO SEAT MORE PURE RADICALS.
I AGREE, AND I PLAN TO.

DON'T HESITATE TO CALL ON ME AGAIN WHEN YOU'RE IN WASHINGTON.
REPUBLICAN PAPERS NOTED HOW MUCH BETTER DUNN WAS TREATED BY GRANT THAN BEAUREGARD, BUT THE DEMOCRATIC PRESS WAS INFURIATED BY THE LIEUTENANT GOVERNOR'S WARM RECEPTION.

DUNN VISITED THE U.S. SENATE NEXT. THE VISIT FROM THE TRAILBLAZING LIEUTENANT GOVERNOR WAS HIGHLY ANTICIPATED.
WITH NO AFRICAN AMERICANS YET IN CONGRESS, HE WAS THE NATION'S HIGHEST-RANKING BLACK ELECTED OFFICIAL.

DUNN MADE A POINT TO GREET ADMIRERS AND WELL-WISHERS IN THE CLOAKROOM UNTIL CHARLES SUMNER, A RADICAL REPUBLICAN SENATOR FROM MASSACHUSETTS, INVITED HIM ONTO THE SENATE FLOOR.

SOME SENATORS GAVE DUNN A DIGNITARY'S WELCOME, THOUGH OTHERS, LIKE GARRETT DAVIS OF KENTUCKY, REFUSED TO MEET HIM.

I WANT NO INTRODUCTION. NOT THAT I HAVE ANY OBJECTION TO THE NIGGER, FOR NO MAN WILL EXTEND MORE PROTECTION THAN I WILL WHEN HE IS IN HIS PROPER PLACE.

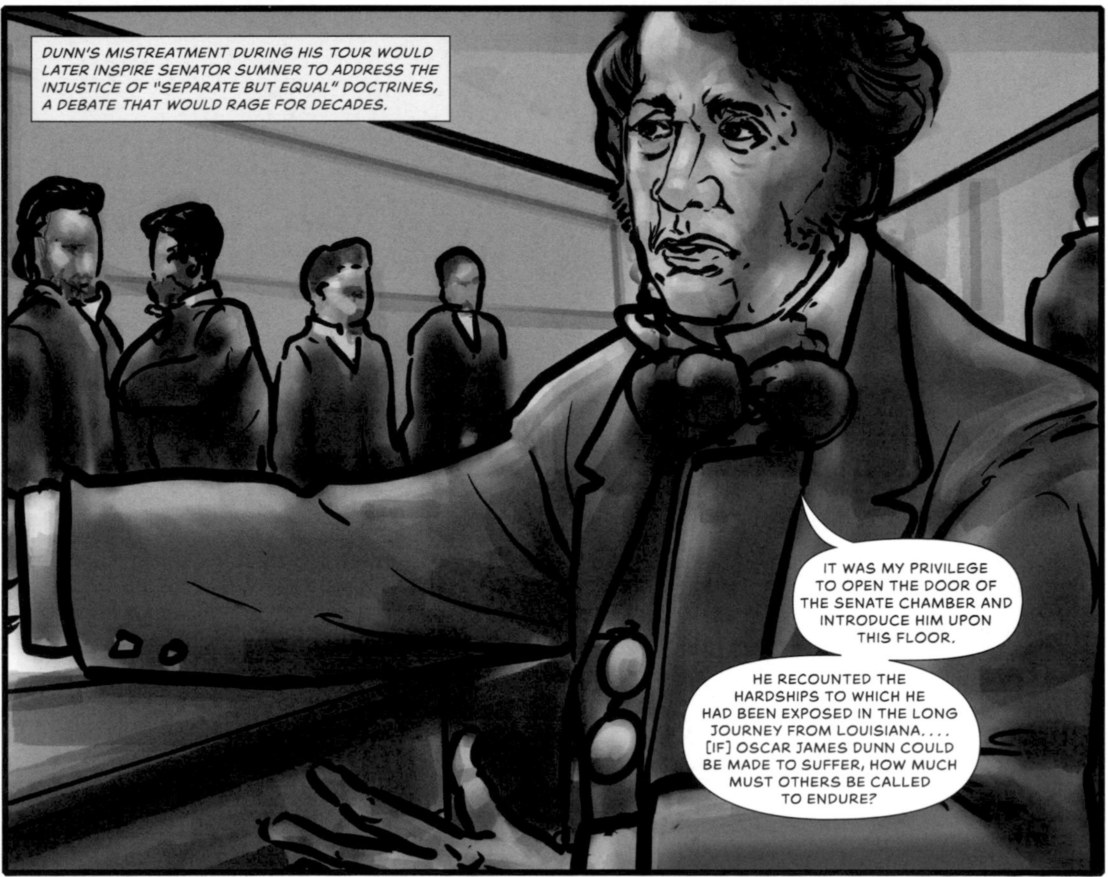
DUNN'S MISTREATMENT DURING HIS TOUR WOULD LATER INSPIRE SENATOR SUMNER TO ADDRESS THE INJUSTICE OF "SEPARATE BUT EQUAL" DOCTRINES, A DEBATE THAT WOULD RAGE FOR DECADES.
IT WAS MY PRIVILEGE TO OPEN THE DOOR OF THE SENATE CHAMBER AND INTRODUCE HIM UPON THIS FLOOR.
HE RECOUNTED THE HARDSHIPS TO WHICH HE HAD BEEN EXPOSED IN THE LONG JOURNEY FROM LOUISIANA. . . . [IF] OSCAR JAMES DUNN COULD BE MADE TO SUFFER, HOW MUCH MUST OTHERS BE CALLED TO ENDURE?

DUNN CONTINUED HIS POLITICAL JUNKET THROUGHOUT THE NORTHEAST.
BOSTON
IN BOSTON, DISTINGUISHED MEMBERS OF THE ABOLITIONIST MOVEMENT, INCLUDING REV. JOSHUA BOWEN SMITH AND WILLIAM LLOYD GARRISON, HELD A DINNER IN DUNN'S HONOR.
PHILADELPHIA
IN PHILADELPHIA, DUNN MET WITH JOSEPH JENKINS ROBERTS, LIBERIA'S FIRST PRESIDENT, AND EBENEZER BASSETT, WHO HAD RECENTLY BEEN APPOINTED BY PRESIDENT GRANT AS THE FIRST BLACK U.S. DIPLOMAT AND RESIDENT MINISTER TO HAITI.

NEW YORK CITY

IN NEW YORK, DUNN WAS FORCED TO SHARE QUARTERS WITH THE WAIT STAFF OF THE METROPOLITAN HOTEL, WHILE HIS WHITE COMPANIONS WERE PERMITTED TO HAVE THEIR OWN HOTEL ROOMS.

AT THE NEW YORK STOCK EXCHANGE, BROKERS HIRED A LOCAL BARBER TO IMPERSONATE DUNN, AND TOURED HIM AROUND THE EXCHANGE LIKE A DIGNITARY.
CAN YOU COMMENT ON THE FINANCIAL FITNESS OF LOUISIANA'S BONDS?
I BELIEVE BONDS ARE CHEAP AT PRESENT PRICES.
UH OH, THE LIEUTENANT GOVERNOR IS GOING TO GO SHORT ON US!
I . . . I MUST ADMIT, I HAVE NO IDEA WHAT YOU'RE TALKING ABOUT.

THE REAL DUNN RECEIVED BETTER TREATMENT AT REV. HENRY WARD BEECHER'S PLYMOUTH CHURCH IN BROOKLYN.
AFTER SUNDAY SERVICE, CONGREGANTS LINED UP TO SHAKE HANDS WITH THE HISTORY-MAKING LIEUTENANT GOVERNOR.

DUNN NEXT TOOK A TOUR OF WHITE AND BLACK NEW YORK PUBLIC SCHOOLS, WHERE HE WAS GREETED WITH ELABORATE ASSEMBLIES AND PERFORMANCES.
THANK YOU SO MUCH FOR THIS WARM WELCOME. I ENCOURAGE YOU ALL TO CONTINUE FURTHERING YOUR EDUCATIONS, AND PLEASE CALL UPON ME IF YOU SHOULD VISIT LOUISIANA.

BEFORE LEAVING NEW YORK, DUNN SENT A MESSAGE INVITING DEMOCRATIC MAYOR ABRAHAM OAKEY HALL TO A SOCIAL VISIT AT HIS HOTEL.

THE MAYOR'S RESPONSE MADE CLEAR THAT RACISM KNEW NO GEOGRAPHIC BOUNDS.
Should you call upon me for any reason other than official purposes, a police officer will put you out of your hotel.

DUNN'S JUNKET PRESENTED A MIXTURE OF INSULTS AND SALUTATIONS, BUT AS HE RETURNED TO NEW ORLEANS, HIS TRIP WAS HAILED AS A STEP FORWARD IN RACE RELATIONS.
DUNN HAD ESTABLISHED HIMSELF AS A NATIONAL POLITICAL STAR.

PART FIVE

IN NEED OF AN EXORCISM

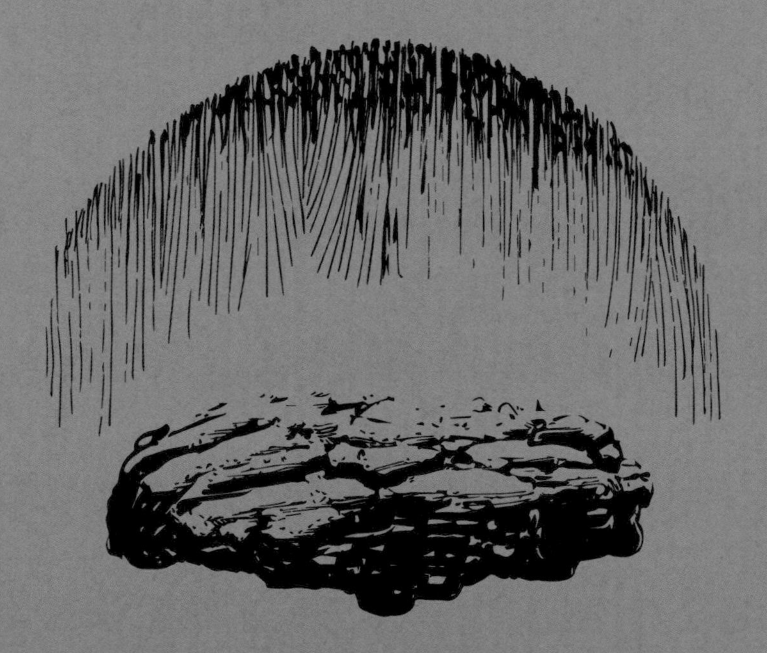

BARELY A MONTH AFTER RETURNING TO NEW ORLEANS, THE LIEUTENANT GOVERNOR LANDED IN JAIL.
HE HAD GOVERNOR WARMOTH TO BLAME.

THE LOUISIANA SUPREME COURT HAD RECENTLY UPHELD THE AUTHORITY OF THE METROPOLITAN POLICE IN THE CITIES SURROUNDING NEW ORLEANS . . .
. . . CLEARING THE WAY FOR WARMOTH, WITH AS MANY AS 400 FEDERAL TROOPS AND POLICE, TO TAKE OVER NEIGHBORING JEFFERSON CITY, A STRONGHOLD OF EX-CONFEDERATES AND A HAVEN OF OPPOSITION TO THE STATE GOVERNMENT.

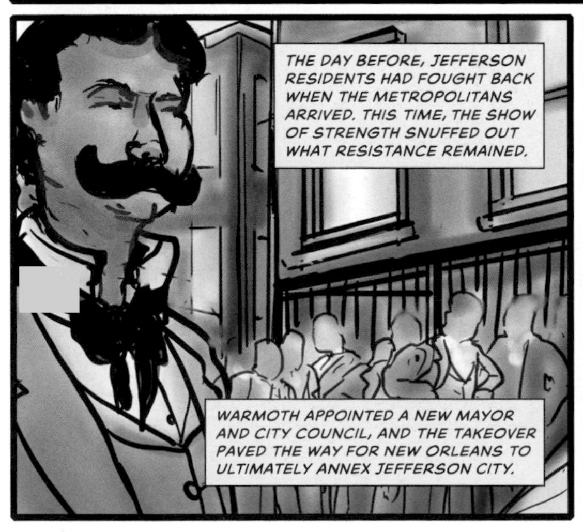
THE DAY BEFORE, JEFFERSON RESIDENTS HAD FOUGHT BACK WHEN THE METROPOLITANS ARRIVED. THIS TIME, THE SHOW OF STRENGTH SNUFFED OUT WHAT RESISTANCE REMAINED.
WARMOTH APPOINTED A NEW MAYOR AND CITY COUNCIL, AND THE TAKEOVER PAVED THE WAY FOR NEW ORLEANS TO ULTIMATELY ANNEX JEFFERSON CITY.

THE DEPOSED MAYOR OF JEFFERSON SUED, AND JUDGE COOLEY--THE SAME DEMOCRATIC JUDGE WHO RULED AGAINST THE METROPOLITANS BEFORE--FOUND THE POLICE IN CONTEMPT OF COURT.

IN THE COMING DAYS, DUNN BORE THE BULK OF THE BLAME FOR THE POLICE ACTIONS.

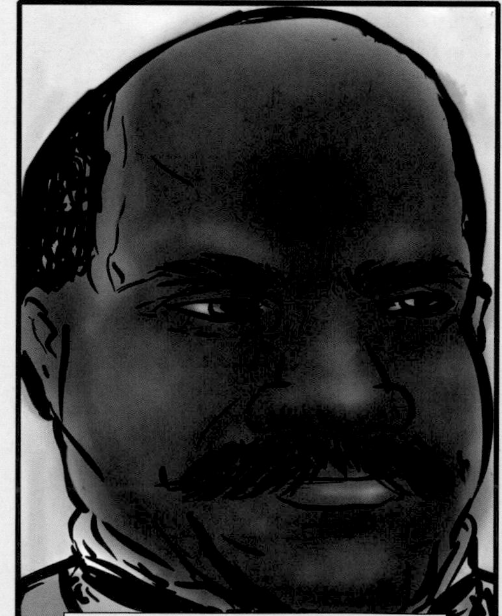

HOPING TO REGAIN CONTROL OVER THE FORCE, DUNN DEMANDED THAT MORE AFRICAN AMERICANS BE GRANTED POSITIONS OF AUTHORITY WITHIN THE METROPOLITANS.

RADICALS AND DEMOCRATS ALIKE WERE BEGINNING TO QUESTION WARMOTH'S CONSOLIDATION OF POWER THROUGH APPOINTMENTS, DISMISSALS, AND USE OF THE METROPOLITANS AS HIS OWN PRIVATE ARMY.

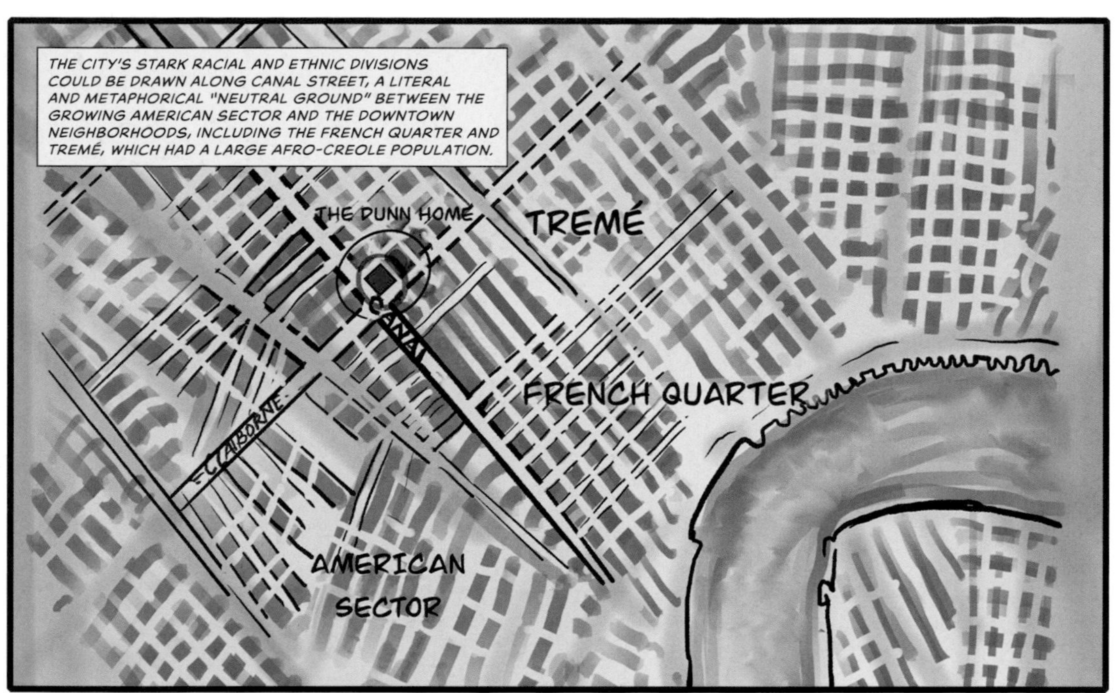
THE CITY'S STARK RACIAL AND ETHNIC DIVISIONS COULD BE DRAWN ALONG CANAL STREET, A LITERAL AND METAPHORICAL "NEUTRAL GROUND" BETWEEN THE GROWING AMERICAN SECTOR AND THE DOWNTOWN NEIGHBORHOODS, INCLUDING THE FRENCH QUARTER AND TREMÉ, WHICH HAD A LARGE AFRO-CREOLE POPULATION.
THE DUNN HOME
TREMÉ
CANAL
CLAIBORNE
FRENCH QUARTER
AMERICAN SECTOR

NEAR THE END OF 1869, DUNN PURCHASED A NEW, LARGE HOUSE LOCATED DIRECTLY ALONG THIS DIVIDING LINE, STRADDLING TWO WORLDS.

IN A CONSPICUOUS GESTURE TO HIS FIERCEST RIVALS, DUNN DRAPED THE HOUSE IN BLACK AFTER THE DEATH OF FORMER CONFEDERATE GEN. ROBERT E. LEE IN 1870. DEMOCRATS PRAISED HIM FOR IT.

TURNERS' HALL, NEW ORLEANS
THOUGH HE WON ADMIRATION FROM POLITICAL RIVALS, DUNN COULDN'T ESCAPE RACISM IN HIS SOCIAL LIFE.

IN MARCH 1870, MEMBERS OF THE NEW ORLEANS TURNERS' ASSOCIATION, A GERMAN SOCIAL ORGANIZATION, INVITED DUNN AS A SPECIAL GUEST TO A MASQUERADE BALL.

PLEASE WELCOME LIEUTENANT GOVERNOR **OSCAR J. DUNN**!
WHAT A **DISGRACE!**
HOW **DARE** THEY TRY TO FORCE HIM ON US!

THE ORGANIZATION'S LEADERSHIP ADOPTED RESOLUTIONS CONDEMNING HIS INVITATION AS A "VIOLATION OF DECENCY" AND STATING THAT A SMALL GROUP OF MEMBERS FOR "SELFISH AND PERSONAL REASONS" TRIED TO ADVOCATE "SOCIAL EQUALITY OF THE RACES."
THE SCANDAL REACHED THE NATIONAL TURNERS' ASSOCIATION, WHICH SUPPORTED THE MEMBERS WHO HAD INVITED DUNN AND THREATENED TO EXPEL THE NEW ORLEANS CHAPTER FOR ITS TREATMENT OF DUNN AND THOSE MEMBERS.

TO COMBAT THE RACIAL TERROR THAT HAD PLAGUED THE 1868 ELECTION, WARMOTH WORKED WITH THE STATE LEGISLATURE TO PASS VOTER REGISTRATION AND ELECTION LAWS THAT PUT HIM SOLELY IN CHARGE OF THE STATE'S ELECTORAL MACHINERY.
HE INTENDED TO PROTECT BLACK VOTERS, BUT THE MOVE DOUBLED AS AN UNPRECEDENTED EXPANSION OF EXECUTIVE POWER.

HE CONSOLIDATED POWER IN OTHER WAYS, TOO, MAKING CONTROVERSIAL DISMISSALS AND APPOINTMENTS TO OFFICIAL POSITIONS, REPLACING POLITICAL RIVALS WITH ALLIES.

HIS ADMINISTRATION INITIALLY SOUGHT TO DIG THE CITY AND STATE OUT OF DEBT, BUT AS IT COZIED UP TO WEALTHY BUSINESSMEN, IT WAS TAINTED BY CORRUPTION.

LOBBYISTS FOR LEVEE, CANAL, AND RAILROAD INTERESTS, ACCORDING TO WARMOTH HIMSELF, "CROWDED THE HALLS OF THE LEGISLATURE, AND THRONGED THE AVENUES LEADING TO THE CAPITOL, TAKING OUT MEMBER AFTER MEMBER, SUGGESTING BRIBES."
REPUBLICANS AND DEMOCRATS, BLACK AND WHITE, PARTICIPATED.

DUNN'S INTEGRITY WAS NOTED IN THE PRESS, ALBEIT IN RACIST TERMS. THE NEW YORK HERALD WROTE: "HE REFUSED A $10,000 BRIBE TO SIGN A RAILROAD BILL. HIS CHARACTER IS AS SPOTLESS AS HIS FACE IS BLACK."

SIR, MY CONSCIENCE IS **NOT** FOR SALE.
STAYING OUT OF THE FRAY HIMSELF, DUNN GREW INCREASINGLY FRUSTRATED WITH WARMOTH'S LEADERSHIP.

THOUSANDS OF DOLLARS MEANT FOR FREEDMEN'S BUREAU SCHOOLS IN SEVERAL PARISHES VANISHED WITHOUT EXPLANATION.

MANY POLITICIANS USED THEIR OFFICES TO ENRICH THEMSELVES. IN HIS ROLE ON THE NEW ORLEANS PARK COMMISSION, P. B. S. PINCHBACK PROFITED FROM INFLATED PURCHASES OF LAND THAT HE CO-OWNED. HE ALSO MADE HUGE SUMS SPECULATING IN STATE BONDS.
HE LATER ADMITTED, "I BELONGED TO THE GENERAL ASSEMBLY, AND KNEW ABOUT WHAT IT WOULD DO.... MY INVESTMENTS WERE MADE ACCORDINGLY."

WARMOTH FOUGHT BACK AGAINST SOME OF THE CORRUPTION--VETOING PARTICULARLY SCANDALOUS BILLS PASSED BY THE LEGISLATURE AND TURNING DOWN NUMEROUS BRIBES HIMSELF.
BUT HE, TOO, PROFITED FROM HIS POSITION, MAKING A GREAT DEAL OF MONEY SPECULATING IN STATE BONDS AND TREASURY NOTES. IT WAS REPORTED THAT WARMOTH MADE $1 MILLION DURING HIS TERM AS GOVERNOR, ON AN $8,000 ANNUAL SALARY.

WARMOTH MUST GO!
IN JANUARY 1870, A MOB GATHERED IN LAFAYETTE SQUARE EXPRESSING OUTRAGE AT THE RAMPANT CORRUPTION.
THE LEGISLATORS LINE THEIR POCKETS WHILE WE SUFFER!
THERE ARE MANY PERSONS IN THE LEGISLATURE WHO HAD BEEN RECENTLY ENFRANCHISED AND ARE IGNORANT OF THE MANIPULATIONS OF THE LOBBYMEN.
YOU CHARGE THE LEGISLATURE WITH PASSING CORRUPTLY MANY BILLS LOOKING TO THE PERSONAL AGGRANDIZEMENT OF INDIVIDUALS AND CORPORATIONS.
LET ME SUGGEST TO YOU THAT THOSE INDIVIDUALS AND CORPORATIONS ARE YOUR VERY BEST PEOPLE.
WARMOTH DEFLECTED THE BLAME.

WARMOTH WOULD LATER MAKE A BLUNT ADMISSION TO A CHICAGO TRIBUNE REPORTER.
I DON'T PRETEND TO BE HONEST. I ONLY PRETEND TO BE AS HONEST AS ANYBODY IN POLITICS.
WHY, DAMN IT, EVERYBODY IS DEMORALIZED DOWN HERE. CORRUPTION IS THE FASHION.

IN EARLY 1870, AFTER CONTROVERSIALLY DISMISSING THE STATE AUDITOR, WARMOTH LANDED IN FRONT OF A GRAND JURY, WHERE HE REFUSED TO ANSWER QUESTIONS RELATED TO CORRUPTION.

SOLDIERS' JOY CHAPEL, NEW ORLEANS
THE CITY, IT COULD'VE BEEN SAID, WAS IN NEED OF AN EXORCISM. IN THE SPRING OF 1870, IT GOT ONE.
THE NEW YORK HERALD REPORTED THAT 400 SPECTATORS, INCLUDING DUNN, PACKED INTO A CHURCH TO WITNESS THE EXORCISM OF REV. JOHN TURNER.
TURNER, WHO OFFICIATED AT DUNN'S WEDDING, WAS ALSO A MEMBER OF HIS MASONIC LODGE AND THE CHAPLAIN FOR THE STATE LEGISLATURE.
WOOF! WOOF!
MEOW!
TURNER, THE STORY WENT, HAD BEGUN INVOLUNTARILY MAKING CAT AND DOG SOUNDS.
FAILING TO FIND A CONVENTIONAL CURE, HE CALLED UPON A WOMAN KNOWN AS MADAME LOTT, THE SISTER OF A STATE LEGISLATOR AND REPORTEDLY A VOODOO PRACTITIONER.
"VOODOO" HERE REFERS TO THE RELIGION UNIQUE TO THE SOUTHERN U.S. THAT SHARES ROOTS WITH OTHERS IN THE AFRICAN DIASPORA. THE TERM IS OFTEN MISAPPLIED TO THE KIND OF SENSATIONAL ACTS THE CROWD CAME TO SEE THIS DAY.
THE FAMOUS VOODOO PRACTITIONER MARIE LAVEAU STILL HELD REMARKABLE INFLUENCE IN NEW ORLEANS, BUT WAS GETTING OLDER.
THIS EVENT WAS BILLED AS MADAME LOTT'S "HOUR OF FORTUNE."

MEOW!
THE WHITE PRESS TRIED TO DISCREDIT BLACK LEADERS BY ASSOCIATING THEM WITH SUCH SCENES. THE ACCOUNT OF DUNN'S ATTENDANCE AT THE EXORCISM WAS REPEATED IN PAPERS ACROSS THE COUNTRY. TO THIS DAY, IT IS DIFFICULT TO ASSESS ITS VALIDITY.

AS MADAME LOTT GOT CLOSER TO TURNER, SHE SWOONED . . .

. . . AND SANK TO THE FLOOR.

AN ASSISTANT EMERGED FROM THE CROWD AND SPRINKLED MADAME LOTT'S FACE WITH WATER.
SHE ROSE AGAIN AND CONTINUED HER WALK TOWARD TURNER.
THIS MAN HAS BEEN BEWITCHED BY 12 INDIVIDUALS, NINE MEN AND THREE WOMEN.
NINE OF THE INDIVIDUALS RESPONSIBLE ARE CURRENTLY IN THIS CHURCH, AND THREE LEFT SHORTLY AFTER MY ENTRANCE!

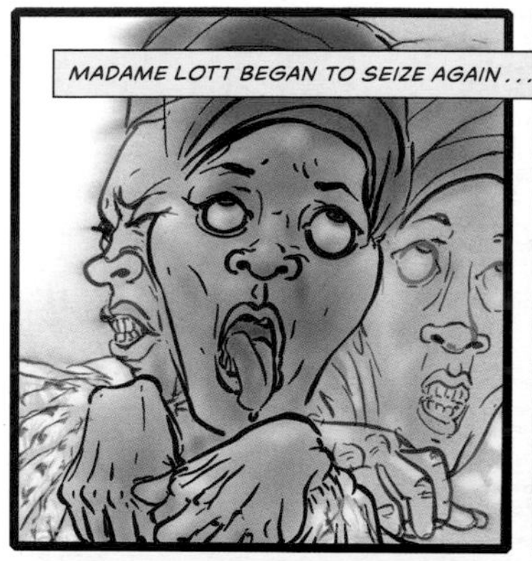
MADAME LOTT BEGAN TO SEIZE AGAIN . . .

. . . BUT, THIS TIME, ROSE TO HER FEET WITHOUT ASSISTANCE.

SHE USED A WAND TO EXTRACT A MOUSE-LIKE CREATURE FROM A CRACK IN THE FLOOR . . .

. . . THEN EXITED TO THE CHURCH YARD.

IN THE YARD, SHE PULLED A MINIATURE COFFIN FROM BENEATH A BRICK . . .

. . . AND THEN RETURNED TO THE SANCTUARY.

MADAME LOTT TOSSED THE CREATURE AND COFFIN INTO THE FLAMES OF THE CHURCH STOVE.

I AM FREE OF THE CURSE!

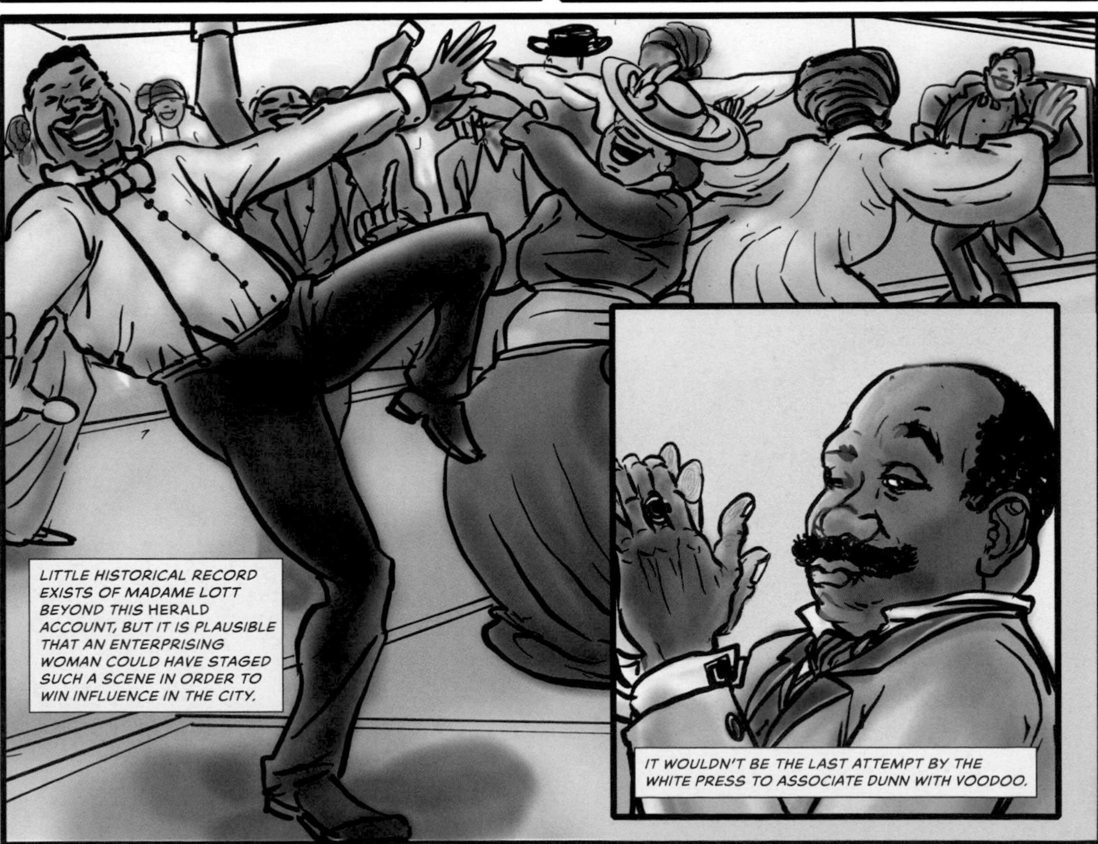
LITTLE HISTORICAL RECORD EXISTS OF MADAME LOTT BEYOND THIS HERALD ACCOUNT, BUT IT IS PLAUSIBLE THAT AN ENTERPRISING WOMAN COULD HAVE STAGED SUCH A SCENE IN ORDER TO WIN INFLUENCE IN THE CITY.
IT WOULDN'T BE THE LAST ATTEMPT BY THE WHITE PRESS TO ASSOCIATE DUNN WITH VOODOO.

PART SIX

NO GREATER DIVIDE

DUNN WORKED CLOSELY WITH HIS AFRO-CREOLE ALLIES IN THE FIGHT FOR CIVIL RIGHTS, BUT HE DISAGREED WITH THEM ON ASPECTS OF THE INTEGRATION DEBATE.

AFRO-CREOLE LEADERS, MANY OF THEM IDENTIFYING AS PART OF AN ELITE ANTEBELLUM CLASS, ENVISIONED FULL INTEGRATION ACROSS SOCIETY, WHILE DUNN WAS A FIERCE ADVOCATE OF BLACK PATRONAGE OF BLACK LODGES . . .

. . . CHURCHES . . .

. . . AND BUSINESSES.

AS WITH THE PEOPLE'S BAKERY PROJECT, DUNN BELIEVED SOLIDARITY WITHIN THESE FRATERNAL, RELIGIOUS, AND SOCIAL ENTITIES FORMED THE FOUNDATION OF BLACK EMPOWERMENT.

DUNN AGREED WITH HIS AFRO-CREOLE COUNTERPARTS, HOWEVER, ON INTEGRATING VITAL SERVICES LIKE RAILROADS . . .

. . . AND PUBLIC SCHOOLS.

EDUCATION HAD ALWAYS PLAYED A VITAL ROLE IN DUNN'S LIFE . . .

. . . AND HIS WIFE, ELLEN'S. SHE'D RECEIVED AN EDUCATION PRIOR TO THE CIVIL WAR, AND THEY BOTH HAD EXPERIENCE AS TEACHERS.

DUNN HAD TRIED AND FAILED TO MANDATE THE INTEGRATION OF PUBLIC SCHOOLS WHEN HE WAS ON THE CITY COUNCIL, AND HE WAS A FORCE BEHIND THE 1868 LAW THAT FORBADE SCHOOL SEGREGATION.
BUT FOR TWO YEARS, SCHOOLS HAD USED LAWSUITS AND OTHER TACTICS TO AVOID INTEGRATION, AND WARMOTH WASN'T PUSHING THE ISSUE.

BY 1870, HOWEVER, DUNN'S PURE RADICAL ALLIES HAD TAKEN CONTROL OF THE SCHOOL BOARD, AND CHANGE WAS ON THE HORIZON.

MECHANICS' INSTITUTE
DUNN'S POLITICAL MOMENT ARRIVED, AND THE DIVIDE IN THE LOUISIANA REPUBLICAN PARTY WAS FULLY EXPOSED, AT THE 1870 PARTY CONVENTION.
DUNN AND WARMOTH WERE BOTH NOMINATED FOR THE PRESIDENCY OF THE CONVENTION.

IT IS THE FIRST TIME, I BELIEVE IN THE HISTORY OF THE UNION . . . THAT A GOVERNOR AND LIEUTENANT GOVERNOR HAVE BEEN CANDIDATES AGAINST EACH OTHER FOR THE PRESIDENCY OF THE CONVENTION.
DUNN WAS ELECTED 54-43, IN AN EMBARRASSING BLOW TO WARMOTH.

I LIKE THE GOVERNOR VERY WELL.
I THANK YOU, GENTLEMEN OF THE CONVENTION, FOR THE COMPLIMENT YOU HAVE PAID ME IN ELECTING ME OVER HIM.

WE SEE ONE CLASS OF REPUBLICANS FORCED TO ASK ANOTHER CLASS OF REPUBLICANS FOR THEIR RIGHTS.
I AM REMINDED OF THE REVOLUTIONARY ORATOR WHO SAID, "WE ASK FOR PEACE, PEACE, AND THERE IS NO PEACE." SO WITH THE COLORED; THEY ASK FOR PROTECTION, PROTECTION, AND THERE IS NO PROTECTION.
HOSTILITIES TOWARD WARMOTH ERUPTED ON THE CONVENTION'S LAST DAY. PURE RADICALS, FRUSTRATED WITH THE ENFORCEMENT OF THE CIVIL RIGHTS LAW, CALLED HIM OUT FOR REFUSING TO SUPPORT A RESOLUTION THAT WOULD MAKE CIVIL RIGHTS VIOLATIONS CRIMINAL OFFENSES.

WARMOTH DEFENDED HIS ACTIONS.
FROM ALL THAT HAS BEEN SAID, IT MIGHT BE THOUGHT THAT I AND I ONLY AM PREVENTING COLORED MEN FROM BEING TREATED AS THE EQUALS OF WHITES. . . .
IF MY SIGNATURE WOULD ACCOMPLISH ALL THAT IS EXPECTED FROM THE BILL I WOULD SIGN IT TODAY!
PUT YOUR SIGNATURE TO IT AND WE WILL ENFORCE THE LAW!
THE RESOLUTION WAS NOT INTRODUCED FOR THE GOOD OF THE REPUBLICAN PARTY.
IT WAS INTRODUCED TO PRODUCE DISCORD.
IT CAME FROM A CLIQUE OF MALCONTENTS, HEADED BY THE NEW ORLEANS TRIBUNE, WHO WERE OPPOSED TO ME BECAUSE I WOULD NOT GIVE OFFICE TO EVERY MAN THEY WANTED ME TO APPOINT.
THE TRIBUNE HAD CLOSED SHOP ONLY MONTHS EARLIER.
THE OPPOSITION CAME FROM MEN WHO ENTERED THE REPUBLICAN PARTY WHEN THE PATH WAS EASY AND PRETTY . . .
. . . FROM MEN WHO HAD BOUGHT AND SOLD NEGROES . . .
. . . FROM MEN WHO HAD SERVED IN THE CONFEDERATE ARMY . . .
. . . AND FROM A FEW OTHERS WHO CONSIDERED THEMSELVES THE CREAM OF THE REPUBLICAN PARTY.

THESE MEN SHOULD BE PUT OUT OF THE PARTY. HARMONY WOULD THEN BE SECURED!

POSTMASTER CHARLES W. LOWELL ACCUSED WARMOTH OF USING THE POLICE TO BEAT CITIZENS BUT NOT TO ENFORCE CIVIL RIGHTS, ELICITING OBJECTIONS FROM THE CROWD THAT DUNN OVERRULED.
THE GOVERNOR COULD ENFORCE THE RIGHTS OF COLORED MEN. . . .
WE DON'T WANT TO HEAR ANY MORE OF YOUR DEMAGOGUERY AND NONSENSE!
I HAVE HEARD A GREAT DEAL OF WHAT THE GENTLEMAN CALLS NONSENSE ALREADY, AND I SHALL LISTEN TO THIS.
THE STATEMENT THAT I USED THE METROPOLITAN FORCE FOR THAT PURPOSE IS A FALSEHOOD! THE MAN WHO REPEATS IT IS AS BIG A LIAR AS THE MAN WHO SAID IT.
THE CONVENTION ENDED AWKWARDLY AFTER THE GOVERNOR'S ERUPTION.
DESPITE INTERNAL STRIFE, REPUBLICANS PERFORMED WELL IN THE LOUISIANA ELECTIONS THAT FALL.
WITH WARMOTH IN CHARGE OF ELECTION RETURNS, VOTER INTIMIDATION WAS SIGNIFICANTLY DOWN FROM THE 1868 ELECTIONS.

FEELING THREATENED BY DUNN AND THE PURE RADICALS, WARMOTH TRAVELED TO WASHINGTON TO ASK PRESIDENT GRANT TO REMOVE THEIR ALLIES--INCLUDING POSTMASTER LOWELL AND US MARSHAL STEPHEN B. PACKARD--FROM INFLUENTIAL FEDERAL POSITIONS AT THE US CUSTOMHOUSE IN NEW ORLEANS.

WARMOTH PLANNED TO PLEDGE LOYALTY TO GRANT IN THE UPCOMING ELECTION IN EXCHANGE FOR HAVING HIS ALLIES APPOINTED TO CUSTOMHOUSE POSITIONS.
GRANT, HOWEVER, HAD A WELL-KNOWN DISTRUST OF WARMOTH.

DURING THE CIVIL WAR, WARMOTH, A LIEUTENANT COLONEL, HAD TAKEN A LEAVE OF ABSENCE AFTER BEING WOUNDED AT VICKSBURG.
UPON HIS RETURN, GENERAL GRANT DISHONORABLY DISCHARGED HIM FOR MALINGERING--EXAGGERATING HIS INJURY--AND SPREADING FALSE ACCOUNTS OF UNION LOSSES.

WARMOTH HAD HAD TO MAKE A PERSONAL PLEA TO PRESIDENT LINCOLN TO BE REINSTATED.

NOW WITH GRANT THE PRESIDENT AND WARMOTH A GOVERNOR, TENSION REMAINED. GRANT GRUDGINGLY AGREED TO NOMINATE A WARMOTH SUPPORTER IN PLACE OF LOWELL . . .

. . . BUT THE SENATE REJECTED THE NOMINATION, AND LOWELL KEPT HIS JOB. WARMOTH WAS FURIOUS.

NOT LONG AFTER WARMOTH'S VISIT, DUNN AND LOUISIANA SENATOR WILLIAM PITT KELLOGG VISITED GRANT IN WASHINGTON, WHERE THE PRESIDENT SHARED HIS PERSONAL OPPOSITION TO WARMOTH'S RECOMMENDATIONS.
DUNN'S PURE RADICAL FACTION WOULD INCREASINGLY ALIGN AND OVERLAP WITH GRANT'S ALLIES IN THE NEW ORLEANS CUSTOMHOUSE, UNITED AGAINST WARMOTH.

BY CHRISTMAS 1870, A COURT HAD RULED DECISIVELY THAT THE SCHOOLS SHOULD BE DESEGREGATED WITHIN THE MONTH, THREE YEARS AFTER DUNN FIRST INTRODUCED A SCHOOL INTEGRATION BILL ON THE CITY COUNCIL.
NEW ORLEANS WAS ABOUT TO EMBARK ON A HISTORIC INTEGRATION EFFORT UNLIKE ANY OTHER IN THE NATION.

TO INSPIRE OTHER BLACK PARENTS, THE DUNNS ENROLLED THEIR DAUGHTERS FANNY AND EMMA, AS WELL AS AN ADOPTED CHILD NAMED CHARLOTTE KENNEDY, AS THE FIRST BLACK CHILDREN ADMITTED TO THE MADISON GIRLS' SCHOOL.

ELEVEN BLACK BOYS ENROLLED AT TWO WHITE SCHOOLS AT THE SAME TIME. IT'S UNKNOWN WHETHER THE DUNNS' SON, CHARLES, WAS ONE OF THEM.

MANY TEACHERS RESIGNED IN PROTEST . . .
. . . AND WHITE ENROLLMENT PLUNGED AS PARENTS WITHDREW THEIR STUDENTS. THE NUMBER OF PRIVATE AND PAROCHIAL SCHOOLS IN THE CITY BOOMED TO ACCOMMODATE THE EXODUS OF WHITE STUDENTS FROM PUBLIC SCHOOLS.

BUT AFTER THE INITIAL OUTBURST, MANY WHITE PARENTS QUIETLY RE-ENROLLED THEIR STUDENTS IN THE INTEGRATED SCHOOLS.

OVER THE NEXT FEW YEARS, THE NEW ORLEANS INTEGRATION EXPERIMENT APPEARED TO BE WORKING.
AS MANY AS A THOUSAND BLACK STUDENTS AND SEVERAL THOUSAND WHITE STUDENTS ATTENDED DESEGREGATED SCHOOLS TOGETHER IN THE CITY. NOTHING LIKE IT WAS TAKING PLACE ANYWHERE ELSE IN THE COUNTRY.

MEANWHILE, RACIAL TENSIONS AMONG REPUBLICANS BUBBLED OVER AGAIN IN EARLY 1871 WHEN ONE OF LOUISIANA'S U.S. SENATE SEATS OPENED UP. AT THE TIME, SENATORS WERE SELECTED BY STATE LEGISLATURES.
THOUGH DUNN WAS AN EARLY CONTENDER, P. B. S. PINCHBACK, WHO'D STAYED OUT OF THE FRAY DURING THE RAUCOUS CONVENTION, EMERGED AS THE PREFERRED CANDIDATE OF BLACK LEGISLATORS.

WARMOTH SUPPORTED JOSEPH R. WEST, A CONSERVATIVE UNION VETERAN, WHO BECAME THE FAVORITE AMONG WHITE LEGISLATORS OF BOTH PARTIES. THE NEW YORK HERALD REPORTED THAT WEST WAS WILLING TO SPEND AS MUCH AS $500,000 FOR THE SEAT.
WHEN IT BECAME CLEAR WEST WOULD HAVE THE VOTES TO WIN, PINCHBACK ASSAILED HIS FELLOW REPUBLICANS.
WE SAID, WHEN WE STARTED, THAT WE WERE IN FAVOR OF RECOGNIZING THE POLITICAL RIGHTS OF ALL MEN. . . .
I BELIEVED, AND I SO STATED, THAT THEY WOULD BE WILLING TO SEE THE COLORED MAN HOLD UNIMPORTANT PLACES, BUT I DID NOT BELIEVE, WHEN IT CAME TO A SQUARE VOTE, THAT THEY WOULD SUPPORT HIM FOR IMPORTANT OFFICES. . . .
I AM, UNFORTUNATELY, THE INSTRUMENT BY WHICH THIS LESSON HAS BEEN TAUGHT THE PEOPLE OF LOUISIANA.
I AM THE GOAT DRAWN UP TO THE ALTAR TO BE SACRIFICED.

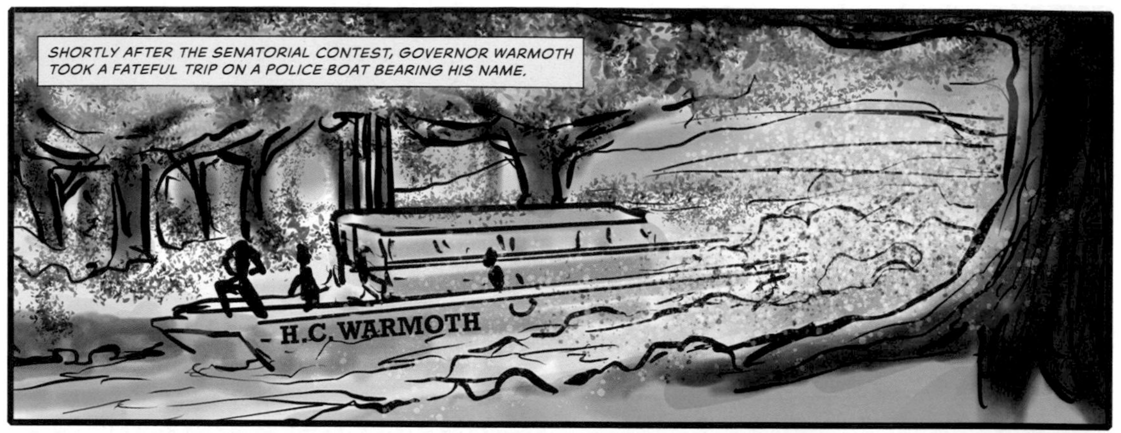
SHORTLY AFTER THE SENATORIAL CONTEST, GOVERNOR WARMOTH TOOK A FATEFUL TRIP ON A POLICE BOAT BEARING HIS NAME.
H.C. WARMOTH

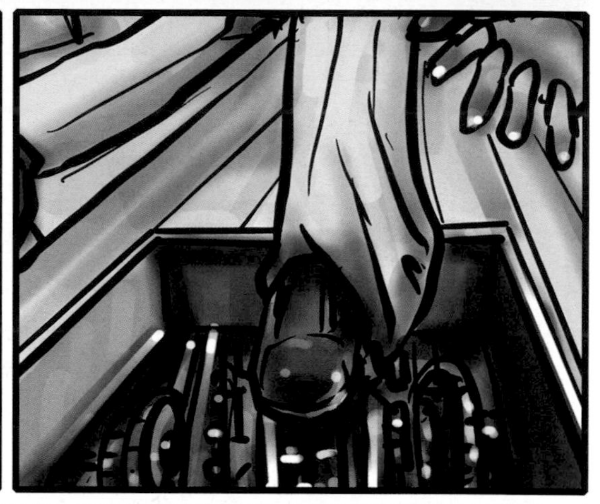

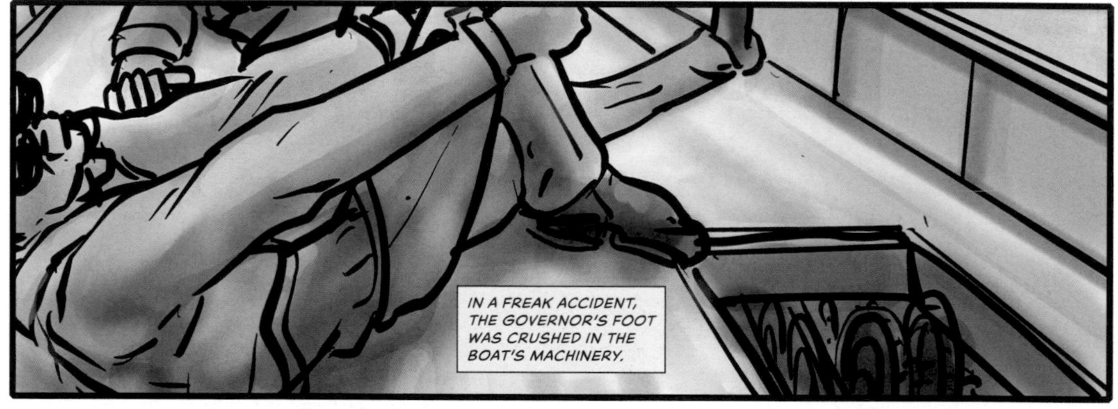
IN A FREAK ACCIDENT, THE GOVERNOR'S FOOT WAS CRUSHED IN THE BOAT'S MACHINERY.

WARMOTH'S INJURY REQUIRED SURGERY, FOLLOWED BY A PROLONGED RECOVERY AT HOME.

THE GOVERNOR'S ABSENCE AND INJURY WERE THE SUBJECTS OF INTENSE RUMOR.
I HEAR HE MIGHT DIE FROM HIS INJURIES.
I HEARD OSCAR DUNN PLANS TO TAKE OVER.
WHAT IF THIS IS SOME RUSE ORCHESTRATED TO PUT ME IN A COMPROMISED POLITICAL POSITION?
THEN WHO WILL RUN THE STATE?
WITH WARMOTH'S STATUS UNCLEAR, DUNN MAY HAVE BEEN RELUCTANT TO ASSUME THE GOVERNOR'S RESPONSIBILITIES AT FIRST. BUT IN MAY, WARMOTH LEFT THE STATE FOR AN EXTENDED CONVALESCENCE, PUTTING DUNN IN A DIFFICULT POSITION.
DUNN MADE HIS DECISION: HE WOULD STEP UP AND BECOME **THE FIRST BLACK ACTING GOVERNOR IN U.S. HISTORY.**

DUNN IMMEDIATELY HAD TO WEIGH EXECUTIVE ACTION ON A MATTER OF LIFE OR DEATH.
TWO SPANISH MEN WERE SCHEDULED TO BE EXECUTED FOR A WELL-PUBLICIZED, GRISLY MURDER, AND THE SPANISH, FRENCH, BELGIAN, AND ENGLISH CONSULS ASKED DUNN TO COMMUTE THE SENTENCES.

WERE I A WHITE MAN, I WOULD CONSIDER MYSELF FREE TO ACT, BUT AS I AM A NEGRO, NO END OF ABUSE WILL BE THROWN UPON ME.
THE GOVERNOR HAS LEFT THE STATE . . . TO THROW THIS RESPONSIBILITY ON ME. I WILL NOT ASSUME IT.
CHASTENED AFTER TAKING THE HEAT FOR THE POLICE ACTIONS IN JEFFERSON, DUNN MIGHT HAVE WANTED TO AVOID BEING BLAMED FOR ANOTHER CONTROVERSIAL DECISION.

THE FATE OF THE TWO MEN WAS SEALED.

MEANWHILE, HORACE GREELEY, THE EDITOR OF THE NEW-YORK TRIBUNE, HAD EMERGED AS A CHALLENGER TO PRESIDENT GRANT FOR THE UPCOMING 1872 ELECTION.
MANY REPUBLICANS FELT OSTRACIZED BY GRANT, AND GREELEY ARGUED THAT FEDERAL INTERVENTION IN THE SOUTH HAD LASTED LONG ENOUGH--THAT IT WAS TIME TO END RECONSTRUCTION.

TO DRUM UP FAVOR FOR HIS BID AGAINST GRANT, GREELEY CAME TO NEW ORLEANS, WHERE HE MET WITH DUNN AND OTHER LOCAL LEADERS.
IF AND WHEN I BECOME PRESIDENT, I SAY WE COLONIZE THE COLORED POPULATION TO PUBLICLY OWNED LANDS, AND SETTLE THE RACIAL DISCORD THAT WAY.

THE WHITE AND COLORED POPULATIONS MUTUALLY NEED EACH OTHER. AND, UNDERSTAND THIS, WITHOUT THE SUPPORT OF LOUISIANA'S COLORED PEOPLE, YOU WILL **NEVER** BE PRESIDENT.
DUNN AND GREELEY DID NOT SEE EYE TO EYE, AND THE PRESIDENTIAL HOPEFUL MOVED ON TO FIND SUPPORT ELSEWHERE.

PASS CHRISTIAN, MISSISSIPPI
AFTER RETURNING BRIEFLY TO HIS DUTIES, WARMOTH EXPERIENCED A RELAPSE AND LEFT THE STATE AGAIN, THIS TIME TO STAY AT A WATERFRONT RESORT, WHERE HE REMAINED BEDRIDDEN.

WITH WARMOTH AWAY AGAIN, A PETTY DISPUTE HIGHLIGHTED THE QUESTION: "WHO WAS IN CHARGE?"
A COURT CLERK HAD APPLIED FOR A LEAVE OF ABSENCE, AND AFTER CONSULTING THE LAW, DUNN ASKED WARMOTH'S SECRETARY, O. D. BRAGDON, TO APPROVE IT. BRAGDON REFUSED.

DO YOU DISOBEY ON YOUR OWN RESPONSIBILITY?
I'M ACTING UNDER ORDERS OF GOVERNOR WARMOTH.

BRAGDON THEN LOCKED THE EXECUTIVE OFFICE . . .

. . . AND LEFT FOR PASS CHRISTIAN TO SEE WARMOTH.

DUNN HIRED A LOCKSMITH TO OPEN THE EXECUTIVE OFFICE.
GOVERNOR'S OFFICE

SOON, THOUGH, BRAGDON RETURNED TO NEW ORLEANS AND THE EXECUTIVE OFFICE--CATCHING DUNN BY SURPRISE.

I HAVE INSTRUCTIONS FROM GOVERNOR WARMOTH TO TAKE CHARGE OF HIS PRIVATE PAPERS.
YOUR SERVICES AS PRIVATE SECRETARY WILL NOT BE REQUIRED!
IF GOVERNOR WARMOTH HAS ANY PRIVATE PAPERS HERE, THEY SHOULD REMAIN AS INVIOLATE AS IF THEY WERE LOCKED UP IN HIS OWN HOME.

ON JULY 10, 1871, THE COMMERCIAL BULLETIN PUBLISHED A PROCLAMATION BY DUNN ANNOUNCING THAT HE HAD A CONSTITUTIONAL RESPONSIBILITY TO STEP IN AS EXECUTIVE DURING WARMOTH'S ABSENCE.
I do hereby assume the duties devolving upon me as governor of the state of Louisiana.

DUNN MOVED SWIFTLY, FILLING VACANCIES INCLUDING A JUDGESHIP...
Recorder of Mortgage
...THE RECORDER OF MORTGAGES...
...AND THE SUPERINTENDENT OF CHARITY HOSPITAL.

DUNN ALSO REQUESTED THE RESIGNATIONS OF MANY WARMOTH-SUPPORTING OFFICIALS.

THE LONG-SIMMERING FEUD BETWEEN THE ACTING GOVERNOR AND THE ABSENTEE GOVERNOR HAD REACHED A FEVER PITCH.

NEWSPAPERS FUELED PUBLIC DEBATE, SPECULATING ON WHAT HAD MOTIVATED DUNN'S ACTIONS.

I SHALL NOT BE TOLD THAT I MUST DO ANYTHING!
IT WAS REPORTED THAT, FOR YEARS, DUNN HAD TAKEN ISSUE WITH WARMOTH'S REPEATED ATTEMPTS TO COERCE HIM TO SUPPORT HIS POLICIES.

AFTER THEIR MANY RUN-INS, ONE NEWSPAPER REPORTED THAT WARMOTH HAD PLACED DUNN'S HOME UNDER SURVEILLANCE.

IT EVEN ALLEGED THAT WARMOTH--PRIOR TO HIS INJURY--HAD CONDUCTED MANY OF THESE RECONNAISSANCE MISSIONS HIMSELF.

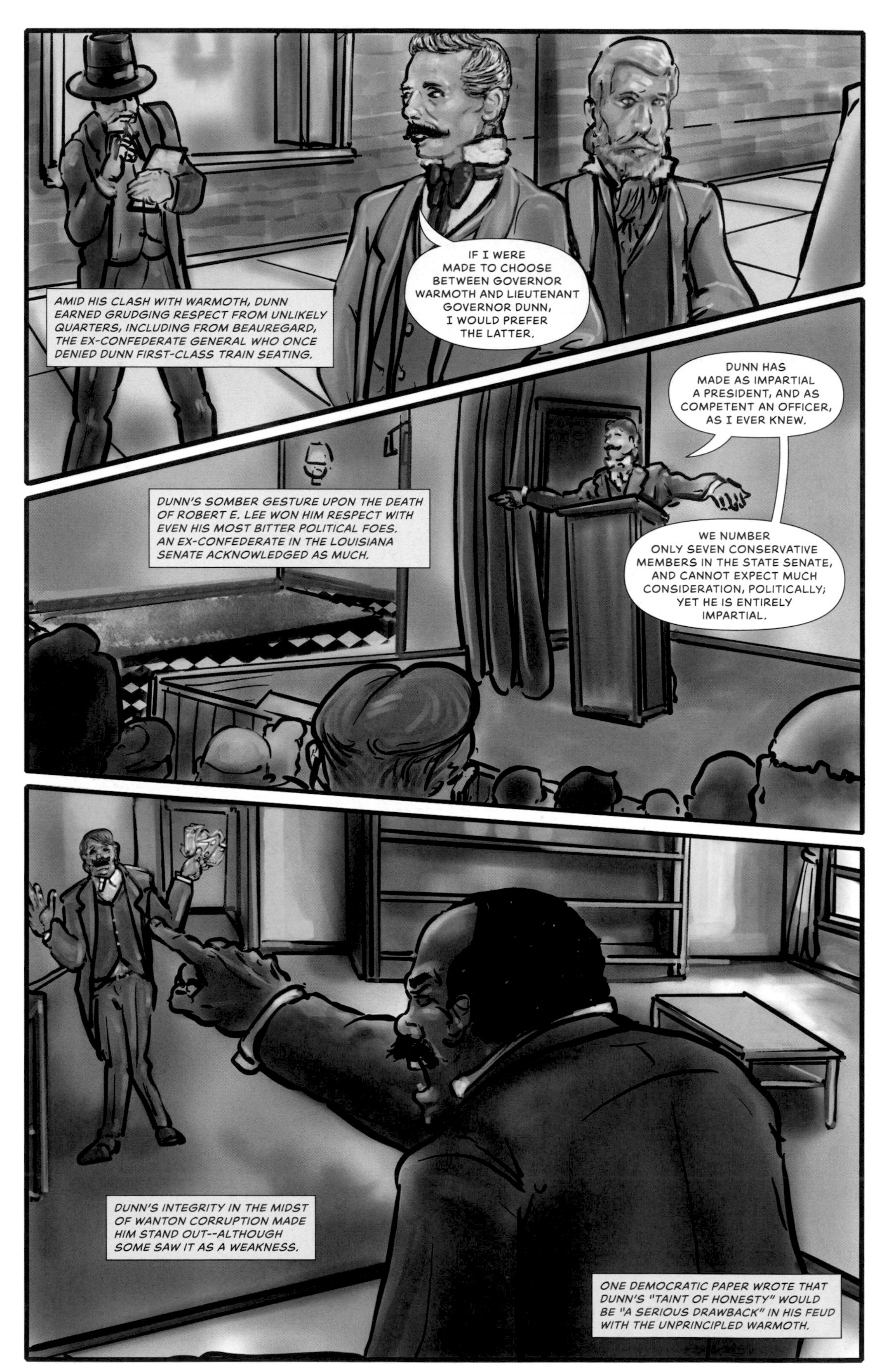
AMID HIS CLASH WITH WARMOTH, DUNN EARNED GRUDGING RESPECT FROM UNLIKELY QUARTERS, INCLUDING FROM BEAUREGARD, THE EX-CONFEDERATE GENERAL WHO ONCE DENIED DUNN FIRST-CLASS TRAIN SEATING.
IF I WERE MADE TO CHOOSE BETWEEN GOVERNOR WARMOTH AND LIEUTENANT GOVERNOR DUNN, I WOULD PREFER THE LATTER.
DUNN'S SOMBER GESTURE UPON THE DEATH OF ROBERT E. LEE WON HIM RESPECT WITH EVEN HIS MOST BITTER POLITICAL FOES. AN EX-CONFEDERATE IN THE LOUISIANA SENATE ACKNOWLEDGED AS MUCH.
DUNN HAS MADE AS IMPARTIAL A PRESIDENT, AND AS COMPETENT AN OFFICER, AS I EVER KNEW.
WE NUMBER ONLY SEVEN CONSERVATIVE MEMBERS IN THE STATE SENATE, AND CANNOT EXPECT MUCH CONSIDERATION, POLITICALLY; YET HE IS ENTIRELY IMPARTIAL.
DUNN'S INTEGRITY IN THE MIDST OF WANTON CORRUPTION MADE HIM STAND OUT--ALTHOUGH SOME SAW IT AS A WEAKNESS.
ONE DEMOCRATIC PAPER WROTE THAT DUNN'S "TAINT OF HONESTY" WOULD BE "A SERIOUS DRAWBACK" IN HIS FEUD WITH THE UNPRINCIPLED WARMOTH.

WITH DUNN TIGHTENING HIS EXECUTIVE GRIP, WARMOTH, STILL HOBBLED, MADE A SURPRISING RETURN TO THE CITY ON JULY 18, 23 DAYS AFTER LEAVING THE STATE.

WARMOTH DENOUNCED DUNN'S AUTHORITY--CLAIMING HE'D ONLY BEEN ON VACATION--AND SCOLDED HIM IN A PUBLIC STATEMENT.
I can but regard any act performed by you, in the capacity of Acting Governor, as an intrusion, calling for immediate revocation and rebuke.

DUNN FIRED BACK.
In the future, as in the past, I shall fearlessly assume and conscientiously perform the duties devolving upon me under the constitution.... Permit me respectfully to decline accepting your Excellency as my exemplar in either modesty, courtesy, propriety, or official duty.

WITH A STATE REPUBLICAN CONVENTION JUST WEEKS AWAY, WARMOTH ESCALATED HIS ATTACKS ON DUNN'S POLITICAL NETWORK, DISMISSING POLITICAL APPOINTEES AND POLICE OFFICERS RUMORED TO BE DUNN SUPPORTERS.
HE THEN DEPLOYED THE SAME KIND OF INTIMIDATION TACTICS ONCE USED AGAINST REPUBLICANS BY WHITE DEMOCRATS.

WARMOTH USED COVERT METROPOLITAN POLICE UNITS, COMPOSED OF MEN ALLEGED TO HAVE PARTICIPATED IN THE 1866 MASSACRE, TO DISRUPT PURE RADICAL WARD CLUB MEETINGS.

UNDERCOVER POLICE WOULD INFILTRATE THE CLUBS . . .

. . . BECOME DISORDERLY AFTER MEETINGS WERE CALLED TO ORDER . . .

. . . AND TURN VIOLENT.

THEN, UNIFORMED METROPOLITANS WOULD SHOW UP AND ARREST CLUB MEMBERS WHO HAD BEEN DRAWN INTO THE FRAY. SCORES OF PURE RADICALS WERE BEATEN AND ARRESTED.

VIOLENCE ERUPTED ONCE AT A CLUB MEETING WHERE DUNN HAD BEEN SCHEDULED TO SPEAK.
DUNN'S CRITICS ACCUSED HIM OF WIELDING INAPPROPRIATE INFLUENCE THROUGH ALLIES WHO CONTROLLED PRINTING CONTRACTS IN RURAL PARISHES--USING THE PRESS TO SCARE VOTERS INTO SENDING DUNN-FRIENDLY DELEGATES TO THE CONVENTION.
DUNN RAISED ALARMS ABOUT WARMOTH IN A LETTER HE WROTE TO A POLITICIAN IN OPELOUSAS.
An effort is being made to sell us out to the Democrats... and we must nip it right in the bud.
WARMOTH'S CAMP WOULDN'T GO DOWN QUIETLY. WROTE ONE ANONYMOUS SUPPORTER: "THE GOVERNOR WOULD HAVE CONTROL OF THE CONVENTION--OR BLOOD."
THE CHAOS WOULD COME TO A HEAD, ONCE AND FOR ALL, AT THE CONVENTION IN AUGUST.

THE STAKES AT THE 1871 LOUISIANA REPUBLICAN CONVENTION WERE HIGH: IF WARMOTH'S CAMP COULD SECURE CONTROL OF THE PARTY'S CENTRAL COMMITTEE, IT WOULD ENSURE HE WOULD BE NOMINATED FOR ANOTHER TERM AS GOVERNOR.
IF DUNN'S CAMP HAD CONTROL, WARMOTH WOULD FACE IMPEACHMENT.

WARMOTH WANTED THE CONVENTION HELD AT THE MECHANICS' INSTITUTE, HIS HOME TURF, SO THAT HE COULD BETTER DEPLOY POLICE IF THINGS DIDN'T GO HIS WAY.
IT WASN'T HIS CALL, THOUGH--IT WAS UP TO PARTY LEADERS--SO WARMOTH RENTED OTHER SUITABLE HALLS IN THE CITY TO LIMIT THE PARTY'S OPTIONS.

WARMOTH'S PLAN BACKFIRED. FEARING POLICE VIOLENCE, PARTY LEADERSHIP CHOSE THE U.S. CIRCUIT COURTROOM INSIDE THE CUSTOMHOUSE--HEADQUARTERS FOR DUNN'S POWERFUL POLITICAL ALLIES.

PURE RADICALS REPORTED RECEIVING CREDIBLE THREATS OF VIOLENCE.
IN ORDER TO PREVENT THAT, U.S. MARSHAL STEPHEN B. PACKARD, THE LEADER OF THE DUNN-FRIENDLY CUSTOMHOUSE FACTION, DEPUTIZED FEDERAL MARSHALS AND SOME 40 U.S. INFANTRYMEN FOR THE EVENT.

THE PARTY ALSO REQUIRED DELEGATES TO PRESENT ADMISSION TICKETS TO POSTMASTER LOWELL. PACKARD AND LOWELL WERE THE MEN WARMOTH HAD RECENTLY TRIED AND FAILED TO HAVE REMOVED FROM OFFICE.

ON THE MORNING OF AUGUST 9, 1871, WARMOTH'S SUPPORTERS ENTERED THE CUSTOMHOUSE TO FIND ITS ROTUNDA FILLED WITH HEAVILY ARMED SOLDIERS.

WARMOTH ARRIVED BETWEEN 10 AND 11 A.M., AND DESPITE HAVING A TICKET WAS INFORMED THAT THE COURTROOM WOULD NOT BE READY TO RECEIVE DELEGATES UNTIL 11:30.

JUST THEN, ACCORDING TO WARMOTH, A MAN EXITED THE COURTROOM, AND THE OPEN DOOR REVEALED A SECRET MEETING UNDERWAY INSIDE.

HAVING BEEN REFUSED ADMITTANCE TO THE HALL DESIGNATED BY THE CENTRAL COMMITTEE FOR HOLDING A CONVENTION, I PROPOSE WE NOW ADJOURN TO TURNERS' HALL AND HOLD A CONVENTION THERE.
IN LATER ACCOUNTS, DUNN'S SUPPORTERS DIDN'T MENTION A SECRET MEETING. THEY ASSERTED THAT WARMOTH LEFT AFTER BEING TOLD TO WAIT.

THE NEXT DAY, TWO SEPARATE CONVENTIONS COMMENCED, EACH DENOUNCING THE OTHER AS AN ILLEGITIMATE "BOLTER" CONVENTION.
WARMOTH'S CONVENTION RAILED AGAINST THE PRESENCE OF FEDERAL TROOPS AT THE CUSTOMHOUSE. DUNN'S CONVENTION CONDEMNED WARMOTH'S CORRUPTION AND THE VIOLENCE PERPETRATED BY HIS SUPPORTERS.

IF IT SHOULD GO TO THE PEOPLE OF THIS COUNTRY THAT PRESIDENT GRANT HAS SANCTIONED THE CALLING OF A REPUBLICAN CONVENTION IN THE UNITED STATES CUSTOMHOUSE TO BE CONTROLLED BY THE UNITED STATES MARSHAL, PACKED BY UNITED STATES OFFICIALS, AND SURROUNDED BY THE UNITED STATES ARMY . . . THE AMERICAN PEOPLE WILL REPUDIATE HIM.
TURNERS' HALL

CUSTOMHOUSE
POSTMASTER LOWELL CHASTISED WARMOTH FOR STARTING A ROGUE CONVENTION.
WARMOTH AND HIS PARTY ARE BOLTERS, AND WARMOTH HAS ALWAYS BEEN AN ENEMY OF PRESIDENT GRANT. BE BOLD AND UNITED!

TURNERS' HALL
EVER THE POLITICAL MANEUVERER, PINCHBACK CAST HIS LOT WITH THE WARMOTH CONVENTION, WHERE HE WAS NAMED PERMANENT CHAIRMAN.
IS IT POSSIBLE WE ARE TO BE PUT DOWN BY THE GOVERNMENT WE HAVE SUSTAINED?
IF THAT BE THE CASE, THE SOONER THIS GOVERNMENT IS TORN DOWN AND A MONARCHY BUILT UPON ITS RUINS, THE BETTER!

THE GOVERNOR RECEIVED BRIBES, STOLE THE PUBLIC MONEY, AND IS THE GREATEST LIVING PRACTICAL LIAR.
SPEAKER OF THE LOUISIANA HOUSE GEORGE W. CARTER CASTIGATED WARMOTH.
CUSTOMHOUSE

I WILL NOT BE MADE THE TOOL OF ANYONE, NOT EVEN OF GOVERNOR WARMOTH. LET THE COLORED PEOPLE UNDERSTAND THAT DISTINCTLY. I THINK AND ACT FOR MYSELF.
DUNN ADDRESSED CRITICISM THAT HE WAS BEING USED BY FEDERAL OFFICIALS.

THE CUSTOMHOUSE CONVENTION RESOLVED TO ENDORSE PRESIDENT GRANT, REQUEST FEDERAL ASSISTANCE IN PRESERVING PEACE IN THE CITY, SUSTAIN PUBLIC SCHOOL INTEGRATION, AND REDUCE THE STATE DEBT--WHICH HAD BALLOONED UNDER WARMOTH.
SPEAKER CARTER READ ALOUD A FORMAL DENUNCIATION OF THE GOVERNOR.

H. C. WARMOTH . . . HAS FORFEITED OUR CONFIDENCE, HAVING SHOWN CLEARLY THAT HE WOULD SACRIFICE THE REPUBLICAN PARTY TO ADVANCE HIMSELF, AND CAN NO LONGER BE SAFELY FOLLOWED AS A REPUBLICAN LEADER.

WARMOTH, MEANWHILE, SENT 20 MEN, INCLUDING PINCHBACK, TO PERSONALLY DELIVER THEIR GRIEVANCES TO GRANT WHILE HE WAS ON VACATION AT HIS SUMMER COTTAGE.
DUNN'S CAMP SENT A SUMMARY OF THEIR RESOLUTIONS TO PRESIDENT GRANT.
LONG BRANCH, NEW JERSEY

WARMOTH'S MEN URGED GRANT TO DENOUNCE DUNN'S CONVENTION AND ITS USE OF FEDERAL TROOPS AND TO RECOGNIZE THEIRS AS THE LEGITIMATE VOICE OF THE REPUBLICAN PARTY IN LOUISIANA.

THEY RECEIVED A COLD RECEPTION.
I DON'T SEE WHAT HARM THE PRESENCE OF UNITED STATES SOLDIERS COULD DO TO A REPUBLICAN CONVENTION.
IF YOU'LL ONLY REVIEW OUR REPORT--
I'LL TAKE YOUR REPORT AND INVESTIGATE THE FACTS THOROUGHLY BEFORE TAKING ANY ACTION.
HE NEVER DID.

NEW ORLEANS, SEPTEMBER 1871
THE FEUD BETWEEN DUNN AND WARMOTH IN LOUISIANA MIRRORED THE NATIONAL CLASH BETWEEN GREELEY AND GRANT.
GREELEY ENTERED THE LOUISIANA FRAY BY CALLING FOR THE REMOVAL OF THE GRANT-FRIENDLY CUSTOMHOUSE OFFICIALS INVOLVED IN THE CONVENTION DEBACLE.
DUNN RESPONDED WITH A LENGTHY OPEN LETTER TO GREELEY, SETTING THE RECORD STRAIGHT ON THE CONVENTION, AND ON WARMOTH HIMSELF.

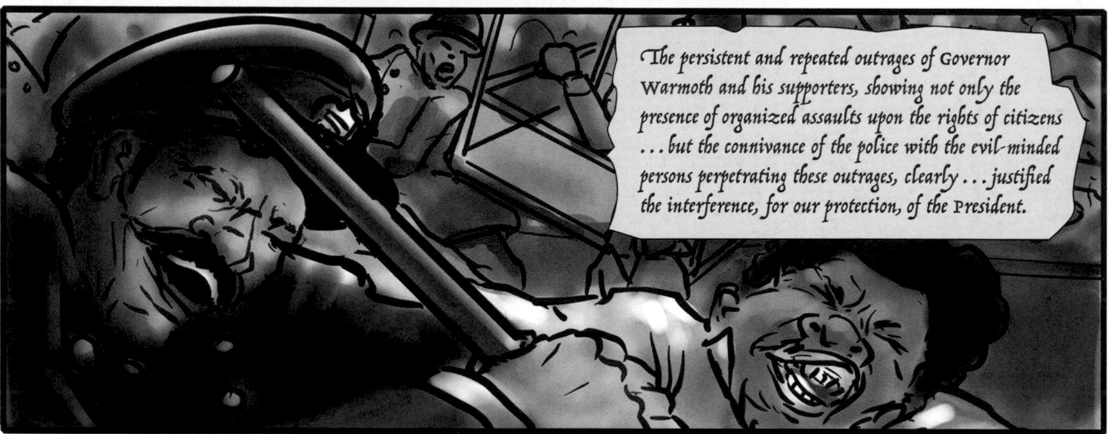
The persistent and repeated outrages of Governor Warmoth and his supporters, showing not only the presence of organized assaults upon the rights of citizens . . . but the connivance of the police with the evil-minded persons perpetrating these outrages, clearly . . . justified the interference, for our protection, of the President.

DUNN DESCRIBED WARMOTH AS "THE FIRST KU-KLUX GOVERNOR OF THE PARTY HE HAS DISGRACED, AND IS NOW TRYING TO DESTROY."

HE BOLDLY CHALLENGED GREELEY'S AUTHORITY, TURNING THE CANDIDATE'S OWN WRITINGS--ON FARMING AND OTHER TOPICS--AGAINST HIM.
If your agricultural data and conclusions are not more reliable than . . . the conclusions reached by you relative to Louisiana politics, the man who reads your book and follows the teachings thereof will never make a successful farmer.

We want for ourselves and the people of all parties better laws on the statute books and better men to administer the same....

The people gravely and earnestly are fighting for their personal and political rights, against the encroachments of impudent and unfaithful public servants....

DUNN POINTED OUT THAT GREELEY HIMSELF HAD ARGUED THAT THE "CARPET-BAG SCOUNDRELISM" OF SOME REPUBLICANS IN THE SOUTH HAD HARMED THE PARTY--AND ARGUED THAT WARMOTH EXEMPLIFIED THE PROBLEM.

The young man who now occupies the executive chair of Louisiana, whose crimes against his party and his people you charitably ignore and whose championship you so boldly assume, is preeminently the prototype and prince of the tribe of carpetbaggers, who seem to be your pet aversion.

Respectfully,
Oscar J. Dunn
DUNN'S LETTER LAID BARE THE FRACTURE IN LOUISIANA AND THE REPUBLICAN PARTY WRIT LARGE. IT WAS AN ALARM AND A BATTLE CRY.
IT WASN'T ENOUGH.

PART SEVEN

COLLAPSE

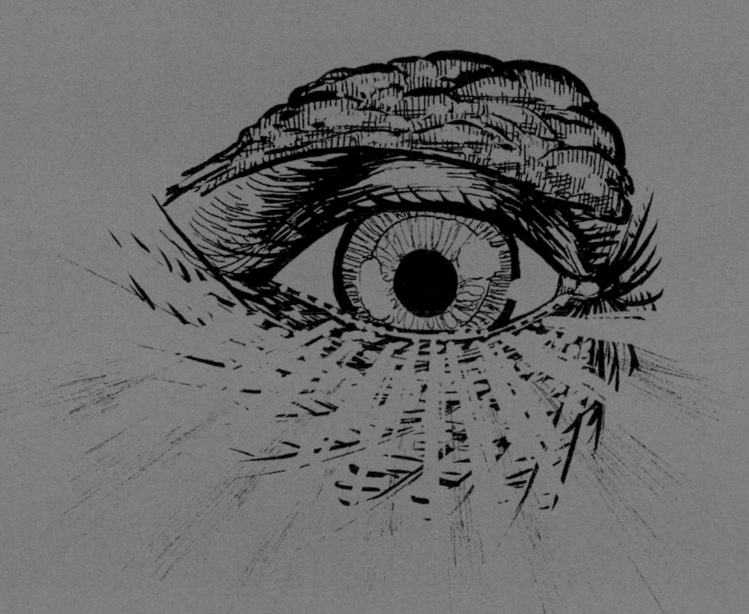

ON ALL SAINTS' DAY, A HOLY DAY WHEN MANY NEW ORLEANIANS HONOR THEIR DEAD, A FRIEND DELIVERED AN OMINOUS MESSAGE TO DUNN.
PINCHBACK, WHO HAD TAKEN WARMOTH'S SIDE IN THE EXECUTIVE FEUD, INTENDED TO ATTACK DUNN IN HIS "DOMESTIC RELATIONS."
THE FRIEND SAID DUNN'S "GREAT FRAME QUIVERED WHEN HE RECEIVED THE DASTARDLY MESSAGE."
WHAT DID PINCHBACK KNOW?

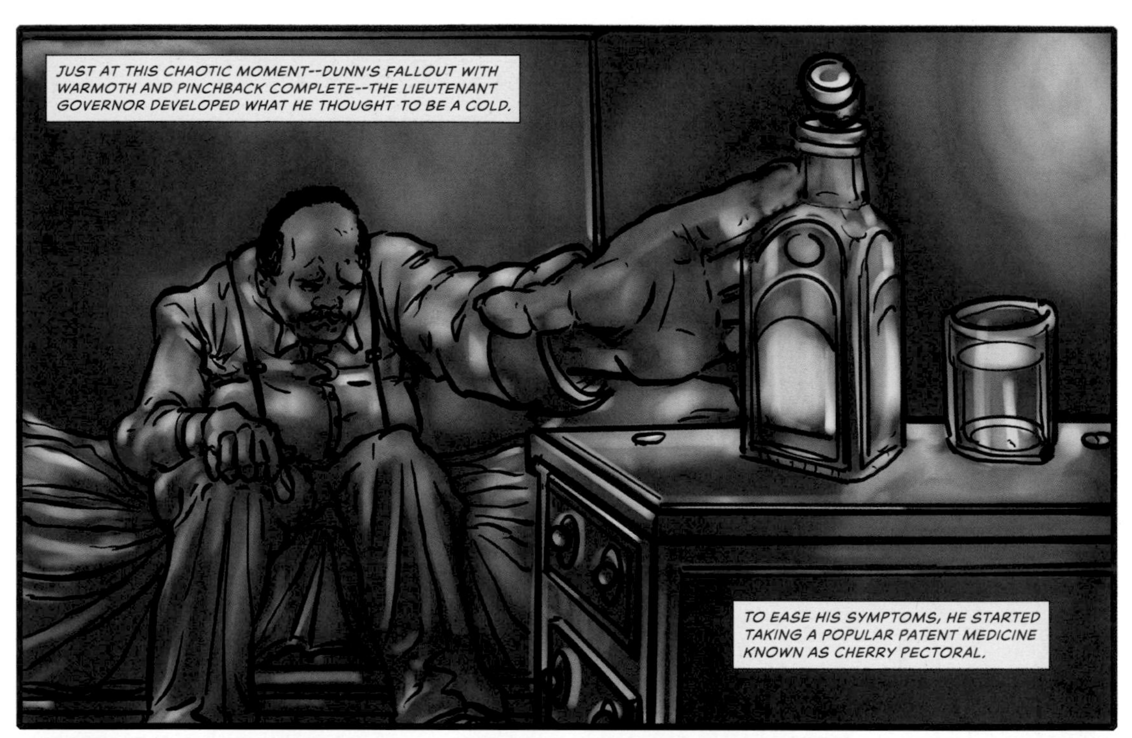
JUST AT THIS CHAOTIC MOMENT--DUNN'S FALLOUT WITH WARMOTH AND PINCHBACK COMPLETE--THE LIEUTENANT GOVERNOR DEVELOPED WHAT HE THOUGHT TO BE A COLD.
TO EASE HIS SYMPTOMS, HE STARTED TAKING A POPULAR PATENT MEDICINE KNOWN AS CHERRY PECTORAL.

ALTHOUGH SICK, DUNN CONTINUED TO MAKE SPEECHES TO HIS CONSTITUENCY AND RALLY THE SUPPORT OF PURE RADICALS.

HIS DEMEANOR SWUNG WILDLY IN THESE SPEECHES, FROM HIGH SPIRITS . . .

. . . TO DEPRESSION.

SPEAKING AT ONE CHURCH, DUNN TOOK ON A SOMBER AND REFLECTIVE TONE.
I URGE YOU TO BE TRUE CHRISTIANS; TO BE HONEST IN ALL YOUR TRANSACTIONS; TO DO NO WRONG THING . . . TO TAKE NOTHING THAT DID NOT BELONG TO YOU, TO PAY YOUR SOCIETY DUES AND ALWAYS BE JUST.

I MAKE NO PROFESSIONS OF RELIGION MYSELF, BUT I ENDEAVOR TO DO RIGHT AND LIVE HONESTLY.
DUNN SPOKE FOR NEARLY AN HOUR, TAKING TIME TO ADDRESS THE GREATEST REGRET OF HIS CAREER.
I DO NOT FEEL WELL, AND HAVE NOT BEEN WELL FOR SEVERAL DAYS. THIS MIGHT BE THE LAST TIME I SHOULD EVER ADDRESS YOU, AND THEREFORE I URGE YOU TO WEIGH WELL MY WORDS, REMEMBER MY ADVICE, AND HEED IT.
I DID ONE THING FOR WHICH I WILL NEVER FORGIVE MYSELF. SOMETIME DURING THE YEAR 1865, GOVERNOR WARMOTH SENT ME WORD THAT HE WOULD BE PLEASED TO SEE ME AT HIS OFFICE. . . .
I INVITED HIM TO BE PRESENT AT THE NEXT MEETING OF THE FRIENDS OF UNIVERSAL SUFFRAGE. I PRESENTED GOVERNOR WARMOTH TO THE MEMBERS OF THE ORGANIZATION, AND UPON MY PROPOSITION HE BECAME A MEMBER.

A FEW WEEKS LATER, ON A WARM NOVEMBER MORNING, DUNN AWOKE IN GOOD SPIRITS.
HE SPENT THE AFTERNOON WITH HIS CUSTOMHOUSE ALLY, U.S. MARSHAL PACKARD.

AFTER HIS VISIT WITH PACKARD, HE CAME HOME FOR DINNER.

AFTER DINNER, DUNN BEGAN VOMITING PROFUSELY. THE FITS OF VOMITING CONTINUED THROUGH THE NIGHT AND INTO THE FOLLOWING AFTERNOON.

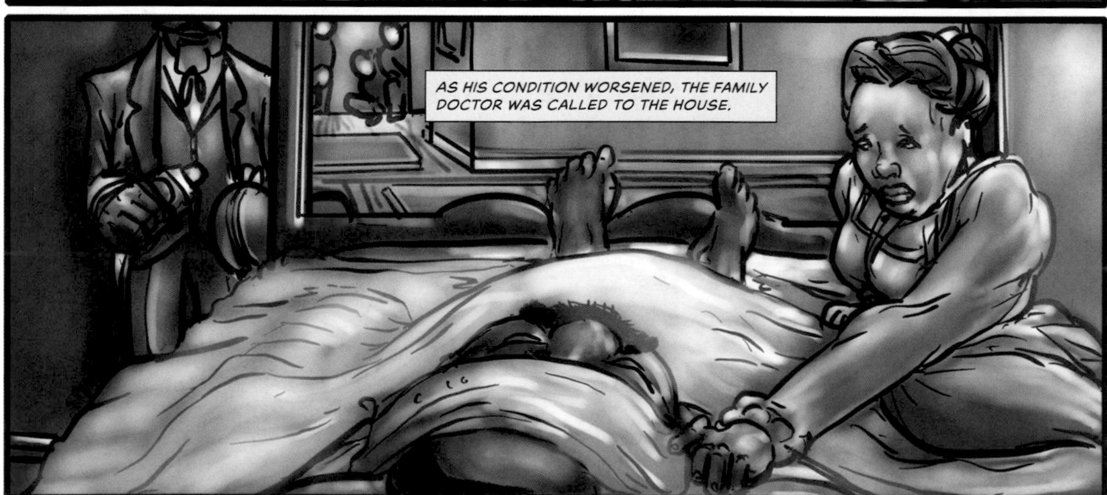
AS HIS CONDITION WORSENED, THE FAMILY DOCTOR WAS CALLED TO THE HOUSE.

A NUMBER OF PROMINENT FIGURES CAME TO CHECK ON THE BEDRIDDEN DUNN, INCLUDING GOVERNOR WARMOTH.
THE WEATHER COOLED SIGNIFICANTLY, AND THE LIEUTENANT GOVERNOR'S CONDITION BECAME GRAVE.

BY 2 A.M. ON NOVEMBER 21, DUNN WAS UNCONSCIOUS. PACKARD CAME TO CHECK ON HIM AND CALLED ANOTHER DOCTOR.

THAT DOCTOR DECLARED THAT DUNN WAS SUFFERING FROM "CONGESTION OF THE BRAIN AND LUNGS," CAUSED BY THE VOMITING. DUNN'S BREATHING GREW INCREASINGLY STAGGERED.
SEVERAL MORE DOCTORS VISITED TO CONSULT ON HIS ILLNESS THAT DAY, INCLUDING DR. ROUDANEZ, THE FORMER TRIBUNE OWNER.

ELLEN DUNN WAS STUNNED AND HEARTBROKEN, "MOANING AS IF HER HEART WOULD BREAK." FRIENDS CONSOLED HER AS THE HOURS PASSED.

ON NOVEMBER 22, 1871, AS BELLS IN THE CITY TOLLED THE HOUR OF 6 A.M., OSCAR DUNN TOOK HIS LAST BREATH.

DUNN'S SUDDEN DEATH AT THE AGE OF 49, AMID A HEATED POLITICAL FEUD, ALARMED HIS CONSTITUENCY AND FUELED RUMORS OF FOUL PLAY THAT VERY DAY.
THEY'VE POISONED THE GOVERNOR!

I'VE BEEN NURSING FOR THIRTY YEARS, AND I'VE NEVER SEEN PNEUMONIA LIKE THAT.

THE RUMOR SPREAD LIKE WILDFIRE.
THEY'RE SAYING HE WAS POISONED?
A STRONG, HEALTHY MAN LIKE THAT--IT JUST DOESN'T ADD UP.

THEY'VE POISONED OSCAR DUNN!
CHECK HIM FOR ARSENIC!

THAT EVENING, AT LEAST THREE PHYSICIANS REQUESTED TO PERFORM AN AUTOPSY, BUT A FAMILY SPOKESMAN NAMED JAMES LEWIS REFUSED.
I CAN ASSURE YOU, DOCTORS, THE FAMILY IS SATISFIED THAT THE DECEASED HAS DIED A NATURAL DEATH.

THE NEXT MORNING, SPEAKER CARTER CLAIMED THAT HE HAD BEEN POISONED AS WELL.
HIS OWN DOCTOR DOUBTED HE'D BEEN POISONED--BUT THE CLAIM INFLAMED THEORIES THAT THERE WAS A PLOT TO ASSASSINATE MEMBERS OF DUNN'S POLITICAL CAMP.

WITH RUMORS CIRCULATING ABOUT A BLACK REVOLT, SEVERAL NEWSPAPERS PRINTED A SIGNED STATEMENT FROM DUNN'S DOCTORS MAINTAINING THAT HE HAD DIED OF NATURAL CAUSES.
SEVEN DOCTORS HAD ATTENDED TO DUNN, BUT ONLY FOUR SIGNED THE STATEMENT. THE MOST CONSPICUOUS MISSING SIGNATURE WAS THAT OF DR. ROUDANEZ, WHO HAD BECOME AN ALLY OF DUNN'S.

RUMORS PERSISTED FOR DECADES.
THE MOST OUTRAGEOUS THEORY APPEARED IN THE NEW YORK TIMES IN 1894: THAT MADAME LOTT, THE VOODOO PRACTITIONER AND SISTER OF A POLITICAL RIVAL OF DUNN'S, HAD "CONJURED" HIM.

THE STORY SAID THAT, AFTER HIS DEATH, A WAX FIGURE STUCK WITH PINS HAD BEEN FOUND UNDER HIS PILLOW, ATTACHED TO A SLIP OF PAPER THAT SAID, IN FRENCH, "O. J. DUNN WILL SURELY DIE."
THE TALE CAME AMID A TREND OF RACIST EDITORIALS ABOUT VOODOO, AND WAS RIDDLED WITH INACCURACIES, BUT IT DEMONSTRATES THAT INTRIGUE AROUND DUNN'S DEATH LINGERED FOR DECADES.

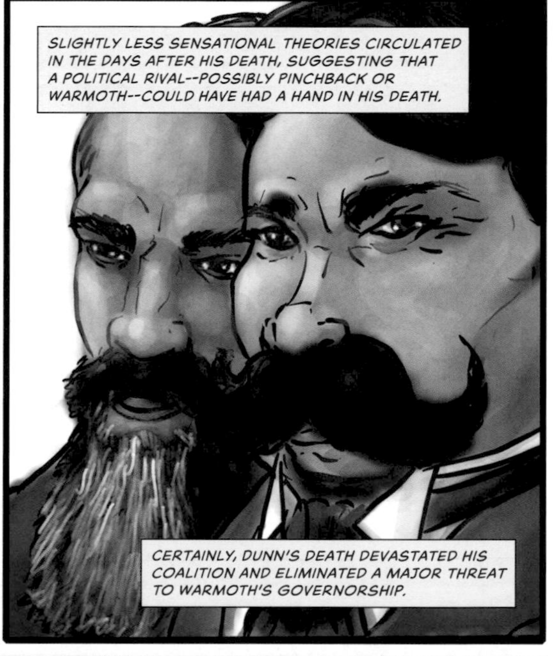
SLIGHTLY LESS SENSATIONAL THEORIES CIRCULATED IN THE DAYS AFTER HIS DEATH, SUGGESTING THAT A POLITICAL RIVAL--POSSIBLY PINCHBACK OR WARMOTH--COULD HAVE HAD A HAND IN HIS DEATH.
CERTAINLY, DUNN'S DEATH DEVASTATED HIS COALITION AND ELIMINATED A MAJOR THREAT TO WARMOTH'S GOVERNORSHIP.

DUNN'S FAVOR IN THE EYES OF PRESIDENT GRANT, WHOSE DISDAIN FOR WARMOTH WAS WELL KNOWN, HAD ALSO BEEN GROWING.
IN THE AFTERMATH OF DUNN'S DEATH, IT WAS REPORTED THAT GRANT HAD BEEN CONSIDERING HIM AS A POSSIBLE RUNNING MATE FOR THE 1872 ELECTION-- **AS AMERICA'S FIRST BLACK VICE PRESIDENT.**

a secret that would harrow your soul
PINCHBACK'S THREAT TO DUNN ON ALL SAINTS' DAY DEMONSTRATED HOW BITTER THEIR RIVALRY HAD BECOME. **BUT WHAT WAS THE SECRET?**

IT'S POSSIBLE PINCHBACK DISCOVERED THAT DUNN HAD BOARDED WITH ELLEN AND HER LATE HUSBAND, PETER MARSHALL, PRIOR TO MARSHALL'S DEATH.
PINCHBACK COULD HAVE ALLEGED THAT DUNN AND ELLEN HAD ENGAGED IN AN ADULTEROUS RELATIONSHIP--COULD HAVE EVEN QUESTIONED THE LEGITIMACY OF ELLEN'S CHILDREN.

ANOTHER HYPOTHESIS IS THAT THE THREAT DISTRESSED DUNN SO MUCH THAT HE TOOK HIS OWN LIFE.

NEW ORLEANS, NOVEMBER 23, 1871
THE DAY OF OSCAR DUNN'S FUNERAL, A HUGE CROWD GATHERED OUTSIDE HIS HOME.

A LONG LINE FORMED AS WELL-WISHERS--FRIENDS AND RIVALS, REPUBLICANS AND DEMOCRATS, BLACK AND WHITE--WAITED THEIR TURN TO PAY RESPECT TO THE DECEASED.

A MASSIVE PROCESSION ASSEMBLED TO CARRY THE BODY TO ST. JAMES A.M.E. CHURCH.

REV. JAMES LYNCH, MISSISSIPPI'S SECRETARY OF STATE, DELIVERED DUNN'S EULOGY.
THERE NOW LIES BEFORE US THE REMAINS OF THE FIRST COLORED MAN WHO EVER HELD AN EXECUTIVE OFFICE IN THIS COUNTRY. . . . THE AFFLICTION IS THE NATION'S, AND THE NATION WILL MOURN.
IN LIEUTENANT GOVERNOR DUNN IT HAS BEEN SHOWN THAT THE COLORED MAN, CRUSHED TO THE EARTH BY A TYRANNIC POWER, COULD, WHEN HIS SHACKLES WERE BROKEN, RISE TO DIGNITY, USEFULNESS, AND THE LOFTIEST PATRIOTISM.

AS MANY AS 20,000 PEOPLE LINED CANAL STREET TO OBSERVE THE FUNERAL PROCESSION. THE LOCAL PRESS REGARDED IT AS ONE OF THE LARGEST FUNERAL GATHERINGS IN THE HISTORY OF NEW ORLEANS.
THE CORTÈGE INCLUDED HUNDREDS OF CARRIAGES . . .

. . . FREEMASONS . . .

. . . MEMBERS OF LOCAL BENEVOLENT SOCIETIES . . .

. . . INFANTRYMEN . . .

. . . MARCHING BANDS . . .

. . . REPRESENTATIVES FROM WARD CLUBS . . .

CARROLLTON
. . . POLICE . . .

. . . AND VARIOUS OTHER DIGNITARIES.

AN ENTIRE CITY MOURNED WITH DUNN'S BEREAVED FAMILY.

CARROLLTON
POLICE

THE PROCESSION WRAPPED AROUND THE HENRY CLAY MONUMENT AT THE BASE OF CANAL STREET BEFORE PROCEEDING TOWARD DUNN'S FINAL RESTING PLACE.

ST. LOUIS CEMETERY NO. 2

WHEN THE PROCESSION REACHED ITS DESTINATION, DUNN'S MASONIC BRETHREN COMPLETED THE BURIAL CEREMONIES.

DUNN'S FRIENDS AND FOLLOWERS LINGERED IN THE CEMETERY, REMINISCING ABOUT HIS LIFE INTO THE NIGHT.

WARMOTH WASTED NO TIME IN CALLING A SPECIAL SESSION TO CHOOSE A NEW LIEUTENANT GOVERNOR. HE NEEDED TO MOVE QUICKLY, BEFORE THE LEGISLATURE COULD IMPEACH HIM AND POSSIBLY ELEVATE SPEAKER CARTER TO THE GOVERNORSHIP.
HIS CHOICE--ELECTED OVER THE OBJECTIONS OF DUNN ALLIES, AND ALLEGEDLY THANKS TO SOME BRIBERY--WAS P. B.S. PINCHBACK.

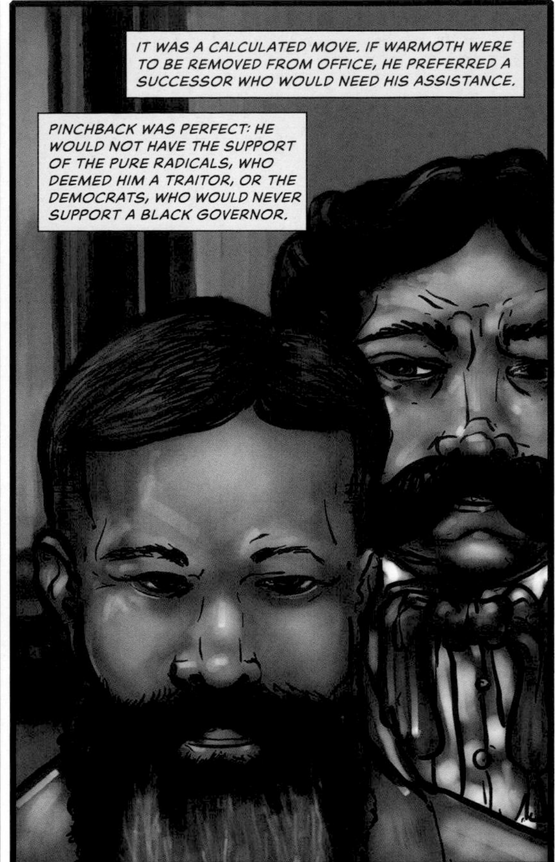
IT WAS A CALCULATED MOVE. IF WARMOTH WERE TO BE REMOVED FROM OFFICE, HE PREFERRED A SUCCESSOR WHO WOULD NEED HIS ASSISTANCE.
PINCHBACK WAS PERFECT: HE WOULD NOT HAVE THE SUPPORT OF THE PURE RADICALS, WHO DEEMED HIM A TRAITOR, OR THE DEMOCRATS, WHO WOULD NEVER SUPPORT A BLACK GOVERNOR.

BUT, BY THEN, WARMOTH HAD MADE TOO MANY ENEMIES. HE'D LONG BEFORE ALIENATED BLACK VOTERS AND--IN SUPPORTING GREELEY FOR PRESIDENT--THE GRANT-ALIGNED CUSTOMHOUSE REPUBLICANS. DEMOCRATS WERE EAGER TO END HIS CORRUPT ADMINISTRATION, TOO.
WARMOTH COULDN'T EVEN MUSTER THE SUPPORT TO CAMPAIGN FOR REELECTION IN 1872.

ONE MAN CONTINUED TO ALLEGE FOUL PLAY IN DUNN'S DEATH: THE LAWYER AND JOURNALIST MAJ. THOMAS MORRIS CHESTER. HE HAD A FATEFUL ENCOUNTER WITH PINCHBACK ON NEW YEAR'S DAY 1872.
WHAT SHALL WE DO WITH HIM, GOVERNOR PINCHBACK?
AS CHESTER WAS LEAVING A FRIEND'S HOUSE THAT EVENING, A GROUP OF DRUNKEN MEN AMBUSHED HIM.

DON'T WORRY, I'LL PROTECT YOU, MAJOR.

I'D RATHER DIE THAN OWE ANY PROTECTION TO A MAN LIKE YOU!

SOMEONE SHOT CHESTER ABOVE THE LEFT EYE. HE BLACKED OUT AND COULD NOT REMEMBER THE SHOOTER, BUT LATER CHARGED PINCHBACK AND OTHERS WITH ATTEMPTED MURDER.

PINCHBACK ADMITTED BEING PRESENT PRIOR TO THE SHOOTING BUT DENIED CULPABILITY, AND ANOTHER MAN WAS JAILED FOR JUST TWO DAYS. AN ARREST WARRANT ISSUED FOR PINCHBACK WENT NOWHERE--HE WAS, LIKE HIS PREDECESSOR DUNN, NOW THE PRESIDENT OF THE POLICE BOARD.

THAT FALL, PRESIDENT GRANT WON REELECTION, BUT LOUISIANA'S ELECTIONS WERE MARKED BY CHAOS AGAIN.
TWO CANDIDATES FOR GOVERNOR, DEMOCRAT JOHN McENERY AND REPUBLICAN WILLIAM PITT KELLOGG, AND TWO SETS OF LEGISLATORS CLAIMED VICTORY. FEDERAL TROOPS, UNDER JUDICIAL ORDERS, TOOK POSSESSION OF THE STATEHOUSE.
U.S. MARSHAL PACKARD REFUSED TO ALLOW WARMOTH SUPPORTERS INTO THE STATEHOUSE.

BY A VOTE OF 58-6, WARMOTH WAS IMPEACHED AND SUSPENDED FROM OFFICE.

FEDERAL TROOPS BROKE INTO THE GOVERNOR'S OFFICE . . .

. . . AND P. B. S. PINCHBACK TOOK OVER AS ACTING GOVERNOR.
ALTHOUGH DUNN SERVED AS ACTING GOVERNOR 18 MONTHS EARLIER, PINCHBACK WOULD BE REMEMBERED AS THE FIRST BLACK GOVERNOR IN U.S. HISTORY. HE HELD THE OFFICE FOR JUST 36 DAYS--UNTIL THE END OF WARMOTH'S TERM, WHEN KELLOGG WAS SEATED IN HIS PLACE. THE LEGISLATURE THEN DROPPED ITS IMPEACHMENT CHARGES AGAINST WARMOTH.

PINCHBACK REMAINED POLITICALLY ACTIVE. HE HELPED CONVINCE STATE LEADERS TO ESTABLISH THE PUBLIC, HISTORICALLY BLACK SOUTHERN UNIVERSITY--BUT, IN EXCHANGE, HE SUPPORTED A NEW CONSTITUTION IN 1879 THAT SANCTIONED SEGREGATION.
HE LATER MOVED TO WASHINGTON, D.C., WHERE HE DIED IN 1921.

WARMOTH, BRIEFLY THE FACE OF THE LOUISIANA RADICAL MOVEMENT, SOON BOUGHT A PLAQUEMINES PARISH SUGAR PLANTATION, WHERE HE WOULD LIVE FOR A NUMBER OF YEARS.
HE EVENTUALLY RETURNED TO NEW ORLEANS, AND POLITICS, AND DIED IN THE CITY IN 1931.

AFTER DUNN'S DEATH, ELLEN AND THE KIDS FELL ON HARD TIMES.
TO SETTLE DEBTS, A NUMBER OF THE FAMILY'S ASSETS WERE AUCTIONED OR SOLD.

ULTIMATELY, THEIR FAMILY HOME HAD TO BE SOLD AT A SHERIFF'S AUCTION.

BUT IN A TURN OF GOODWILL, THE BUYER SOLD IT BACK TO ELLEN, ASSUMING THE DEBT AS A LOAN.

WHEN THE NATIONAL CONVENTION OF COLORED CITIZENS CAME TO NEW ORLEANS IN 1872, LOCAL LEADERS--INCLUDING PINCHBACK--ARRANGED FOR THE PROCEEDS OF ADMISSIONS TO THE KEYNOTE SPEECH, GIVEN BY ABOLITIONIST AND STATESMAN FREDERICK DOUGLASS, TO BE DONATED TO THE DUNN FAMILY.

CONVENTION DELEGATES ADOPTED A RESOLUTION TO HONOR OSCAR DUNN AND VISITED ELLEN AT HOME TO PAY THEIR RESPECTS.

MAYOR BENJAMIN FRANKLIN FLANDERS APPOINTED ELLEN AS KEEPER OF THE CITY ARCHIVES.
THE STATE LEGISLATURE ALSO PASSED ACTS TO GRANT HER A STIPEND--WHICH SHE LIKELY USED TO PAY OFF HER HOME LOAN--AND TO GUARANTEE PAYMENT OF DUNN'S SALARY THROUGH THE REMAINDER OF HIS TERM.

ELLEN LATER BECAME THE "CHIEF COUNTRESS" AT THE U.S. MINT. IN 1875 SHE ALSO MARRIED JAMES HENRI BURCH, AN OLD MASONIC FRIEND OF DUNN'S, CHANGING HER NAME TO ELLEN DUNN BURCH.

ELLEN DUNN BURCH SPENT THE REST OF HER LIFE IN CIVIL SERVICE AND WAS CONSULTED BY THE LIKES OF DOUGLASS, PRESIDENT GRANT, AND OTHER NATIONAL LEADERS ON THE CONDITION OF BLACK PEOPLE IN THE SOUTH. SHE DIED IN 1885.
RECORDS REGARDING THE FATES OF THE DUNN CHILDREN ARE SCARCE.

IN 1873 GOVERNOR KELLOGG APPROVED ACT 57, PASSED BY THE LEGISLATURE, WHICH SET ASIDE $10,000 TO ERECT A MONUMENT HONORING OSCAR DUNN.

THE MONUMENT WAS NEVER BUILT. TO THIS DAY, NOBODY KNOWS WHY, BUT THE LOOMING COLLAPSE OF RECONSTRUCTION AND INCREASING GOVERNMENTAL CHAOS IN LOUISIANA MAY HAVE HAD SOMETHING TO DO WITH IT.

DURING MARDI GRAS 1873, THE MISTICK KREWE OF COMUS MOCKED RECONSTRUCTION FIGURES WITH ITS PARADE THEME, "THE MISSING LINKS TO DARWIN'S ORIGIN OF SPECIES."

THE KREWE PORTRAYED GENERAL BUTLER AS A HYENA, WARMOTH AS A SNAKE, AND A BLACK LEADER--POSSIBLY DUNN, POSSIBLY A GENERIC CARICATURE--AS A GORILLA PLAYING A STRINGED INSTRUMENT AND, IN ANOTHER TABLEAU, PUTTING ON A CROWN.

DEMOCRATIC RESENTMENT OVER THE OUTCOME OF THE 1872 ELECTIONS AND THE PRESENCE OF FEDERAL TROOPS FESTERED.
IN APRIL 1873, IN GRANT PARISH, A WHITE PARAMILITARY GROUP ATTACKED A COURTHOUSE OCCUPIED BY BLACK MILITIAMEN, IN WHAT BECAME KNOWN AS THE COLFAX MASSACRE.

THE WHITE TERRORISTS MURDERED AS MANY AS 150 BLACK MEN, POSSIBLY THE WORST SCENE OF RACIAL VIOLENCE DURING RECONSTRUCTION.
We, the white people of Louisiana embracing the Democratic party, the Conservative party, the White man's party...
IN 1874, LOUISIANA DEMOCRATS OPENLY ENDORSED WHITE SUPREMACY IN THEIR PARTY PLATFORM.
A PARAMILITARY ORGANIZATION CALLED THE WHITE LEAGUE SPRANG UP ACROSS THE STATE. IN NEW ORLEANS, IT ROSE UP AGAINST THE REPUBLICAN STATE GOVERNMENT IN AN INSURRECTION KNOWN AS THE BATTLE OF LIBERTY PLACE.
THE WHITE LEAGUE TOOK OVER CITY HALL AND THE STATEHOUSE, AND ONLY SURRENDERED CONTROL OF THE CITY AFTER PRESIDENT GRANT SENT NAVAL SHIPS AND FEDERAL TROOPS TO RESTORE ORDER. DOZENS WERE KILLED AND MANY MORE INJURED.

BY 1876, REPUBLICANS ON THE NATIONAL LEVEL HAD LARGELY LOST INTEREST IN SUSTAINING RECONSTRUCTION, AND SOUTHERN DEMOCRATS WERE ACTIVELY FIGHTING TO END IT.
IN ORDER TO SECURE THE ELECTORAL VOTES NECESSARY TO WIN THAT YEAR'S PRESIDENTIAL ELECTION, REPUBLICAN RUTHERFORD B. HAYES STRUCK A COMPROMISE, AGREEING TO REMOVE FEDERAL TROOPS FROM THE SOUTH, INCLUDING LOUISIANA, ONCE AND FOR ALL.

IN 1877, WHITE NEW ORLEANIANS CELEBRATED THE DEPARTURE OF FEDERAL TROOPS BY FIRING 100 GUNS AT THE FOOT OF CANAL STREET. RECONSTRUCTION WAS OVER.

DEMOCRATS CLOSED RANKS IN LOUISIANA AND SOON BEGAN PASSING LAWS THAT DISENFRANCHISED BLACK PEOPLE--ROLLING BACK MOST OF THE GAINS MADE DURING RECONSTRUCTION.
IN 1891, A NEW MONUMENT WOULD BE ERECTED ON CANAL STREET--NOT OF DUNN, BUT IN HONOR OF THE WHITE LEAGUE REBELLION AT LIBERTY PLACE. IT REMAINED ON PUBLIC DISPLAY UNTIL 2017.

IN 1915, NEW ORLEANS OFFICIALS UNVEILED A STATUE OF GENERAL BEAUREGARD.
IT ALSO STOOD UNTIL 2017.
MEANWHILE, A GENERATION OF HISTORIANS DECLARED RECONSTRUCTION A FAILED PERIOD DEFINED BY CORRUPTION, DEEMPHASIZING ITS CIVIL RIGHTS ACHIEVEMENTS.
DUNN WAS CAST AS A PUPPET, SUBSERVIENT TO THE LOATHED CARPETBAGGER WARMOTH.
AFTER DUNN'S DEATH, ONE NEWSPAPER WROTE THAT "WHEN A FUTURE HISTORIAN SHALL RECORD THE TRANSITION OF THE COLORED RACE FROM BONDAGE TO FREEDOM . . . DUNN WILL NOT BE LOST IN THE MULTITUDE BUT WILL APPEAR HIGH ABOVE HIS FELLOWS, IN HIMSELF A TYPE OF THAT VERY TRANSITION."
WITHIN A FEW DECADES, THAT MEMORY APPEARED LOST.
HISTORIANS LIKE W. E. B. DU BOIS LATER HIGHLIGHTED THE ACHIEVEMENTS OF DUNN AND OTHER BLACK LEADERS OF THE ERA, BUT RECONSTRUCTION REMAINS ONE OF THE MOST MISUNDERSTOOD PERIODS OF U.S. HISTORY.

PART EIGHT

MONUMENTS OF MOURNFUL HEARTS

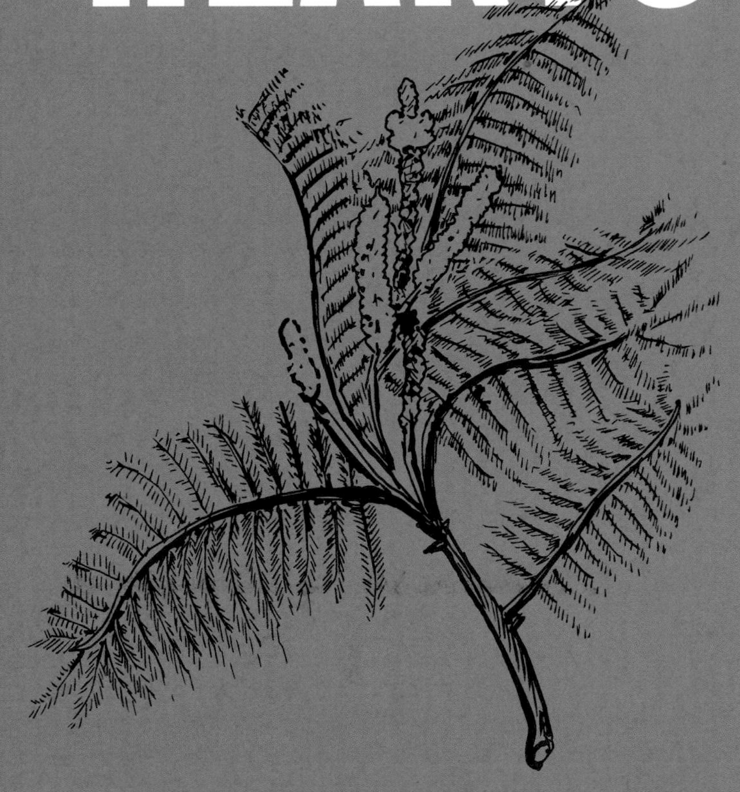

CONGO SQUARE, NEW ORLEANS
TWO WEEKS AFTER DUNN'S DEATH, HIS FRIENDS HELD A COMMEMORATION CEREMONY FOR HIM ON A BLUSTERY DECEMBER EVENING.

NONE SPOKE MORE PASSIONATELY THAN THOMAS MORRIS CHESTER--WHOSE WORDS THIS NIGHT MIGHT HAVE PROVOKED THE NEW YEAR'S DAY ATTACK.

A GREAT MAN HAS FALLEN IN LOUISIANA! BUT YESTERDAY HE MOVED AMONG US IN ALL THE GRANDEUR OF AN INCORRUPTIBLE OFFICIAL--A SPOTLESS PATRIOT, AN EXALTED CITIZEN, AND A POLISHED GENTLEMAN.

MEN OF EVERY SHADE OF POLITICAL OPINIONS . . . HAVE DIVESTED THEMSELVES OF PREJUDICE, AND TESTIFIED TO THE PURITY OF HIS PRIVATE AND PUBLIC CHARACTER.
YE WHO PURSUED HIM WITH SUCH UNRELENTING FURY, GO TO YONDER CITY OF THE DEAD AND LOOK UPON YOUR GHASTLY WORK. . . .

I ARRAIGN YOU, ONE AND ALL, TO ANSWER BEFORE THE BAR OF PUBLIC OPINION FOR ***THE MORAL MURDER OF OSCAR JAMES DUNN.***

CHESTER CONTINUED.
HE PASSED AWAY UNIVERSALLY VENERATED AND LAMENTED, TO THAT IMMATERIAL WORLD, WHERE HE IS SAYING TONIGHT, "*I FOUGHT A GOOD FIGHT UPON THE BANKS OF THE MISSISSIPPI*..."

"I KEPT THE FAITH OF THE REPUBLICAN PRINCIPLES; I RESISTED TEMPTATION IN WHATEVER PHASE IT PRESENTED ITSELF; I REFUSED TO COMPROMISE WITH FRAUD; I EXECRATED WHITE TREASON AND ANATHEMATIZED BLACK TRAITORS...."
SUCH A MAN CAN NEVER DIE, WHERE PRIVATE VIRTUE AND PUBLIC RECTITUDE ARE REVERED...

HE WILL LIVE IN THE AFFECTION OF THE PEOPLE--IN THE MORAL EXCELLENCE OF THOSE WHO WILL EMULATE HIS VIRTUES...

IN THE BRIGHT PAGE OF THE NATION'S HISTORY...

NEW ORLEANS, 1976
IN THE MONUMENTS OF MOURNFUL HEARTS TOWERING BEYOND THE CLOUDS. . . .

THERE HAVE BEEN NO BLACK GOVERNORS OR LIEUTENANT GOVERNORS.
BUT--
HOW COULD SHE NOT KNOW?
BRIAN MITCHELL
OSCAR JAMES DUN
1826 — 1871
LT. GOV. LA 1868 — 1871
GRAND MASTER PRINCE HALL
LA MASONS 1864— 67
CHESTER CONTINUED.
OUR CHAMPION IS DEAD! LONG LIVE OUR CHAMPION!
MONUMENTAL

EXTRACT from the Reconstructed Constitution OF THE

WILSON

MAHIER

CROMWELL

BONNEFOI

MOSES

MURREL

GARDINER

VALFROIT

BURREL

MORRIS

ISABELLE

SCOTT

LEROY

LEWIS

ANTOINE

DESLONDE

BILL OF RIGHTS.

ARTICLE 13.

All persons shall enjoy equal rights and privileges upon any conveyance of a public character; and all places of business or of public resort, shall be deemed places of a public character, and shall be opened to the accommodation and patronage of all persons, without distinction or discrimination on account of race or COLOR.

PUBLIC EDUCATION.

ARTICLE 135.

All children of this State shall be admitted to the Public Schools or other Institutions of learning sustained or established by the State in COMMON, *without distinction of* RACE COLOR *or* PREVIOUS CONDITION. *There shall be no separate schools or institutions of learning established exclusively for any Race by the State of Louisiana.*

ROBERTS

DUPART

O. J. DUNN

LIEUT. GOVERNOR OF LOUISIANA

POLLARD

ISABELLE

RIGGS

FRANCOIS

MARTIN

MONROE

WILLIAMS

BUTLER

MEADOWS

PINCHBACK

POINDEXTER

STATE OF LOUISIANA.

WITH PORTRAITS of the Distinguished Members of the Convention & Assembly. A. D. 1868.

In the Senate, Thursday, September third, Pinchback rose to a question of privilege, and said: I want to tell them to cease. I want to tell them they have nearly reached the end of their string. The next outrage of the kind which they commit will be the signal for the dawn of retribution—a retribution of which they have not dreamed; a signal that will cause ten thousand torches to be applied to this city, for patience will then have ceased to be a virtue, and this city will be reduced to ashes.

HISTORIOGRAPHY

RECONSTRUCTED NARRATIVES

WITH SUFFICIENT GENERAL AGREEMENT AND DETERMINATION AMONG THE DOMINANT CLASSES, THE TRUTH OF HISTORY MAY BE UTTERLY DISTORTED AND CONTRADICTED AND CHANGED TO ANY CONVENIENT FAIRY TALE THAT THE MASTERS OF MEN WISH.

—W. E. B. Du Bois, *Black Reconstruction in America* (1935)

MONUMENTAL joins an exciting new wave of books, films, and other media reviving interest in Reconstruction, one of the most misunderstood eras in American history. In his 2019 book *Stony the Road: Reconstruction, White Supremacy, and the Rise of Jim Crow*, scholar Henry Louis Gates Jr. argues that Reconstruction has such contemporary relevance because its central questions—about citizenship and voting rights, the government's role in fighting terrorism, and the relationship between political and economic democracy—continue to vex American society today.[1] Filled with hidden histories like Dunn's, Reconstruction remains a black box to much of the public—certainly compared to the Civil War, which has been perpetually commemorated, particularly in the South, through the adulation of its leading figures.

In 1980 historian John Hope Franklin observed that every generation has written its own history of Reconstruction and that, in their accounts of the era, historians have told us as much about their own generation's racial struggles as about Reconstruction itself.[2] It follows

EXTRACT FROM THE RECONSTRUCTED CONSTITUTION OF THE STATE OF LOUISIANA WITH PORTRAITS OF THE DISTINGUISHED MEMBERS OF THE CONVENTION AND ASSEMBLY; 1868; lithograph; *THNOC, 1979.183*

that the racism of some of the earliest and most influential crafters of Reconstruction history have contributed to America's collective failure to comprehend the era and its significant African American leaders. Historians and popular media have wrestled over the facts, narratives, and consequences of Reconstruction ever since.

***THE BIRTH OF A NATION* POSTER**; ca. 1936; *courtesy of the Library of Congress, Prints and Photographs Division, LC-DIG-ppmsc-04380*

The first generation of scholars to write formal histories of the era and examine Reconstruction's Black leadership, known as Traditionalists, were white men entrenched in Jim Crow America.[3] These historians, including influential Columbia University professors William Archibald Dunning and John William Burgess and their protégés, characterized Reconstruction as a colossal failure and branded its Black leadership as corrupt, ignorant, and ill prepared. In the analyses of "Dunning School" historians and their peers, Southern whites who resisted federal intervention and the expansion of African American rights emerged as the heroes. Despite rebelling against federal authority and often deploying violence and intimidation to invoke their will, these "Redeemers"—and particularly a powerful faction of white planters and Democratic politicians known as Bourbons—were enshrined in Traditionalist histories as having saved Southern society by restoring the region's antebellum social and racial hierarchy. In his 1907 history *Reconstruction, Political and Economic, 1865–1877*, Dunning wrote: "The end was single—the rescue of the states from the scandalous misrule of the carpet-baggers and negroes."[4]

This scholarship was reinforced by negative portrayals of Black people in literature and on the movie screen. These fictional accounts have helped shape public perceptions of Reconstruction and, because of their influence via popular culture, merit discussion alongside academic works. In the novels *The Leopard's Spots* (1903) and *The Clansman* (1905), Thomas Dixon told stories of how the Ku Klux Klan saved the South from complete devastation by Black and white Radical Republicans. *The Clansman* described a state legislature composed largely of Black men, its chambers stinking of "vile cigars, stale whiskey, and the odor of perspiring Negroes."[5] Dixon portrayed Republican leaders, both Black and white, as lazy, vulgar, and thieving.[6] D.W. Griffith immortalized *The Clansman* by adapting it to film as *The Birth of a Nation* (1915). The movie became one of the most popular films in American history, and by 1946 it had been seen by over 200 million viewers worldwide. President Woodrow Wilson hosted Dixon and Griffith for a private screening of the film at the White House.[7]

Many of the earliest objections to Traditionalist interpretations came from African Americans themselves. One of the most vocal critics was John R. Lynch, a former Mississippi congressman, whose book *The Facts of Reconstruction* (1913) refuted Traditionalist claims that Black politicians had mismanaged state governments. His Revisionist perspective maintained that they had "never dominated a State, nor . . . controlled the Republican organization of any State to the exclusion of the white men." Therefore, he argued, they could not be held responsible for many of the political actions and outcomes decried by Traditionalists. Lynch also offered the passage of the Fourteenth Amendment, which granted citizenship rights and equal protection to all people born or naturalized in the US, and the Fifteenth Amendment, which expanded voting rights to nonwhite men, as hallmarks of the era's success. In a tone unprecedented for its time, Lynch directly challenged Traditionalist historian James Ford Rhodes by declaring Rhodes's seven-volume *History of the United States from the Compromise of 1850 to the Final Restoration of Home Rule at the South in 1877* (1893–1906) as "the most biased, partisan and prejudiced historical work" he had ever read.[8] Lynch's writings were largely ignored by Traditionalist scholars but served as seminal works for subsequent Revisionist historians.

Between 1924 and 1935, historians Alrutheus Ambush Taylor, Francis Butler Simkins, Robert Hilliard Woody, Howard K. Beale, and W. E. B. Du Bois published works that continued in the Revisionist model exemplified by Lynch. In the work of this second wave of Revisionists, Reconstruction's Black leadership replaced the Redeemers as heroes of the era. Du Bois, for example, described Oscar Dunn as an "unselfish, incorruptible leader." These Revisionists viewed Reconstruction's Black leaders as harbingers of change and equality. They emphasized the era's successes—the expansion of public education, civil rights, male suffrage, and the economic reconstruction of Southern states—over its failures. Whereas Traditionalists had blamed Black people and white Radicals for Reconstruction's failure, the new Revisionist historians put the responsibility upon the Bourbon elite, southern Democrats, greedy carpetbaggers, and white Republicans who abandoned their Black counterparts. Like Lynch, they were unafraid to call out the biases of their forebears. Du Bois went so far as to dedicate the final chapter of his essential *Black Reconstruction in America, 1860–1880* (1935) to "The Propaganda of History," excoriating top Traditionalist scholars, one by one.[9] Much like Lynch, the new Revisionists failed to garner widespread support for their iconoclastic interpretations of Reconstruction.[10]

Not until the sweeping social and political reformations of the civil rights movement of the 1950s and '60s did Revisionists gain traction. As Black people emerged victorious from the struggle to reaffirm the rights they had won during the Civil War and Reconstruction, it was easy for many to compare the contemporary fight with its antecedent. Historian C. Vann Woodward even dubbed the era the "Second Reconstruction."[11] Renewed interest in America's nineteenth-century Reconstruction breathed new life into the Revisionist movement and its interpretations of the era's Black leadership. Historian Joel Williamson led this revival of Revisionism with his pioneering study of Reconstruction in South Carolina. Williamson's research depicted Black people as active participants in the campaigns for suffrage, equal rights, public education, and access to land. He contradicted Traditionalists' views that Reconstruction's Black leaders were ignorant and childlike. Williamson's study also disputed the early Revisionists' contentions that Black people had played a small role politically within Reconstruction governments. Williamson and other post–civil rights Revisionists challenged the assertions of the Traditionalist historians and, one after another, their interpretations replaced established Traditionalist conclusions.[12] The transition was not universally welcomed, though, as some contemporary Traditionalists refused to accept the movement's radical new ideas. Historian E. Merton Coulter denounced Revisionist assessments of Reconstruction, arguing that "no amount of revision can write away the grievous mistakes made in this abnormal period of American history."[13]

A cohort of Post-Revisionist historians soon emerged that rejected the generalizations of the Traditionalists and the Revisionists. They maintained that Reconstruction could not be fairly assessed by applying fault entirely to one race, Black or white. They critiqued Reconstruction's Black leadership and the Bourbon elite for their contributions to the era's tensions. Post-Revisionists focused their attentions on Reconstruction as a political process that transformed both Black and white communities in the South. Their research found complex political networks operating in response to social, political, and economic situations that were often specific to a particular geography.[14]

An important study in the early Post-Revisionist movement was historian Thomas Holt's *Black Over White: Negro Political Leadership in South Carolina during Reconstruction* (1977). In contrast to Williamson, who contended that the Republican Party had been ineffectual because its Black leaders had distanced themselves from their white counterparts by conceding to the demands of their Black constituency, Holt provided a new conservative image of Reconstruction's Black leadership. Holt showed that internal tensions within the Black community may have played a role in Reconstruction's failure. His revelation that South Carolina's Reconstruction Black community was fragmented and factionalized opened a new area of debate regarding Reconstruction politics, one that *Monumental* explores in the relationship between New Orleans's Afro-Creole and Anglo-African communities.

Louisiana's unique history in this regard has granted scholars an invaluable field for study. Post-Revisionist historians John W. Blassingame and David Rankin analyzed the complex array of factors that stratified New Orleans's Black leadership. These factors included place of birth, social status before and after the war, geography, occupation, age, skin color, wealth, and literacy, as well as cultural and religious affiliations. Rankin's research, detailed in a 1974 article in the *Journal of Southern History* and titled "The Origins of Black Leadership in New Orleans during Reconstruction," was largely quantitative, revealing that the majority of Black politicians were

Afro-Creoles who bore little resemblance to the average Black voter in Reconstruction Louisiana, who was more likely than not an English-speaking, Protestant, formerly enslaved person. Rankin maintained that many of these Afro-Creole politicians had never been enslaved, were connected by blood to some of the city's oldest white families, were literate, spoke French, and worshipped in Catholic churches.

Conversely, Blassingame's research in *Black New Orleans, 1860–1880* (1973) was largely qualitative and provided glimpses into New Orleans politics and culture. Although Blassingame acknowledged the factors that Rankin employed in making his generalizations about Black politicians, he also provided a far more detailed and balanced assessment of the city's amalgamated Black community. His intricate portrayal revealed that though Afro-Creoles and Anglo-Africans were often divided by antebellum prejudices and conflicting interests, they were capable of working collaboratively on mutually important issues.

Charles Vincent's *Black Legislators in Louisiana during Reconstruction* (1976) assessed the political effectiveness of Louisiana's Black leaders by examining their ability to pass legislation that would benefit their constituency. Like many Revisionists before him, Vincent maintained that Black legislators had successfully provided an array of social and fiscal reforms that benefited the state's Black and white citizens alike. Despite the text's detail on political matters, Vincent's research failed to examine the roles that factionalism and ethnicity played within the Black leadership.

In the 1980s, a number of books grappled with the broader Black experience during Reconstruction. One of the most noted was Eric Foner's *Reconstruction: America's Unfinished Revolution, 1863–1877* (1988). Foner's tome, a Pulitzer Prize finalist, was the culmination of the Revisionist and Post-Revisionist writing that preceded it and gained international accolades for successfully blending social and political history. Foner's narrative centered on the perspectives of freedmen themselves. The two most important themes that Foner identified were the impact of an emancipated labor force in the South and the freedmen's developing ideas about equal opportunity, freedom, and citizenship. Foner's evenhanded evaluation of complex economic, social, and political issues throughout the South during Reconstruction served as a model for several subsequent books.[15]

The election of Barack Obama as the first African American US president, in 2008, inspired another wave of scholarly and popular interest in the Reconstruction era and its Black leadership. The reaction to his presidency—both during and after his term in office—has likewise spurred comparisons to the efforts by Redeemers to undo the gains made by African Americans during Reconstruction. "The eruption of the expression of white supremacist ideology in what increasingly appears to be a determined attempt to roll back the very phenomenon of a Black presidency," Gates wrote in *Stony the Road*, "is just one reason that the rise and fall of Reconstruction and the surge of white supremacy in the former Confederate states following the end of the Civil War are especially relevant subjects for Americans to reflect upon at this moment in the history of our democracy."[16] Along with *Stony the Road*, Gates produced the award-winning 2019 PBS documentary *Reconstruction: America after the Civil War*, but he isn't alone in examining Reconstruction anew in the wake of Obama's election and presidency.

PRESIDENT BARACK OBAMA, WITH FAMILY, TAKING THE OATH OF OFFICE;
January 20, 2009; photograph by Chuck Kennedy; *courtesy of the Associated Press*

Foner's *The Second Founding: How the Civil War and Reconstruction Remade the Constitution* (2019) argued that the passage of the Reconstruction amendments and the intervention of the federal government in the South to protect the rights of vulnerable African Americans forged a new relationship between citizens and the federal government so profoundly different from what preceded it that it constituted a second founding of the nation. Like *Stony the Road*, it grappled with the effort to dismantle the rights guaranteed by those amendments during the Jim Crow era and into modern times. *Before Obama: A Reappraisal of Black Reconstruction Era Politicians* (2012), edited by Matthew Lynch, was a two-volume compendium of biographical essays that largely celebrated the unheralded work of Black lawmakers in the Reconstruction South. It included a chapter about Dunn by Linda English that provided one of the more thorough recent assessments of his career. English wrote that by being universally praised for his integrity and acumen, Dunn defied the stereotypes Traditionalists attempted to apply to Reconstruction's Black leaders, which may have been a reason why they overlooked him. She noted that Dunning's *Reconstruction, Political and Economic, 1865–1877*, omitted Dunn entirely, and argued that "the historical disregard of Dunn and his contributions to Louisiana by critics of Radical Reconstruction is a telling indicator of the shortcomings of their arguments."[17]

Historians Justin A. Nystrom and Philip Dray have also contributed scholarship about Black politicians in Reconstruction Louisiana in the last decade, though both provide only limited sketches of Dunn. Nystrom's *New Orleans after the Civil War: Race, Politics, and a New Birth of Freedom* (2010) acknowledged the racial complexity that existed in New Orleans politics but, unlike Revisionists and early Post-Revisionists, he maintained that many Black politicians entered the political arena for the same reason as their white counterparts: financial gain. Dray's *Capitol Men: The Epic Story of Reconstruction through the Lives of the First Black Congressmen*

DUNN DEFIED THE STEREOTYPES TRADITIONALISTS ATTEMPTED TO APPLY TO RECONSTRUCTION'S BLACK LEADERS, WHICH MAY HAVE BEEN A REASON WHY THEY OVERLOOKED HIM.

(2008), similar to *Before Obama*, recounted stories of a handful of Black Reconstruction leaders, tracing their paths to political power and difficulties as the nation's first group of Black politicians following the Civil War.

Monumental joins this Obama/Post-Obama generation of Reconstruction analysis, and it has also been influenced by robust local and national conversations about the commemoration of Civil War and Reconstruction history in public spaces. These were largely sparked by the 2015 mass shooting at "Mother Emanuel" AME Church in Charleston, South Carolina, when a white supremacist who evinced pride in the Confederacy and its flag murdered nine Black churchgoers. National outrage following the shooting was accompanied by cries to remove statues honoring Confederate leaders, memorials, and flags. New Orleans became ground zero in this debate in 2015 when its city council voted 6–1 to remove four statues and monuments commemorating Confederate leaders and the 1874 white supremacist rebellion at Liberty Place. When the monuments came down in 2017, New Orleans Mayor Mitch Landrieu delivered a powerful speech on the topic where he stated that the monuments were "not just innocent remembrances of a benign history" but rather celebrated "a fictional, sanitized Confederacy: ignoring the death, ignoring the enslavement, ignoring the terror that it actually stood for."[18]

The debates over these public spaces continue, with creative movements suggesting new ways to commemorate the past, like New Orleans's own Paper Monuments, a community-driven project that empowered citizens to participate in the debate through public proposals, events, and a citywide poster campaign. In 2020 the New Orleans City Council established an advisory committee to rename streets, parks, and other places that honor white supremacists. On the national level, President Obama did his part to draw attention to Reconstruction on January 12, 2017, in the final days of his second term, when he issued a proclamation establishing the Reconstruction Era National Monument in Beaufort, South Carolina, just 70 miles from Mother Emanuel.

We have come a long way from the Dunning School. The study, and authorship, of Reconstruction history is being democratized at an incredible pace through myriad platforms—books, yes, but also documentaries, podcasts, and more. *Monumental* strives to merge a top-down perspective, in its portrayal of Dunn, with a bottom-up spirit, à la Foner's *Reconstruction*, in no small part through the use of illustration to make visible the communities that nurtured him. It joins a rich tradition of graphic histories and has been influenced by a range of predecessors, from Trevor Getz's groundbreaking scholarship in *Abina and the Important Men* (2012) to the late Rep. John Lewis's riveting autobiographical account of the civil rights movement in his award-winning *March* trilogy (2013–16). Through painstaking attention to detail, *Monumental* offers new possibilities for the medium. Our intent is that it will serve as an introduction to Dunn and Reconstruction in Louisiana for younger readers while remaining worthy scholarship that fills important gaps, as we continue to improve our collective understanding of this vital American era and its people.

1. Gates, *Stony the Road*, 5–6.
2. Franklin, "Mirror for Americans," 1–14.
3. Dunning, *Reconstruction, Political and Economic*; Bowers, *Tragic Era*; Rhodes, *History of the United States*.
4. Dunning, *Reconstruction, Political and Economic*, 267.
5. Dixon, *Clansman*, 264–69.
6. Jones, "Images," 321.
7. Benbow, "Birth of a Quotation," 531; Litwack, "*Birth of a Nation*," 136.
8. J. Lynch, *Facts of Reconstruction*, 321; J. Lynch, "Some Historical Errors," 345.
9. Du Bois, *Black Reconstruction*, 711–28.
10. Taylor, *Negro in South Carolina*; Simkins and Woody, *South Carolina during Reconstruction*; Du Bois, *Black Reconstruction*; Beale, *Critical Year*.
11. Woodward, "Political Legacy," 240.
12. Williamson, *After Slavery*; Stampp, *Era of Reconstruction*; Cox and Cox, *Politics, Principle, and Prejudice*; McPherson, *Struggle for Equality*; Franklin, *Reconstruction*; Roark, *Masters without Slaves*; Woodward, *Strange Career*.
13. Coulter, *South during Reconstruction*, xi, 86, 336.
14. Litwack, *Been in the Storm*; McPherson, *Ordeal by Fire*; Current, *Those Terrible Carpetbaggers*.
15. Perman, *Major Problems*; Dykstra, *Bright Radical Star*; Saville, *Work of Reconstruction*; Schwalm, *Hard Fight*; Cimbala, *Guardianship*; Richardson, *Death of Reconstruction*; Blight, *Race and Reunion*.
16. Gates, *Stony the Road*, 5–6.
17. M. Lynch, *Before Obama*, 82–83.
18. Landrieu, "Truth."

LT. GOV. DUNN; ca. 1871; drawing by Alfred Rudolph Waud; *THNOC, The L. Kemper and Leila Moore Williams Founders Collection, 1965.90.311.5*

Lt. Genl. Dunn
ARW
N.O. 1871

PRIMARY SOURCES

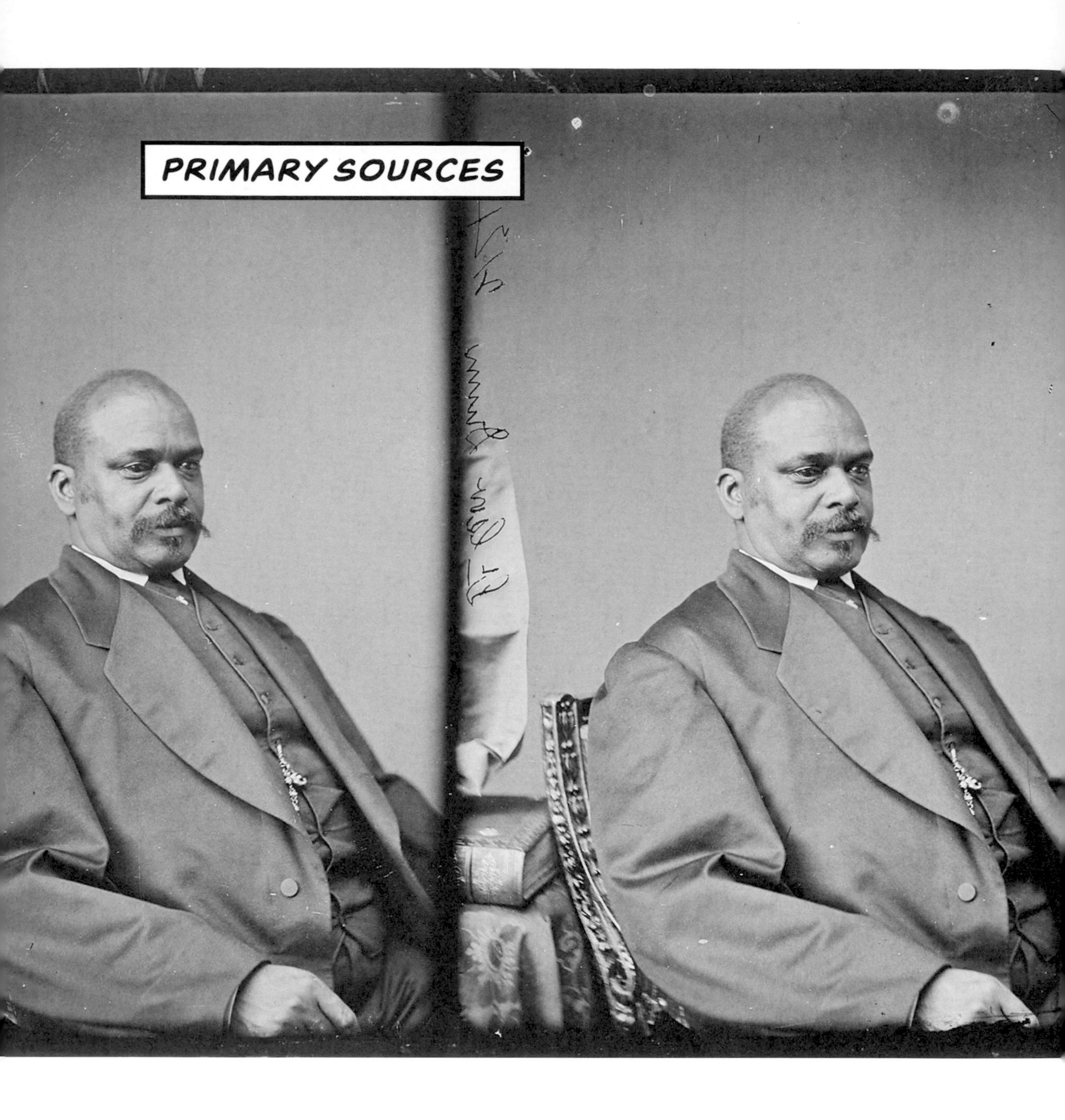

LIEUT. GOVERNOR DUNN, LA; ca. 1869; stereograph by Brady National Photographic Art Gallery (Washington, DC); *courtesy of the National Archives, photo no. 111-B-3733*

FINDING OSCAR DUNN

OSCAR DUNN left no known personal diary or collection of letters, and his sudden death robbed him of the chance to properly reflect on his career as his rivals Henry Clay Warmoth and P. B. S. Pinchback were able to do later in life. Outside of what can be gleaned from official documents and testimony, much about his personal life, particularly his youth, remains unknown. My research for this book, however, uncovered new primary sources that add valuable detail and correct significant errors that have been woven into Dunn's biography.

The bulk of what was previously known about Dunn is summarized in seven academic papers: Marcus Christian's "Men of Worth in Louisiana" and "The Theory of the Poisoning of Oscar James Dunn"; A. E. Perkins's "Oscar James Dunn," "James Henri Burch and Oscar James Dunn in Louisiana," and "Some Negro Officers and Legislators in Louisiana"; Charles Vincent's "Negro Legislators in Louisiana During Reconstruction" (later adapted as a book); and David Rankin's "The Origins of Black Leadership in New Orleans during Reconstruction." The studies generally agree on his political record and reputation for integrity, but fail to create a similarly clear picture of his life before office. They provide conflicting accounts of Dunn's origin and prewar enslaved status, and some mistakenly state that he served in the military during the war, an error likely originating from a single newspaper source that conflated part of his biography with Pinchback's. (I debunked this, in part, by comparing dates in ledgers from Dunn's Masonic lodge with Louisiana Native Guard muster rolls. For more, see pages 225–26.)

Two rediscovered sources, published shortly after Dunn's death, reveal rare details about Dunn's antebellum life: a eulogy given by Dunn's lifelong friend and Masonic brother James Henri Burch, and a lengthy biographical sketch that appeared in the short-lived *Weekly National Republican* of New Orleans, which includes vital background from John Parsons, another friend and Masonic brother of Dunn's. The only other known source containing information about Dunn's early life—one that has been heavily relied upon by historians over the years—is a limited account by James Dryden, a former employer of Dunn's. (Another sketch, written by William Wells Brown in 1874, provides scant unique detail.[1])

I located public records that confirm Dunn's enslavement and his emancipation. A record from 1831 in the New Orleans Notarial Archives details commission merchant George P. Bowers's sale of nine-year-old Oscar, his mother, Maria, and sister, Jane, to James Dunn, who became Oscar's stepfather.[2] A New Orleans City Archives record shows that James Dunn emancipated Maria, Oscar, and Jane in 1832, contradicting a thread in some scholarship that Dunn had been enslaved when he abandoned his plastering job in 1841.[3] (For more, see page 225.)

Another recovered source is a biographical article about Dunn's wife, Ellen Dunn Burch. The article, published in the *St. Paul Daily Globe* in 1885, contains excerpts from an interview conducted with Dunn Burch, and is the sole known account of her life. In it, she discusses her marriage to Dunn, her family's origin, and her life after Dunn's death.

Other new sources provide critical insights regarding Dunn's political career. I found, in the holdings of the Minnesota Historical Society, a speech given by noted African American journalist Maj. Thomas Morris Chester, entitled "Remember Dunn, and Follow Ingraham!"[4] It provides a wealth of information about Dunn's political tensions and final days, including the allegation that Pinchback threatened him weeks before his death. During the editing of this book, we also identified an important aspect of Dunn's time in office that had gotten lost in the historical record: that he had served as acting governor prior to Pinchback, who has been commonly referenced as the first Black governor. (For more, see pages 232–33.)

The consensus by previous scholars regarding Dunn's sterling reputation as a politician is supported by many testimonials made during his lifetime. In 1868, the *New Orleans Republican* published a joint resolution from the Radical Republican clubs of Terrebonne Parish, which stated that Dunn was an "honor to his race" as well as "a gentleman, a sound Republican, a Christian, and a talented politician."[5] Praise for Dunn would not be limited to members of his own party: Democratic state senator James Ogden commented that Dunn was "a man who by his dignity, his courtesy and intelligence, had won the respect of his political enemies."[6] A day after his death, the *Courier-Journal* of Louisville wrote that Dunn's popularity was such that President Ulysses S. Grant had been considering him as a running mate in 1872 or 1876.[7] Early biographers overlooked controversies such as his alleged anti–Afro-Creole speech made during the 1868 campaign and allegations by Warmoth, later on, that Dunn unfairly influenced rural voters through his supporters' control of printing contracts. The balance of the record on Dunn during his lifetime is nonetheless very positive, and had a lasting impact on scholarship about him.

It is my hope that *Monumental* will inspire further study, and perhaps lead to the discovery of additional primary sources that can reveal more details about his life and career.

—Brian K. Mitchell

1. "Oscar James Dunn," *Weekly National Republican* (New Orleans), November 22, 1871; Burch, Eulogy; Dryden, Reminiscences; Brown, *The Rising Son*, 490–91.
2. Orleans Parish Conveyance Book 7, p. 197, February 5, 1831, New Orleans Notarial Archives. The original act of conveyance denoting Dunn's sale was destroyed in a fire, but a notation and summary can be found here.
3. Petition 40B, VCP320, New Orleans City Archives. Maria is listed as approximately 37 years old; Oscar, 10; and Jane, 8.
4. Chester, "Remember Dunn."
5. "Cheering Words," *New Orleans Republican*, January 30, 1868.
6. Perkins, "Oscar James Dunn," 115; "Louisiana Legislature," *Daily Picayune*, July 8, 1868.
7. "Lieutenant-Governor Dunn," *Courier-Journal* (Louisville, KY), November 23, 1871.

RECORD OF POLICE JURY APPROVING JAMES DUNN'S PETITION TO EMANCIPATE MARIA, OSCAR, AND JANE (detail); December 10, 1832; *courtesy of Louisiana Division/City Archives, New Orleans Public Library*

" On the petition of James Dunn f.M.C. praying tha
the consent of the police jury be granted to emancipa
is wife the mulatto woman Maria aged about
thirty five years and her two children Oscar age
en years & Jane aged Eight years, in consideratio
f her long faithful & important services & on
he Certificate of five citizens attesting the facts
stated in the petition; The police Jury unanimous
declare that they consent to the emancipation
f said mulatto woman Maria & her two childr
Oscar & Jane, without being compelled to leave
he State; Provided their consent be ratified by
he jury at a subsequent meeting agreably to
aw. "

— Sitting of the 8th December 1832.

The police jury take again into consideration the
petition of James Dunn f.M.C. praying that the
consent of the jury be granted to emancipate the
mulatto woman named Maria and her two childr
Oscar & Jane, also the resolution passed at their
sitting of the 6th October last & after deliberating
thereon the police Jury unanimously declare that
hey ratify the consent granted in said sitting for
e emancipation of said Maria & her two children
Oscar & Jane, without being compelled to leave the
tate."

e above extracts to be true copies from the Record
ce Jury of the Parish of Orleans. New-Orlean
r 1832.

A. Trudeau

PART ONE: ORIGINS

1822 Oscar Dunn is born.

1831 **FEBRUARY**: James Dunn purchases Maria, Oscar, and Jane from George P. Bowers.

1832 **DECEMBER**: James Dunn emancipates his wife, Maria, and stepchildren, Oscar and Jane.

1836 Oscar Dunn becomes a plasterer's apprentice.

1841 Around this time, Dunn begins teaching music.

1852 **NOVEMBER**: Dunn becomes an apprentice Freemason.

1860 **JUNE**: The Thomas J. Martin scandal erupts, compelling Dunn to quit teaching music.

PART TWO: WAR AND EMANCIPATION

1860 **NOVEMBER**: Republican Abraham Lincoln is elected president of the United States.

DECEMBER: South Carolina secedes from the United States.

1861 **JANUARY**: Louisiana becomes the sixth Southern state to secede. The Confederacy will grow to include eleven states.

1862 **APRIL**: The Civil War begins. By month's end, federal troops occupy New Orleans.

1863 **JANUARY**: Lincoln signs the Emancipation Proclamation, freeing more than 3 million enslaved people.

1864 **DECEMBER**: Dunn is installed as the Most Worshipful Grand Master of the Eureka Grand Lodge.

1865 **JANUARY**: Congress passes the Thirteenth Amendment, formally abolishing slavery.

MARCH: Congress creates the Freedmen's Bureau.

APRIL: Confederate Gen. Robert E. Lee surrenders, effectively ending the Civil War. Lincoln is assassinated in Washington, DC.

JUNE: Dunn joins the Friends of Universal Suffrage.

NOVEMBER: Dunn opens an intelligence office to help freedmen find fair work.

DECEMBER: Louisiana passes Black Codes that severely restrict the rights of freedmen.

1866 **APRIL**: Congress overrides Pres. Andrew Johnson's veto to pass a civil rights bill.

MAY: Dunn is elected president of the new Freedmen's Aid Association.

PART THREE: THE RIOT AND THE RADICALS

1866 **JULY**: A white mob attacks a convention of mostly Black Republicans in New Orleans, killing about 40 people.

DECEMBER: Dunn marries Ellen Boyd Marshall.

1867 **FEBRUARY**: A congressional committee condemns the massacre by police in New Orleans and recommends establishing a new provisional government in Louisiana.

MARCH: Congress passes the first of a series of Reconstruction Acts that divide Southern states into military districts and establish requirements for readmission to the Union.

JUNE: Louisiana's white Masonic organization opens a French-speaking Black lodge, undercutting Dunn's authority.

AUGUST: Gen. Philip Sheridan appoints Dunn to the New Orleans city council.

SEPTEMBER: The council elects Dunn assistant recorder of the Second District, making him the first Black man to serve in a judicial capacity in Louisiana.

1868 **JANUARY**: Dunn is nominated to run for lieutenant governor on the Republican ticket with Henry Clay Warmoth.

PART FOUR: THE BLACK LIEUTENANT GOVERNOR

1868 **FEBRUARY**: The House of Representatives impeaches President Johnson. He later wins acquittal in the Senate.

APRIL: Louisiana voters approve a new state constitution and elect Warmoth and Dunn, who becomes the nation's first Black lieutenant governor.

JULY: The new Republican-led Louisiana legislature ratifies the Fourteenth Amendment, guaranteeing Black people citizenship rights and equal protection under the law. Louisiana legislators introduce a bill designed to help enforce civil rights.

1868 **SEPTEMBER**: Governor Warmoth vetoes the civil rights bill.

NOVEMBER: Democratic presidential candidate Horatio Seymour wins Louisiana after months of white terror enacted upon its Black citizens. Republican Ulysses S. Grant still wins the election.

1869 **FEBRUARY**: Warmoth approves a weaker version of the state legislature's civil rights bill.

MARCH: Dunn is denied first-class rail accommodations for a trip north by the president of the railroad, Gen. P. G. T. Beauregard.

APRIL: Dunn meets with President Grant and is the first Black public official to visit the White House.

PART FIVE: IN NEED OF AN EXORCISM

1869 **MAY**: Warmoth takes control of Jefferson City.

JUNE: Dunn, as president of the Metropolitan Police Board, is briefly imprisoned after a Democratic judge finds the Metropolitans to be in contempt of court.

DECEMBER: Dunn purchases a new home on Canal Street.

1870 **FEBRUARY**: The Fifteenth Amendment is ratified, prohibiting federal or state denial of voting rights based on race, color, or previous condition of servitude.

MARCH: The Louisiana legislature passes laws that give Governor Warmoth sweeping power over elections.

APRIL: Dunn allegedly attends a public exorcism of Rev. John Turner.

MAY: Congress passes the first of a series of Enforcement Acts meant to deter the white supremacist terror that plagued the 1868 elections.

PART SIX: NO GREATER DIVIDE

1870 **AUGUST**: At the Republican State Convention, Dunn is elected president over Warmoth.

NOVEMBER: Thanks to the new federal and state laws, Louisiana elections are held peacefully. Republicans perform well across the board.

1871 **JANUARY**: Following a court ruling, New Orleans public schools are integrated. Dunn's daughters are the first Black children admitted to the Madison Girls' School.

MARCH: Warmoth injures his foot in a boating accident, requiring surgery.

MAY: Warmoth's injury requires him to leave the state which, according to the state constitution, makes Dunn the first Black acting governor in US history. In his first major decision as acting governor, Dunn declines to commute the death sentences of two Spanish men convicted of murder.

JULY: Dunn announces a series of executive dismissals and appointments.
Warmoth abruptly returns to New Orleans from Mississippi to reclaim his office.

1871 **AUGUST**: Ahead of the Republican state convention, Warmoth uses undercover police to violently break up Radical club meetings. After a dispute with Dunn allies at the convention, held at the US Customhouse, Warmoth holds a rival convention at Turners' Hall. P. B. S. Pinchback joins him.

SEPTEMBER: The dueling conventions send complaints about each other to President Grant. Dunn sends a letter fiercely critical of Warmoth to presidential candidate Horace Greeley.

PART SEVEN: COLLAPSE

PART EIGHT: MONUMENTS OF MOURNFUL HEARTS

1871 **NOVEMBER**: Pinchback allegedly threatens to reveal scandalous information about Dunn. Weeks later, Dunn becomes violently ill and dies, officially of "congestion of the brain and lungs." Approximately 20,000 people witness Dunn's dramatic funeral procession.

DECEMBER: Warmoth works with legislators to replace Dunn with Pinchback.

1872 **APRIL**: Funds raised from a speech given by Frederick Douglass in New Orleans are donated to Ellen Dunn.

NOVEMBER: President Grant is reelected. Louisiana succumbs to chaos as a Democrat and Republican both claim gubernatorial victories.

DECEMBER: Warmoth is impeached, and Pinchback briefly serves as acting governor.

1873 **JANUARY**: Grant orders Louisiana to seat Republican William Pitt Kellogg as governor.

MARCH: Kellogg approves an act that creates an organization and budget to build a monument to Dunn. It is never built.

1874 The paramilitary White League rebels against the Republican state government in the Battle of Liberty Place, resulting in dozens of deaths.

1875 **MARCH**: Louisiana's senate approves funds to erect a new tomb for Dunn. It is never built.

1877 **APRIL**: Pres. Rutherford B. Hayes withdraws federal troops from Louisiana, ending Reconstruction.

1891 **SEPTEMBER**: A monument honoring the white supremacist uprising at the Battle of Liberty Place is erected in New Orleans.

1915 **NOVEMBER**: A monument honoring Confederate Gen. P. G. T. Beauregard is erected in New Orleans.

1976 Author Brian K. Mitchell's teacher asserts that Louisiana has never had a Black lieutenant governor.

2021 *Monumental* is published, 150 years after Dunn's death.

OSCAR DUNN'S NEW ORLEANS

1 Home of George P. Bowers, possible Oscar Dunn birthplace

2 James and Maria Dunn's boardinghouse, where they were attacked in 1834

3 Dunn's residence, 1846

4 Dunn's residence, ca. 1848–60, and home of Peter and Ellen Boyd Marshall (Dunn's future wife)

5 Richmond Lodge No. 4, where Dunn apprenticed as a Freemason in 1852

6 St. James AME Church,* Dunn's church

7 City Hall,* opposite from Lafayette Square

8 Mechanics' Institute, state government offices and site of 1866 massacre

9 Dunn's intelligence office, 1866

10 Dunn's intelligence office, 1867–68

11 Jackson and Great Northern railroad depot, where Dunn was denied first-class seating in 1869

12 Site where Warmoth took over Jefferson City

13 Dunn's residence, 1869–71

14 Turners' Hall,* location of Dunn's 1870 masquerade controversy and Warmoth's rival 1871 convention

15 US Customhouse,* site of 1871 Republican convention

16 St. Louis Cemetery No. 2,* where Dunn was interred in 1871

17 Congo Square,* location of Dunn Commemoration Ceremony

** Still in existence; colored in purple at right*

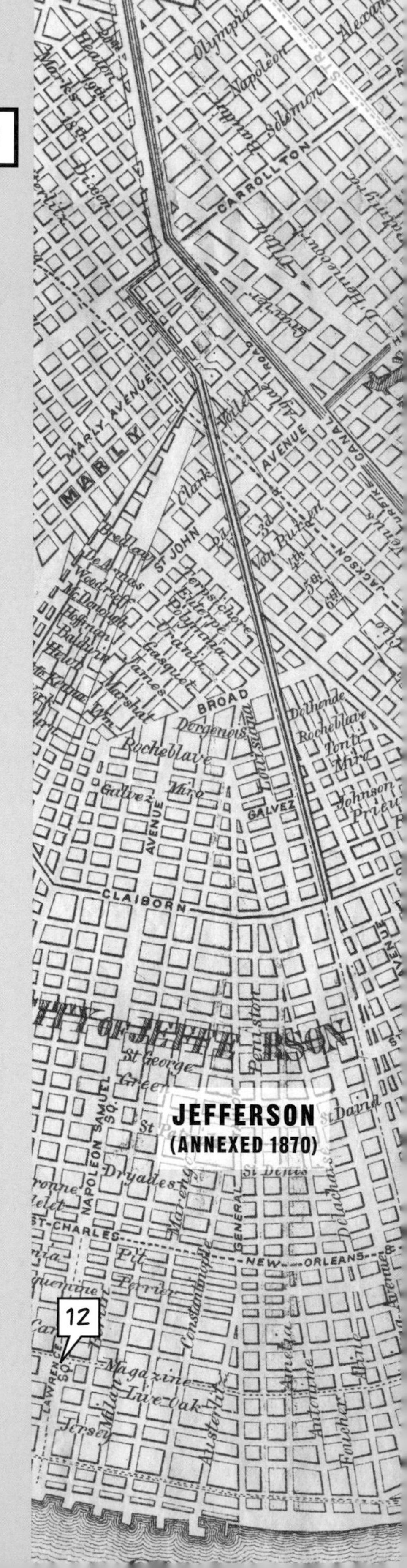

NEW PLAN OF THE CITY AND ENVIRONS OF NEW ORLEANS, COMPILED FOR GARDNERS DIRECTORY (detail); 1869; lithograph by Benedict Simon; *THNOC, The L. Kemper and Leila Moore Williams Founders Collection, 1962.7*

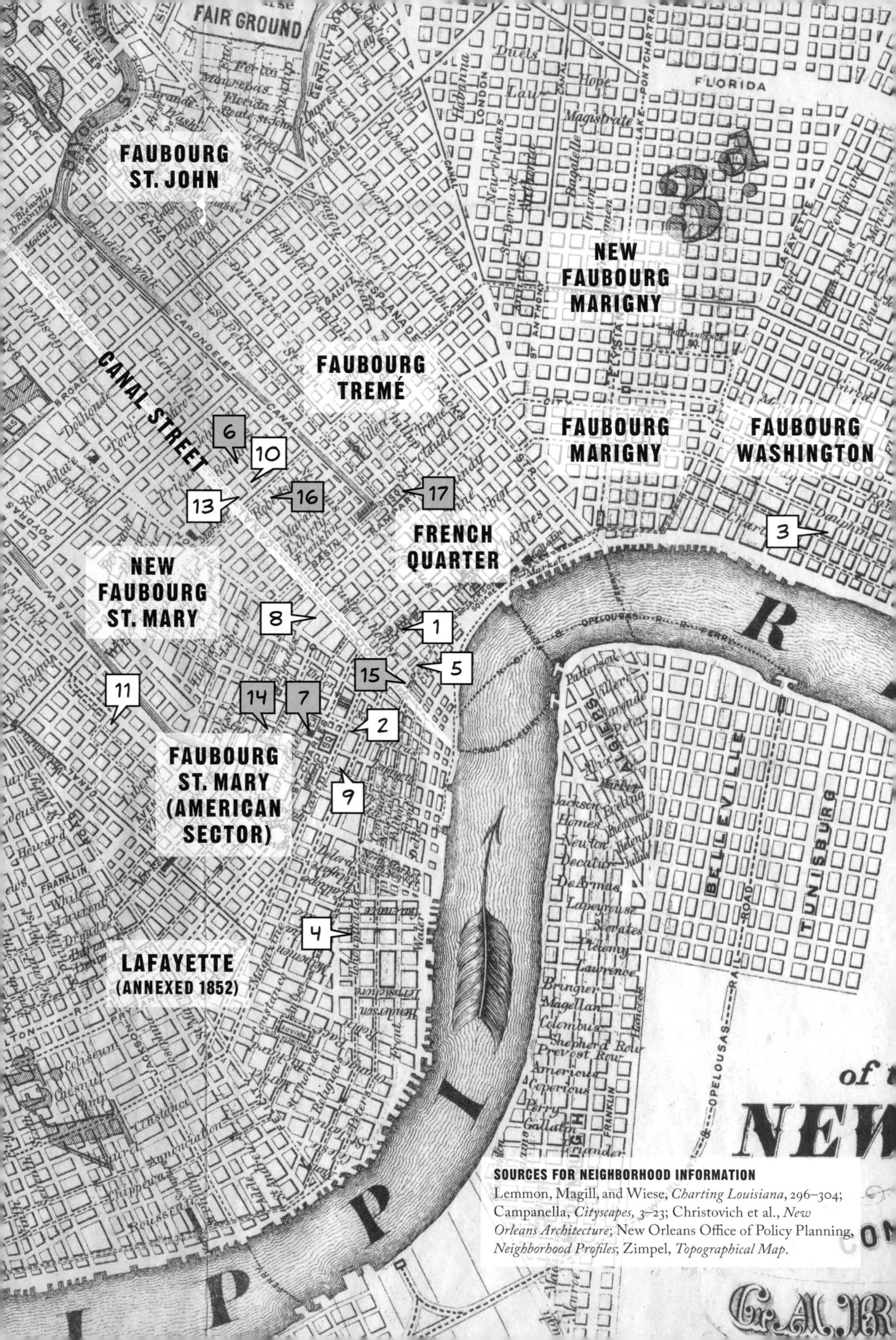

SOURCES FOR NEIGHBORHOOD INFORMATION
Lemmon, Magill, and Wiese, *Charting Louisiana*, 296–304; Campanella, *Cityscapes*, 3–23; Christovich et al., *New Orleans Architecture*; New Orleans Office of Policy Planning, *Neighborhood Profiles*; Zimpel, *Topographical Map*.

AFRO-CREOLE One of two major Black communities in New Orleans during Dunn's lifetime. Many Afro-Creoles were born free or were emancipated by a white father before the Civil War—or had ancestors who had been. They typically spoke French and worshipped in Catholic churches.

ANGLO-AFRICAN The other major Black community in New Orleans during Dunn's lifetime. Before the Civil War most Anglo-Africans were enslaved. They spoke English and worshipped in Protestant churches.

CARPETBAGGER Used derogatorily by ex-Confederates to describe men who had relocated to the South during or after the war and who, it was believed, supported Reconstruction and Republican policies for personal profit.

FAUBOURG A French term meaning "suburb." The New Orleans faubourgs surrounded the French Quarter, the historic center of the city.

FIFTEENTH AMENDMENT Prohibited federal or state denial of voting rights based on race, color, or previous condition of servitude; ratified February 3, 1870.

FOURTEENTH AMENDMENT Granted citizenship rights and equal protection under the law to all people born or naturalized in the United States; ratified July 9, 1868.

FREEDMEN African Americans emancipated during and after the Civil War.

FREEMASONRY A centuries-old fraternal secret society that has member lodges all over the world. Members are known as Freemasons, or just Masons.

FRIENDS OF UNIVERSAL SUFFRAGE A political organization focused on winning voting rights for Black men. It was formed after the Civil War and evolved into the Louisiana Republican Party.

JIM CROW Describes the era and laws that enshrined widespread discrimination against African Americans after the end of Reconstruction and well into the twentieth century.

KNIGHTS OF THE WHITE CAMELLIA A Louisiana white supremacist organization, similar to the Ku Klux Klan operating in other states, that used violence and terror to suppress Republican voting and intimidate African Americans, particularly during the 1868 election season.

METROPOLITANS A police force established by Governor Henry Clay Warmoth with the purpose of combating rampant violence in New Orleans and the surrounding parishes.

PURE RADICAL A predominantly Black subset of the Radical Republican faction distinguished by its members' uncompromising stances on Black rights.

QUADROON An outdated term once used to describe a person considered to be one-quarter Black—sometimes used in reference to Afro-Creoles.

RADICAL A political movement ultimately led by a faction of the Republican Party that advocated for the full extension of social and political rights to Black men and also more punitive measures against the former Confederate states.

RECONSTRUCTION The era of American history dealing with the aftermath of the Civil War and the restoration of the South to the United States.

REDEEMERS A conservative Southern political faction that emerged during Reconstruction that sought to restore white supremacy in the region.

SCALAWAG Used as an epithet by ex-Confederates to describe Southern natives sympathetic to Reconstruction and Republican policies after the Civil War.

THIRTEENTH AMENDMENT Officially abolished slavery, except as punishment for a crime; ratified December 6, 1865.

ACKNOWLEDGMENTS

FOLLOWING OSCAR DUNN'S DEATH, Frederick Douglass recited his famous speech "Self-Made Men" in New Orleans in honor of the late lieutenant governor. "Our best and most valued acquisitions have been obtained either from our contemporaries or from those who have preceded us in the field of thought and discovery," Douglass says in the lecture. "We have all either begged, borrowed or stolen. We have reaped where others have sown, and that which others have strown, we have gathered." This graphic history, while bearing the names of the author, illustrator, and editor on its cover, is the fruit of so many others.

As a child, I was taught that in all endeavors we are to thank our creator. Without breath and faith, nothing is possible. I want to thank the matriarchs of my family for keeping the stories and teachings of our ancestors alive: Mattie Dunn, Ruth Ross, Hattie Mae Dunn, Ruby Decquir, Gwendolyn Rouzan, Judy Dunn-West, and without a question, my mother, Shelia Dunn-Ward.

I offer my eternal thanks to teachers and mentors that are no longer with us and without whom I would not be a historian today: Joe Louis Caldwell, Arnold Hirsch, Jerah Johnson, and Michael Mizell-Nelson. I am similarly grateful to Mary Niall Mitchell, Louis Crust, Trevor Getz, Gwendolyn Midlo Hall, and Raphael Cassimere Jr. for their steadfast support of my research. I owe a debt of gratitude to the following individuals and institutions for providing invaluable leads and research materials: Caryn Cossé Bell and Barbara Trevigne; historian and archivist Greg Osborn; James R. Morgan III for being an indispensable resource and praiseworthy scholar of Prince Hall Freemasonry history; the Williams Research Center at THNOC; the Iowa Masonic Library; the Minnesota Historical Society; the Schomburg Center for Research in Black Culture; the Center for Southeast Louisiana Studies; the New Orleans City Archives; the New Orleans Conveyance Office; the New Orleans Notarial Archives; Tulane University's Louisiana Research Collection; Princeton University Library; and the University of North Carolina at Chapel Hill's Southern Historical Collection.

I would like to thank Laine Kaplan-Levenson for highlighting Dunn on a 2017 episode of her *TriPod* program on WWNO, which helped his story find a national audience as discussions of Lost Cause monuments swept the country. I thank New Orleans Mayor Mitch Landrieu for his courageous stance on the monuments that forever changed the landscape of the city. I am grateful to Jessica Dorman, THNOC's director of publications, and Associate Editor Nick Weldon for suggesting Dunn's story for *TriPod* and being willing to bring my dream of a graphic history to life. I owe so much to Jessica and Nick that I can scarcely find the words to articulate how indebted I am to them. I thank them for having the vision to see the Dunn story's importance to our nation and the people of New Orleans. Thank you for the countless hours of toil and sacrifice to breathe life into the project's pages and thank you for your creativity, passion, and commitment.

If I have been the heart of the project, I would undoubtedly admit that Nick has been its mind. Nick has painstakingly analyzed every image, word, map, and symbol that appears on its pages. *Monumental* would not be possible without our third musketeer, Barrington Edwards. Barrington's artwork is the soul of our project and I thank him for his fervor, zeal, and his willingness to redo his artwork until it matched the vision of others. Forever the peacemaker of our trio, Edwards is the personification of great collaboration. There has not been an instance in this project's tenure that I have felt alone in the endeavor thanks to Nick and Barrington.

Last and in no way least to receive their laurels are my family members who have supported my education, provided me with stories regarding our illustrious ancestors, and graciously offered babysitting services when required. I am and will always be indebted to my wonderful wife, Camille Guess-Mitchell, my son, Mason Alexandre Mitchell, and my daughter, Chloe Grace Mitchell. —*Brian K. Mitchell*

I'M INDEBTED TO Nick and to Brian and to Tana for their faith in my ability to deliver on this project. It took a leap of faith to commit to an artist with more passion than experience.

I am humbled by the unseen hands and dialogue of the folks at The Historic New Orleans Collection that saw the importance of this project and held the vision and standards along the way to getting this to you.

Inordinate appreciation goes out to my friend and inspiration John Jennings for the thoughtful redirection of this project my way and the continuous check-ins along the way. The Boston Comics Roundtable and Dan Mazur have held me up and sharpened my thinking while trying to do this story justice. The Boston Comics in Color family, especially Cagen Luse, has kept me in the appropriately "blerdy" headspace, reminding me how important this work is when I was in the weeds and behind the deadlines. Most importantly my lovely and patient wife and partner Cassandra Takeda held every single one of my struggles, blown elbows, and grumpy studio sessions with grace and love.

Thank you all for this side-by-side fellowship up this mountain.—*Barrington S. Edwards*

MY JOURNEY WITH THIS PROJECT began in 2017, and along the way I have been fortunate to connect with so many helpful and talented people. I echo Brian's gratitude for Laine and the *TriPod* team for being receptive to our suggestion to dedicate an episode to Dunn. Another early moment of serendipity came thanks to the graphic novel virtuoso John Jennings, who was exceedingly generous to a stranger in New Orleans, offering me invaluable advice on the nuts and bolts of illustration and introducing me to Barrington. I also want to thank

James R. Morgan III, Sally Sinor at the New Orleans Notarial Archives, and Christina Bryant at the New Orleans Public Library.

I am grateful for the support of so many of my THNOC colleagues, including: Rebecca Smith and our Reading Room staff for helping me navigate our holdings; Keely Merritt and our photography department, particularly for their help digitizing rare editions of the *Weekly National Republican*; Sean Johnson for his insights regarding Prince Hall Freemasonry; Teresa Devlin and our marketing staff for their work in getting the word out about this book; Jenny Schwartzberg and our education team for their thoughtful development of classroom materials and programming; Siobhán McKiernan, Matthew McKnight, and all of my fellow editors for their assistance in myriad ways; Priscilla Lawrence, our former president and CEO, and Daniel Hammer, her successor, for putting their faith in this book; and our publications director, Jessica Dorman, for being its biggest internal champion.

Our designer, Tana Coman, deserves immense credit for eagerly taking on this unwieldy project, keeping a level head, and always being willing to go beyond her comfort zone. Without many precedents in the "hybrid" graphic history category, she's designed something that deftly marries the gravity of Brian's research with the spirit of Barrington's art, and I'm certain her work will be referenced by other graphic history designers for years to come. We are also indebted to Roan Smith, who aided Tana in finalizing the graphic history pages.

As this project evolved, Barrington's creativity and flexibility never wavered. Capturing the fervor of New Orleans during Reconstruction was a tall task—especially for a Boston native—but he did it with style and grace. Through his artwork he has injected profound emotion and depth into *Monumental* that a more traditional book could never have articulated. Barrington, for your patience, your energy, and passion, I can't thank you enough.

None of this happens without Brian, who has been meticulously piecing together Dunn's story for over a decade—really, for most of his life. Brian is a national treasure, whose courageous work revealing painful truths about racist violence in Arkansas has led to numerous lasting memorials and other recognitions for victims in that state. My hope is that his groundbreaking work on Dunn will have a similar impact. I admire his collegiality, resourcefulness, and storytelling instincts. It has been one of the highlights of my life helping him bring this dream of his to fruition.

Finally, I would like to thank my children, Xavier and Zora, for being constant sources of inspiration, and my wife, Dawn Robinson-Weldon, for being my support and sounding board throughout this endeavor. She also gets credit for coming up with one very important element of this book: the title, *Monumental*. Thanks, love! —*Nick Weldon*

GRAPHIC HISTORY NOTES

ABBREVIATIONS

NOCA New Orleans City Archives

NONA New Orleans Notarial Archives

OJD "Oscar James Dunn," *Weekly National Republican* (New Orleans), November 22, 1871.

WPR *War, Politics and Reconstruction: Stormy Days in Louisiana*, Henry Clay Warmoth, 1930.

MASONIC SYMBOLS

Each part of the graphic history begins with a black-and-white symbol derived from Freemasonry. The fraternity that played such a critical role in Oscar Dunn's life has long used symbolism to educate and inspire its members. The symbols used in this book include a rough ashlar stone (page 19), a trowel (35), a scythe and hourglass (59), a level and plumb (77), a smoldering lump of coal (113), a checkerboard pattern (129), the Eye of Providence (163), and a sprig of acacia (193). We encourage curious readers to research the meanings of these symbols independently, and consider how each one might apply to its part of the story.

PART ONE: ORIGINS

22 Orleans Parish Conveyance Book 7, p. 197, February 5, 1831, NONA. The original act of conveyance denoting the sale of Maria, Oscar, and Jane from George P. Bowers to James Dunn was destroyed in a fire at the office of Notary Greenburg R. Stringer, but a notation and summary can be found here. Oscar's birth year is estimated from this record, which lists him as nine years old.

23 Record 373, Collector of Customs at New Orleans. James H. Caldwell is listed along with three indentured servants, including James, who is described as an 18-year-old "mulatto." Caldwell confirmed James Dunn's free status in the Register of Free Persons of Color (NOCA AA430).

24 Orleans Parish Conveyance Book 7, p. 197, February 5, 1831, NONA; Petition 40B, NOCA VCP320. On December 8, 1832, a police jury approved James Dunn's petition for the emancipation of Maria, Oscar, and Jane (the record is reproduced on page 211 of this book). However, when Oscar Dunn was asked by a congressional committee if he was born free, he replied: "I was, as well as I can recollect. My parents, ever since my recollection, have always been free; but I have been informed that my mother was a slave at one time." H. R. Misc. Doc. 41-154, pt. 1, at 178 (2d Sess. 1870).

After his death, Dunn's friends maintained that he had never been enslaved. Dunn might have been unaware of his former enslavement, or intentionally obscured this fact to avoid being stigmatized. Later in life, his political opponents sought to damage his reputation by alleging he had been enslaved.

25 The Dunns' boardinghouse is listed in *Soards' New Orleans Directory*, 1834, and *Michel's New Orleans Annual and Commercial Register for 1834*. A description of the attack appears in Record 7481, NOCA VCP91.

26 Minute Book 2, NOCA VMZ300. This record, from December 11, 1834, lists the arrests and charges. For more details on the thwarted riot, where white skilled laborers and artisans protested the employment of "slaves in the mechanical arts," see Curry, *Free Black*, 96–97.

27–29 OJD. This biographical sketch, written by an unknown author, contains critical information about Dunn's early life, much of which appears to have been supplied by his lifelong friend, John Parsons. It notes

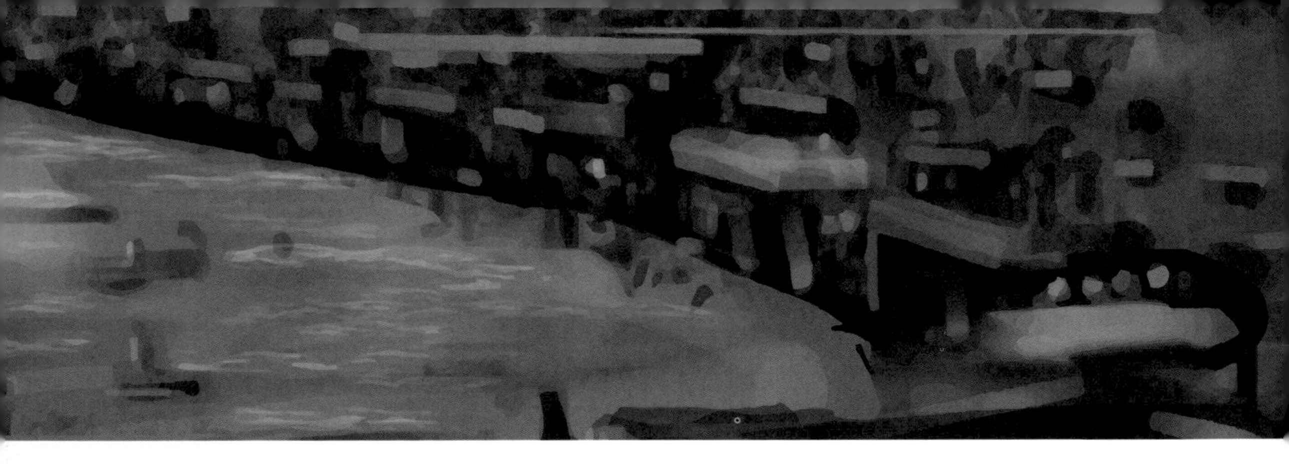

that Dunn "received an ordinary English education" and that he read "with avidity every book that came his way." It details his plastering apprenticeship, his break with his employers, and his early music lessons.

The bounty ad for Dunn appeared in the *Daily Picayune* on December 11, 1841, and featured an illustration commonly used for fugitives from slavery. The ad, however, describes Dunn as an "apprentice to the plastering trade," not a slave. Another ad nearby uses the same illustration but explicitly calls for "the apprehension of the slave N E D," and offers a larger reward of $20. Distinctions existed among apprentices, other indentured servants, and enslaved people (see Lachance, "Index to New Orleans Indentures"). Nonetheless, Dunn's rivals dug up the ad decades later in an attempt to prove he had been enslaved. Later scholars have also mistakenly interpreted the ad as proof of Dunn's enslavement at that time. Parish Court records, cited above, show that Dunn had been emancipated ten years earlier.

30 OJD. The biographical sketch notes that Dunn first moved in with the Marshalls "some twenty-three years ago," and describes him as "an inmate of the house."

"The Late Lieutenant Governor," *Semi-Weekly Louisianian*, November 26, 1871. In a Masonic eulogy published in this article, James Henri Burch detailed Dunn's introduction to Freemasonry and quick rise within the fraternal organization.

31–32 "A Bold Villain," *Daily Picayune*, June 25, 1860; "The Coffee-Colored Lothario," *New Orleans Crescent*, June 26, 1860; "More Developments," *Daily Delta* (New Orleans), June 27, 1860; "Summer Night Amusements," *New Orleans Crescent*, June 29, 1860; "Great Cry and Little Wool," *Daily Picayune*, June 29, 1860; Kein, *Creole*, 93–94. OJD notes: "Martin's conduct brought upon him the wrath of the community at large. No man was more indignant than Mr. Dunn, and the matter had such an effect on him that he abandoned music as a means of support."

PART TWO: WAR AND EMANCIPATION

37 Palmer, "The South," 7. At a pivotal moment between Lincoln's election and the secession of Southern states, the famous New Orleans preacher Benjamin M. Palmer dedicated his Thanksgiving Day sermon to a fiery defense of slavery. Tens of thousands of copies of the speech were disseminated throughout the region. Timothy F. Reilly wrote that Palmer's "unflinching advocacy of slavery . . . perhaps did more to unify the secessionist cause than any other single clerical sermon or political address." Reilly, "Benjamin M. Palmer," 289.

38–39 The Historic New Orleans Collection, *New Orleans during the Civil War*, 27–28, 44–45, 74; Foner, *Reconstruction*, 4. Foner wrote: "Blacks quickly grasped that the presence of occupying troops destroyed the coercive power of both the individual master and the slaveholding community. . . . In the sugar country, where large gangs of slaves labored in some of the South's most wretched conditions, blacks sacked planters' homes and, months before the Emancipation Proclamation, refused to work unless paid wages."

40–41 After Dunn's death, many secondary sources mistakenly attributed a fact of P. B. S. Pinchback's life to Dunn: that he had joined the First Regiment of the all-Black Louisiana Native Guard when it was organized by Union forces in 1862. No records substantiating Dunn's military service have been found. His name does not appear on any known muster rolls of the Native Guard's regiments or in memorial listings after the war (Entry 5514, Muster Rolls, Returns, Regimental Papers;

Wilson, *Black Phalanx*, 176; Hollandsworth, *Louisiana Native Guards*, 119–24; Glatthaar, *Forged in Battle*, 30–311; "Soldiers' and Sailors' Convention," *New Orleans Tribune*, November 10, 1866). Eureka Grand Lodge rolls place Dunn in New Orleans on several dates when the First Regiment was located in either Baton Rouge or Port Hudson (Proceedings of the Most Worshipful Eureka Grand Lodge, 1–16, 10–36; Hollandsworth, *Louisiana Native Guards*, 23–88). After Dunn's death, his family was deeply in debt, but no record exists of his widow drawing a military pension (Orleans Parish Conveyance Book 100, p. 551, November 5, 1872, NONA; Oscar J. Dunn Succession, Record 35,055, NOCA VSB290). The last and perhaps most telling clue that Dunn never served is that none of the friends who gave accounts of his life after his death mentioned a military record ("The Late Lieutenant Governor," *Semi-Weekly Louisianian*, November 26, 1871; "Death of Oscar J. Dunn," *New Orleans Republican*, November 23, 1871; OJD).

A brief history of the Eureka Grand Lodge, its relationship with St. James AME Church, and Dunn's lodge service appears in Thomson and Smith, "Biographical Note."

42 Houzeau, *My Passage*, 25n34; Blassingame, *Black New Orleans*, 212; Nystrom, *After the Civil War*, 202; Thompson, *Exiles at Home*, 227–30; Foner, *Reconstruction*, 49. In his letter to Hahn, Lincoln wrote: "I barely suggest for your private consideration, whether some of the colored people not be let in—as for instance, the very intelligent, and especially those who have fought gallantly in our ranks. . . . But this is only a suggestion, not to the public, but to you alone" (Foner, citing Basler, *Lincoln*, 7:243).

43 Dunn advertised his new intelligence office in the *New Orleans Tribune* from November 26 through December 9, 1865. The OJD sketch says: "Many cases of hardship arose out of the emancipation of the colored race at that time, principally among the aged and the decrepit. . . . In many of these cases the good offices of Mr. Dunn were invaluable." Dunn reported to the Freedmen's Aid Association that he typically garnered $15 a month in pay for men and $10 a month for women ("The Question of Labor," *New Orleans Tribune*, February 22, 1866). These exceeded minimum wages established by the US Treasury Department for Louisiana laborers: $10 a month for "first class" male laborers and $8 a month for "first class" female laborers. "Plantation Regulations," *Black Republican* (New Orleans), April 15, 1865.

44 "Our People and the Great Calamity," *Black Republican* (New Orleans), April 29, 1865; "The Friends of Universal Suffrage," *New Orleans Tribune*, June 16, 1865.

45 Tregle, "Thomas J. Durant," 485; "The Friends of Universal Suffrage," *New Orleans Tribune*, June 18, 1865; "Executive Committee of the Universal Suffrage Party," *New Orleans Tribune*, June 24, 1865.

46 Dufour, "The Age of Warmoth," 337–38; WPR, 5–25. A month after Dunn's death, a newspaper published one of his last speeches, delivered at the Seventh Ward Radical Republican Club, where he lamented inviting Warmoth to join the suffrage group in 1865. "Political Address of Lieutenant-Governor Dunn," *Weekly National Republican* (New Orleans), December 20, 1871.

47 "Correspondence between the Central Executive Committee and Gov. Wells," *New Orleans Tribune*, July 12, 1865. Wells also wrote: "The emancipated slave has much to learn. . . . Should it please Providence to fit him intellectually for an equal place in the body politic with the white citizens of the Republic, at a period much sooner than is now anticipated, I have no doubt all will rejoice."

"The Friends of Universal Suffrage," *New Orleans Tribune*, August 11, 1865; "The Friends of Universal Suffrage," *New Orleans Tribune*, September 1, 1865; "Registration," *New Orleans Tribune*, September 2, 1865. In "Registration," the *Tribune* praised Dunn's efforts: "Next to [Mr. W. R. Crane], Mr. O. J. Dunn has a fair right to our gratitude. With private means only, he organized a machinery covering the whole city of New Orleans, and secured the voluntary and gratuitous concourse of the numerous commissioners and clerks. These two names will ever remain connected with the history of Reconstruction in 1865."

48–49 Central Executive Committee, *Proceedings of the Convention*, 4–5; "Universal Suffrage State Convention," *New Orleans Tribune*, September 26, 1865; "Universal Suffrage State Convention," *New Orleans Tribune*, September 28, 1865; "Convention of the Republican Party of Louisiana," *New Orleans Tribune*, September 30, 1865; "Judge H. C. Warmoth," *New Orleans Tribune*, December 13, 1865.

50 Summers, "Moderates' Last Chance," 54–65; "Platform of the National Democratic Party," *New Orleans Times*, October 18, 1865; Act of December 21, 1865, No. 19, 1865 La. Acts 28–30; An Ordinance Relative to the Police of Negroes Recently Emancipated within the Parish of St. Landry, reprinted in S. Exec. Doc. No. 39-2, at 93–94 (1st Sess. 1865); Du Bois, *Black Reconstruction*, 177–78.

51–52 OJD; "A Noted Colored Lady," *St. Paul Daily Globe*, June 14, 1885. In addition to census data and marriage records, the *Daily Globe* article, derived from an interview with Ellen, fills in important biographical details of her life that haven't been found anywhere else.

53–54 "Louisiana Association for the Benefit of Colored Orphans," *New Orleans Tribune*, December 17, 1865; "A Bakery for the People," *New Orleans Tribune*, December 24, 1865; Vandal, "Black Utopia," 441, 449n46, 451–52. "What was revolutionary in the 1865 black economic program," Vandal wrote about the People's Bakery in New Orleans, "was the fact that for the first time those ideas were implemented by members of an oppressed class or race." He noted that earlier Black cooperative experiments "were usually sponsored by white abolitionists." Dunn, as president, was seen as a bridge between prospective English-speaking freedmen members and the organization's predominantly Francophone, Afro-Creole leadership.

55 "The Question of Labor," *New Orleans Tribune*, February 22, 1866. The *Tribune* published a report Dunn submitted to the Freedmen's Aid Association about his work with laborers and planters. In it Dunn described the kinds of conversations he had with many planters. "I also tell them that if they will take the trouble to win the confidence of the negro by kind treatment," Dunn wrote, "they, the planters, would have no more trouble to obtain plantation laborers."

56 "Economy Hall," *New Orleans Tribune*, May 6, 1866.

PART THREE: THE RIOT AND THE RADICALS

61 Taylor, "An Impossible Task," 205–6; Ficklen, *History of Reconstruction*, 146–56; Bond, *No Easy Walk*, 15–16; Summers, "Moderates' Last Chance," 66–67.

62 "To Be Removed," *Daily Picayune*, March 29, 1866; "Proclamation, by R. K. Howell, President Pro Tem.," *Daily Picayune*, July 10, 1866; Hollandsworth, *An Absolute Massacre*, 4–5; H.R. Rep. 39-16, at 232–33 (2d Sess. 1867). An Afro-Creole painter named Octave Breaux testified that three days before the convention he witnessed two white men discussing "the spilling of blood" and a plan for police to break up the assembly. He immediately told friends and military officers. Other witnesses also testified to having knowledge of the massacre's premeditation and warning others. This Dunn scene is a dramatization; it's not known how he was warned, but he and many other Radicals conspicuously avoided the ill-fated convention.

63–68 H.R. Rep. 39-16, at 35–40, 103, 556 (2d Sess. 1867). The scenes depicting the massacre at the Mechanics' Institute all derive from testimony from the congressional report on the riots. The report outlines in graphic detail a brutal, one-sided attack on Black and white convention attendees and supporters, perpetrated largely by city police and firefighters. The testimony of Charles H. Hughes is representative of many eyewitness accounts: "The police came up and fired into the crowd, and we all took shelter inside the building. After we had been there ten or fifteen minutes there was an awful rush of police inside the hall; they came in firing indiscriminately into the crowd. . . . While the police were charging and firing into the crowd in the hall, some man in the convention jumped up and exclaimed, 'We surrender! We surrender!' The police exclaimed, 'We do not want any prisoners; you have all got to die.'" The report includes an index of "atrocities" which ranged from grotesque murders to petty theft by police.

H.R. Rep. 39-16, at 7–11 (2d Sess. 1867). Durant testified that a man (likely Octave Breaux) warned him of the threats on the convention. Durant was in his office, two blocks from the Mechanics' Institute, that day, and witnessed police shooting Black people in the street. He said, "I secured from a friend, whose name I cannot now mention, such information that my life was marked, that I deemed it very proper to leave the city of New Orleans." He snuck out of his office, took a carriage to Carrollton, and boarded a steamboat headed upriver, never to return.

H.R. Rep. 39-16, at 68–70 (2d Sess. 1867). Dunn testified that he "was indisposed, and did not leave my house" the day of the massacre. He described the harassment Black people endured in New Orleans: "We are insulted on every occasion. . . . In going through the streets it is a common thing to hear them say, 'These negroes think they have their own way now, but they are mistaken; the president is with us, and we will soon drive the negroes and their Yankee friends off.'... If a colored man goes along genteelly dressed they will rub against him and try to pick a quarrel with him." Near the end of his testimony, he said, "They would have killed me five squares off if I had been out on the street, such was the feeling exhibited."

69 Sheridan, *Personal Memoirs*, 429–30. Sheridan detailed the complicity of local authorities in the massacre in a letter he wrote to General Grant on April 19, 1867: "For a period of at least nine months previous to the riot of July 30 [Judge Edmond Abell] had been educating a large portion of the community to the perpetration of this outrage, by almost promising no prosecution in his court against the offenders, in case such an event occurred. The records of his court will show that he fulfilled his promise, as not one of the guilty has been prosecuted." In the same letter he wrote that Louisiana Attorney General Andrew Herron not only failed to indict the perpetrators "but went so far as to attempt to impose on the good sense of the whole nation by indicting the victims." Mayor Monroe, he wrote, "controlled the element engaged in this riot, and when backed by an attorney-general who would not prosecute the guilty, and a judge who advised the grand jury to find the innocent guilty and let the murderers go free, felt secure in engaging his police force in the riot and massacre."

70 "Married," *New Orleans Tribune*, December 30, 1866; OJD. Rev. John Turner officiated the wedding.

71 "Masonic," *New Orleans Tribune*, May 2, 1867; "Masonic," *New Orleans Tribune*, June 23, 1867; "Masonic Union," *New Orleans Tribune*, July 21, 1867; "Union of White and Colored Masons," *New Orleans Republican*, July 23, 1867; "Masonry," *New Orleans Tribune*, July 25, 1867.

72 "Central Executive Committee," *New Orleans Tribune*, November 9, 1866; "No Colored Man Appointed," *New Orleans Tribune*, May 10, 1867; "Central Executive Committee," *New Orleans Tribune*, June 21, 1867; "On Thursday Evening," *New Orleans Tribune*, June 22, 1867; "The New Committee," *New Orleans Tribune*, June 25, 1867; "Mr. O. J. Dunn's Position," *New Orleans Tribune*, July 3, 1867. After Dunn rejected the vice presidency, the committee erroneously announced—at a meeting he was absent from—that he had resigned entirely. On July 3 the *Tribune* ran a letter from Dunn correcting the record, and commented that the party was trying to "get rid of one of the old Radicals and one of the representative men of the colored population."

73 "Sheridan vs. Flanders," *New Orleans Tribune*, July 27, 1867; "Our City Government," *New Orleans Times*, August 2, 1867; "Reconstruction in Louisiana," *New York Times*, August 2, 1867; Tunnell, *Crucible*, 107; Ficklen, *History of Reconstruction*, 187–92; "Local Intelligence," *New Orleans Times*, September 11, 1867; "School Ordinance," *New Orleans Tribune*, October 24, 1867; "The School Question," *New Orleans Tribune*, October 31, 1867; Perkins, "Oscar James Dunn," 108. In Dunn's first judicial appearance he endured racism from both sides. The defendant's counsel, Judge Edmond Abell—the same man removed by General Sheridan for his role in the massacre—filed an exception that "sets forth that Dunn being a negro, is not recognized by the laws of Louisiana as a citizen, and hence is not legally an officer of justice." Dunn overruled him, but the prosecuting witness then refused to take the stand or be sworn in by Dunn. Dunn asked him "if he intended to insult the Court," and when he defiantly stated that he did, Dunn charged him with contempt and fined him $25. "Louisiana," *New York Times*, October 5, 1867.

74 Louisiana, *Official Journal*, 293–310.

75 "The Nominating Convention," *New Orleans Republican*, January 15, 1868; Uzee, "Beginnings," 210–11; Connor, "Reconstruction Rebels," 178–79. The feud over the Louisiana Republican ticket marked the beginning of the end for the *Tribune*, America's first Black-owned daily paper, and planted seeds for many rivalries. Pinchback said Roudanez was "a man who would endanger the safety of his entire race, because he could not have everything just as he wanted it" (Houzeau, *My Passage*, 47–56). In his 1930 autobiography, Warmoth maintained that Roudanez and his fellow *Tribune* proprietors had hoped for an "Africanization of the State" (WPR, 51–58). Roudanez's decision to support a ticket led by Taliaferro, who had once opposed the Thirteenth Amendment and Black suffrage, puzzled his colleagues. Amid the furor, Dunn struggled with his decision to join Warmoth.

PART FOUR: THE BLACK LIEUTENANT GOVERNOR

79–81 Langston, *From the Virginia Plantation*, 288–90. In his autobiography, Langston details the dramatic late-night scene with Dunn. Not long after this visit, Langston founded Howard University's law school in Washington, DC. He later became Virginia's first Black congressman.

"The Nominating Convention," *New Orleans Republican*, January 16, 1868.

82 "Mr. Oscar J. Dunn and the Quadroons of Louisiana," *Opelousas (LA) Courier*, March 28, 1868; Houzeau, *My Passage*, 54n67, 55–56. Jean-Charles Houzeau, a white Radical from Belgium and the editor of the *Tribune*, disagreed with Roudanez's support of the Taliaferro ticket, and resigned in January 1868, leading to a dramatic shift in the paper's voice. Dunn, a longtime friend of the *Tribune*, suddenly became a target. By publishing the unnamed correspondent's account of Dunn's alleged speech, the *Tribune* portrayed him as an enemy of Afro-Creoles. Dunn claimed, in a letter to the *Tribune*, that he had been "grossly misrepresented." The paper refused to print his letter, which ran in the *Republican* instead ("A Card from Hon. O. J. Dunn," *New Orleans Republican*, March 27, 1868), and doubled down by republishing the original account of his speech. There are no known surviving copies of the controversial *Tribune* article, though a contemporaneous *Opelousas Courier* article has been found that contains an apparent excerpt from the original *Tribune* piece. It presents Dunn's alleged statements alongside even more inflammatory commentary from the unnamed correspondent—which perhaps prompted Dunn to assert that the correspondent "successfully attempted to put his own sentiments in my mouth."

83 "Louisiana General Assembly," *New Orleans Republican*, July 10, 1868; "House of Representatives," *New Orleans Republican*, July 11, 1868; "Louisiana General Assembly," *New Orleans Republican*, July 12, 1868; "Civil Government in Louisiana Restored—The Fourteenth Amendment Ratified," *New York Times*, July 15, 1868.

84 WPR, 80–81. Warmoth also said: "The people drank either water caught in cisterns from the dirty roofs of their houses or the dirty unfiltered water of the Mississippi River. Epidemics of yellow and malarial fevers prevailed nearly every year. Houses were unscreened and mosquitoes were as common as the flies that filled the air. The slaughter-houses were so located that all of their offal and filth were poured into the Mississippi River, just above the mains that supplied the people with their drinking-water."

85 Act of September 14, 1868, No. 74, § 14, 1868 La. Acts 85, 87; Dawson, "General Lovell H. Rousseau," 384; Hogue, *Uncivil War*, 66; Louisiana, *Annual Report*, 1869; "Louisiana," *New York Times*, September 6, 1868; Hennessey, "Race and Violence," 78. Lovell Rousseau, the commanding general of Louisiana, reported on the resistance to the multiracial Metropolitan Police: "The community at large refused to recognize or uphold the authority of a body thus constituted. . . . This fact alone rendered the metropolitan police . . . practically worthless, and placed life and property at the mercy of the worst classes in the city." H. R. Exec. Doc. No 40-1, pt. 1, at 305 (3d Sess. 1868).

86 Foner, *Reconstruction*, 337–41.

87–91 "The City," *Daily Picayune*, June 12, 1868; Hennessey, "Race and Violence," 77–79; "The Radical Precession," *Daily Picayune*, September 13, 1868; "Riot on Canal Street," *Daily Picayune*, September 23, 1868; "Louisiana," *New York Times*, September 23, 1868; "Louisiana," *New York Times*, September 24, 1868; "The Riot in New-Orleans; One Negro Killed; Several Persons Wounded; A Democratic Perspective," *New York Times*, September 28, 1868.

92–93 "Veto of the Civil Rights Bill," *New Orleans Republican*, September 26, 1868; "Louisiana," *New York Times*, September 28, 1868; Dufour, "The Age of Warmoth," 345–46; H. R. Misc. Doc. 42-211, at 225–26 (2d Sess. 1872). Days before Warmoth's veto, Dunn presided over the bill's passage during a contentious Senate session. "The Louisiana Legislature," *Daily Picayune*, September 19, 1868.

94 Hennessey, "Race and Violence," 80–84; "Gov. Warmoth's Proclamation," *New York Times*, October 4, 1868; "Louisiana," *New York Times*, October 29, 1868; "The Peril in Louisiana," *New York Times*, October 29, 1868; "General," *New York Times*, November 2, 1868. According to Hennessey, "the most urgent reason for joining a white political organization was the perceived necessity of dealing with the frightening reality of black freedom and citizenship." She wrote that the Innocents, with as many as 1,200 members, were the largest of these groups. They wore red shirts and hats stitched with the "Innocents" name, and carried inflammatory banners, including one depicting a Black man being stabbed with a knife. Though the Innocents were commonly described as ethnically Sicilian, Hennessey noted that the group "also included Americans, Spaniards, Portuguese, Maltese, and Latin Americans" and their leader "was a French Creole." On November 2, a correspondent to the *New York Times* reported that "the 'Innocents' are out and parading the streets in small bands, killing inoffensive black men here and there" and that New Orleans was "in a state of anarchy."

95 Dauphine, "Knights of the White Camelia," 173–190; DeLatte, "St. Landry Riot," 47; "Louisiana," *New York Times*, October 27, 1868; "Butchery of Negroes in St. Bernard Parish—The Arms Stolen in Arkansas in the Hands of New-Orleans Rebels," *New York Times*, October 31, 1868.

96–97 Hennessey, "Race and Violence," 85–86; "Louisiana," *New York Times*, November 2, 1868; "Louisiana," *New York Times*, November 8, 1868; "New Orleans," *National Republican* (Washington, DC), November 30, 1868; "The Police Troubles in New-Orleans—Metropolitan Police Law Declared Unconstitutional," *New York Times*, November 30, 1868. Dunn described the encounter with the man, and addressed the violence surrounding the 1868 presidential election in Louisiana, in testimony to Congress in 1869. H. R. Misc. Doc. 41-154, pt. 1, at 175 (2d Sess. 1870).

98 DeLatte, "St. Landry Riot," 48–49; Du Bois, *Black Reconstruction*, 474; Foner, *Reconstruction*, 342–43; Hennessey, "Race and Violence," 90; Louisiana, *Supplemental Report*, iv. Dunn testified to Congress that he did not vote and had difficulty advising the many Black voters who came to him, "many of whom did not understand my rights and powers, and who would come to me for protection which I could not give, and consequently I avoided them as much as possible." He said he avoided going outdoors at night and had "apprehension" walking in certain areas such as St. Charles Street [now Avenue], where "I have heard threats as I passed that they would put that negro governor out of the way." H. R. Misc. Doc. 41-154, pt. 1, at 178 (2d Sess. 1870).

99 Act of February 23, 1869, No. 38, 1869 La. Acts 37; Editorial, *New Orleans Commercial Bulletin*, February 19, 1869. Warmoth evidently signed the law without fear of it being enforced, writing in his memoir: "The law, of course, was a dead letter. . . . Public sentiment was strongly opposed to it, and the colored people were too wise to undertake to force themselves upon white people who did not want them." WPR, 92.

100–1 "An Outrage," *Davenport (IA) Daily Gazette*, April 12, 1869; "Humbug Chivalry," *Decatur (IL) Weekly Republican*, April 15, 1869. News of Beauregard's treatment of Dunn spread widely, with Republican papers decrying the ex-rebel's "impudence" and mocking his apparent reputation for chivalry. The Democratic press characterized Dunn's request to sit in "the white man's car" as an "ill-advised experiment" and an attempt to "forward a conflict of races." "The Travels of Lynch and Dunn," *Daily Picayune*, April 3, 1869.

102 "Oscar J. Dunn," *New Orleans Crescent*, April 2, 1869. A vehemently racist article in the *Louisville Democrat*, reprinted in the *Crescent*, exemplified the way many white people outside of Louisiana reacted to Dunn's election: "He ought to remember that the little brief authority he is clothed with in the Creole State does not extend beyond the limits of her borders. . . . Decent white people look down upon him with contempt, and would as soon ride in a car, carriage or steamboat with a skunk as such a brainless pretender to decency and official honor."

103 "Africa Heard From," *Evening Courier and Republic* (Buffalo, NY), April 13, 1869; "Lieutenant Governor Dunn," *Semi-Weekly Wisconsin*, April 24, 1869.

104–5 Chernow, *Grant*, 641; "Hearty Reception of a Colored Official at the White House," *New York Herald*, April 3, 1869; "The New Radical Organ," *Fort Wayne Daily Democrat*, April 13, 1869; Simon and Marszalek, *Papers of Ulysses S. Grant*, 19:335.

106–7 "A Colored Lieutenant-Governor," *New York Times*, April 2, 1869; "A Dusky Official Airs His Dignity on the Floor of the Senate," *New York Herald*, April 2, 1869; Sumner, *Equality Before the Law*, 10; Lester, *Charles Sumner*, 510–11.

108 News brief, *Radical Standard* (Carrollton, LA), April 28, 1869; "Complimentary Dinner," *Radical Standard* (Carrollton, LA), May 15, 1869; "Compliments to a Colored Man," *Fall River (MA) Daily Evening News*, April 23, 1869; "Pennsylvania," *New York Herald*, April 26,

1869. Notable attendees at the Boston dinner depicted in the illustration include (faces shown from left to right): Rev. J. B. Smith, Wendell Phillips, William Lloyd Garrison, Lewis Hayden, Robert Morris, Edward G. Walker, and George T. Downing.

109 News brief, *New-York Tribune*, April 23, 1869; "News and Other Items," *Galveston Daily News*, May 9, 1869; "Financial and Commercial," *New York Herald*, April 24, 1869; "Dunn Brown," *Coshocton (OH) Democrat*, May 25, 1869.

110–11 "Plymouth Church Receives Its Idol," *Brooklyn Daily Eagle*, April 26, 1869; "Gov. Dunn Visits the Public Schools," *National Anti-Slavery Standard*, May 15, 1869; "News Notes," *Galveston Daily News*, May 15, 1869.

PART FIVE: IN NEED OF AN EXORCISM

115–16 "New-Orleans," *New York Times*, May 20, 1869; "Lt. Gov. Dunn in Limbo," *Galveston Daily News*, June 16, 1869; "Trial of the Metropolitan Police Board for Contempt," *New Orleans Bee*, June 16, 1869; "A Model Official," *Gettysburg Compiler*, June 25, 1869; "Powers of the Governor of Louisiana—Decisions of the Supreme Court," *New York Times*, August 2, 1869. A dramatic scene unfolded the morning of May 19, 1869, as Warmoth, General Joseph A. Mower, and Metropolitan Police Superintendent George L. Cain marched on horseback down St. Charles Street to seize control of Jefferson ("Capture of Jefferson City," *Daily Picayune*, May 20, 1869). In court, Dunn stated that he had "been informed that the governor has charge of a portion of our force," and other defendants similarly testified to Warmoth's efforts to assert his will through a loyal contingent of the Metropolitan police. H. R. Misc. Doc. 41-154, pt. 2, at 559–66 (2d Sess. 1870).

117 OJD; Orleans Parish Conveyance Book 97, p. 318, December 9, 1869, NONA; "City Intelligence," *New Orleans Commercial Bulletin*, October 19, 1870. Michael A. Ross wrote: "For the leading black politician in Louisiana to have honored Lee was a significant ideological concession. After all, Lee remained a white supremacist after the war." He speculated that Dunn may have extended the gesture "to prove that Republicans could be reasonable without going to the lengths Warmoth had of offering plum patronage positions to the opposition." Ross, "Commemoration of Robert E. Lee's Death," 142.

118–19 *New-Orleans Tägliche Deutsche Zeitung*, March 1, 1870; *Globus*, 288; "A Turner Union Squabble," *New York Herald*, March 25, 1870. The North American Turner Union cited the first plank of its organizational platform in threatening to expel the New Orleans club: "The North American Turner Union purposes, by uniting all societies standing on the following platform, to assist them in their endeavors for educating their members as men of powerful bodies and free minds, and it is its especial aim to bring . . . the endeavor for radical reform in social, political and religious matters to the correct understanding of its members, and to work for the realization of these reforms and for the equal rights of all men." "Trouble Among the Turners," *New York Times*, March 30, 1870.

120 Taylor, *Louisiana Reconstructed*, 174–81; Du Bois, *Black Reconstruction*, 475–77. Warmoth wrote in his memoir: "For the appointment of men of color I was denounced by the opposition as trying to Africanize the State; and for the appointment of conservative white men I was denounced by the 'Pure Radicals' as trying to sell out the Republican Party to the Democrats." WPR, 87–89.

121–22 S. Rep. 42-41, pt. 1, at 202 (2d Sess. 1872); Foner, *Reconstruction*, 388; "Louisiana Politics," *New York Herald*, October 4, 1869; Christian, "Theory of the Poisoning of Oscar J. Dunn," 266n2; Sumner, *Equality Before the Law*, 10; Herbert, *Why the Solid South?* 406; Lonn, *Reconstruction in Louisiana*, 90–91.

123 "Louisiana," *New York Times*, February 4, 1870; Dufour, "The Age of Warmoth," 346–48; "Louisiana," *Chicago Tribune*, February 15, 1872; "Warmoth Before the Grand Jury," *The South-Western* (Shreveport, LA), March 2, 1870.

124–27 "Negro Superstition," *New York Herald*, July 12, 1870; Long, *New Orleans Voudou Priestess*, 128; Gordon, "'Midnight Scenes and Orgies,'" 768, 774. The original account of the exorcism appeared in the *New York Herald*, was republished by newspapers throughout the country, and has been repeated in many books. Little evidence exists, though, of Madame Lott—especially compared to the well-documented Marie Laveau. Further obscuring matters, Long wrote that Herbert Asbury, in his influential 1936 book *The French Quarter*, conflated stories of Lott with those of Malvina Latour, another enigmatic Louisiana Voodoo figure. Gordon noted that similarly sensational "eyewitness and second-hand accounts of Voodoo spectacles appeared regularly in mid- to late-nineteenth-century print culture" and that these "postwar Voodoo articles aimed at discrediting voters of color and Louisiana's interracial legislature."

PART SIX: NO GREATER DIVIDE

131–33 "The Courts," *Daily Picayune*, November 22, 1870; "Mixed Schools," *Daily Picayune*, January 12, 1871. Joseph Logsdon and Caryn Cossé Bell wrote: "Dunn had long supported the radical demands of the black creole leaders to remove all color bars from public life, but he did not feel that the logic of integration extended to the voluntary societies that blacks had fostered within their communities." Logsdon and Bell, "Americanization of Black New Orleans," 248–50.

134–36 "Republican State Convention," *New Orleans Republican*, October 10, 1870; WPR, 92–102; "General Notes," *New York Times*, August 19, 1870; "Radical State Convention," *Louisiana Democrat*, August 24, 1870; Du Bois, *Black Reconstruction*, 478; Pitre, "Collapse of the Warmoth Regime," 164–65.

137–38 "Washington," *New York Times*, December 2, 1870; WPR, 17–22, 102; "Louisiana Affairs," *Daily Picayune*, December 20, 1870; "Congress and the President," *Charleston Daily News*, December 23, 1870; Dray, *Capitol Men*, 110; Simon and Marszalek, *Papers of Ulysses S. Grant*, 21:270–74; "The Louisiana Senatorial Quarrel," *New York Herald*, January 9, 1871.

139 "Mixed Schools," *Daily Picayune*, January 12, 1871; "The Public Schools of New-Orleans—Negro Children as Pupils," *New York Times*, January 18, 1871; Harlan, "Desegregation in New Orleans Public Schools," 665; Vaughn, *Schools for All*, 55. Donald E. DeVore and Joseph Logsdon wrote: "Almost singularly in the nation, the public schools of New Orleans reached for the most difficult objective embodied in the American common school ideal: fundamental racial integration—with black and white students, black and white teachers, and black and white administrators." DeVore and Logsdon, *Crescent City Schools*, 40.

140 Harlan, "Desegregation in New Orleans Public Schools," 663–68. "New Orleans witnessed an extraordinary experiment in interracial education," Eric Foner wrote. "In its first year, white enrollment plummeted and new segregated private and parochial schools sprang into existence. But many participants in this 'white flight' soon returned, and by 1874 several thousand were attending integrated classes." Foner, *Reconstruction*, 366–67.

141 WPR, 106–7; Dufour, "The Age of Warmoth," 350; "The Louisiana Senatorial Quarrel," *New York Herald*, January 9, 1871; "Louisiana Radicals at Loggerheads," *New York Herald*, January 10, 1871; "Debates of the House" and "Debates of the Senate," *New Orleans Republican*, January 12, 1871.

142–43 "Accident to Governor Warmoth," *New Orleans Republican*, March 9, 1871; "Accident to the Governor," *Daily Picayune*, March 9, 1871; News brief, *Weekly Louisianian*, March 12, 1871. Initial reports on Warmoth's well-being conflicted. The pro-Warmoth *Republican* wrote that "the foot was bruised" and that the governor drove himself home from Charity Hospital. The *Daily Picayune* reported that he suffered "a severe gash" and fractured several toes and that hospital attendants transported him to his home, where "opiates had to be administered freely during the evening." The *Louisianian*, overseen by Pinchback, noted after three days that the injury "is still serious enough to require absolute withdrawal from business, and threatens to confine him for some time to his rooms."

144 Castellanos, *New Orleans as It Was*, 118–20; News brief, *New Orleans Republican*, May 5, 1871; News brief, *Weekly Louisianian*, May 21, 1871.

News briefs show that, after his injury, Warmoth left the state twice, leaving Dunn to serve as acting governor for about sixteen days in May 1871 and another twenty-three days from June to July. More than a year and a half later, following Warmoth's impeachment, Pinchback also served as acting governor, for thirty-six days. For this he is commonly—and mistakenly—recognized as America's first Black governor. Warmoth was never removed from office. The conditions that made Dunn and Pinchback acting governor were defined within the same article of the state constitution: "In case of impeachment of the Governor, his removal from office, death . . . resignation or *absence from the State*, the powers and duties of the office shall devolve upon the Lieutenant Governor" (La. Const. of 1868, art. LIII, emphasis added).

Dunn's time as acting governor began with an actual life-or-death decision: almost immediately after Warmoth first left the state, Dunn declined to commute the sentences of the Spanish nationals. The pro-Warmoth *New Orleans Republican* even commented: "We believe that every thinking man . . . will approve the firm stand taken by Governor Dunn in refusing to interfere in a case which has none of the exceptional features such as would warrant the interposition of executive clemency" ("The Condemned Murderers," *New Orleans Republican*, May 12, 1871). For much of Warmoth's time away, newspapers referred to Dunn as acting governor without apparent controversy (e.g., "Official Notices," *New Orleans Republican*, May 16, 1871; News brief, *Daily Picayune*, July 12, 1871). Warmoth only challenged his legitimacy—and returned to Louisiana—when Dunn began making moves Warmoth disagreed with, including a pardon of a man named Harry Hews and appointments and dismissals of several state officials ("Correspondence between Gov. Warmoth and Lieut. Governor Dunn," *New Orleans Bee*, September 1, 1871). Warmoth later tried to delegitimize Pinchback's moment as acting governor in a similar fashion, characterizing it as an intrusion based on a legal technicality (WPR, 112, 213).

145 Foner, *Reconstruction*, 501–10; "Horace Greeley," *Daily Picayune*, May 16, 1871; "Horace Greeley," *Daily Picayune*, May 18, 1871; News brief, *Weekly Louisianian*, June 1, 1871; Dunn, *Lieut. Gov. Dunn to Hon. Horace Greeley*, 1871. The conversation depicted on this page is a dramatization based on an account of a speech Dunn gave in New Orleans after his letter to Greeley went public. "Lieut.-Gov. Dunn's Opinion of Horace Greeley." *New York Times*, May 17, 1872.

146–49 WPR, 112–14; News brief, *New Orleans Republican*, June 25, 1871; "A Breeze at the Governor's Office," *Daily Picayune*, June 28, 1871; "The Gubernatorial Question," *New Orleans Times*, June 29, 1871; "Letter from Bay St. Louis," *New Orleans Times*, July 10, 1871; "Highly Important!" *New Orleans Commercial Bulletin*, July 10, 1871; "Arrival of Governor Warmoth," *New Orleans Republican*, July 19, 1871; "A Radical Row and Rout," *Galveston Daily News*, July 22, 1871; "Eighth District Court," *New Orleans Republican*, August 29, 1871; "The Radical Muddle," *New Orleans Commercial Bulletin*, August 3, 1871.

150 "The Saratoga of the South," *Brooklyn Daily Eagle*, August 21, 1871. In an otherwise racist and biased editorial, the *New Orleans Times* shed a glimmer of insight into the Warmoth-Dunn feud. It ridiculed Republicans for corruption but bemoaned that Dunn's integrity actually handicapped him in such a fight. It satirically suggested what Republican leaders must have thought of Dunn: "What need have we for such a man, who professes principles and ideas so inconsistent with the cardinal doctrines and practices of our party? Let him be gone with . . . his odious cant about duty, honesty, faith, and official dignity and propriety." "The Fight of the Factions," *New Orleans Times*, August 4, 1871.

151 WPR, 114; "Arrival of Governor Warmoth," *New Orleans Republican*, July 19, 1871; "Correspondence between Gov. Warmoth and Lieut. Governor Dunn," *New Orleans Bee*, September 1, 1871; "Louisiana," *Chicago Tribune*, September 1, 1871.

152–53 "The Louisiana Quarrel," *New York Times*, August 28, 1871; Dunn, *Lieut. Gov. Dunn to Hon. Horace Greeley*, 1871; "From New Orleans," *Janesville (WI) Gazette*, September 5, 1871; WPR, 113–14. A number of witnesses testified to Congress about Metropolitan police violently breaking up meetings of Republican clubs that supported Dunn. Several testified that a police-led "mob" that included notorious local gangsters forced Dunn to escape from a meeting at the Tenth Ward Club via a side door. H. R. Misc. Doc. 42-211, at 160–75, 181–96 (2d Sess. 1872).

154–58 WPR, 114–18; "The State Convention," *New Orleans Republican*, August 11, 1871; "What They Say of Each Other," *Ouachita Telegraph*, August 19, 1871; Dufour, "The Age of Warmoth," 352; H. R. Misc. Doc. 42-211, at 126–34 (Packard testimony), 149–54 (details from Customhouse convention), and 299–300 (Warmoth testimony) (2d Sess. 1872).

159 Simon and Marszalek, *Papers of Ulysses S. Grant*, 22:102–3. Decades later, Warmoth remained bitter about the meeting: "The Committee was received by General Grant coldly. He said that he did not see what harm the presence of United States soldiers could do to a Republican Convention. He . . . closed the interview by saying that he would take their report and investigate the facts. It is now fifty years since that time and no reply has ever been received." WPR, 117–18.

160–61 Dunn, *Lieut. Gov. Dunn to Hon. Horace Greeley*, 1871.

PART SEVEN: COLLAPSE

165 Chester, "Remember Dunn." On All Saints' Day, Maj. Thomas Morris Chester, a friend of Dunn's, warned him about Pinchback's message. Chester mentioned this during a passionate speech delivered at a memorial for Dunn two weeks after his death. He didn't name Pinchback, but his innuendo made clear who he was alleging had threatened Dunn. "It was a part of the plan of some of the wandering Machiavelians [*sic*] who recently pilgrimaged to Long Branch," he said—referring to the group that visited President Grant, which included Pinchback—"and to my certain knowledge there was one colored man who undertook this infamous work." Referencing a blurb that questioned Dunn's relationships with his closest allies at the time of his death, Chester also said: "The *Louisianian*, under the immediate and responsible control of a well known colored man"—Pinchback—"... attempts to rob him of the esteem which was so universally accorded while living, and to blur his memory. Such manifestation, over the body of a worthy and lamented citizen, indicates a malignancy of heart."

166–70 "Death of Oscar J. Dunn," *New Orleans Commercial Bulletin*, November 22, 1871; "Lieut. Gov. Dunn," *New Orleans Times*, November 22, 1871; "The Death of Lieutenant Governor Dunn," *New Orleans Times*, November 23, 1871; "Death of Oscar J. Dunn," *New Orleans Republican*, November 23, 1871; "Last Speech of Lieutenant Governor Dunn—Premonition of His Death," *New Orleans Republican*, November 24, 1871; "Political Address of Lieutenant-Governor Dunn," *Weekly National Republican* (New Orleans), December 20, 1871; Christian, "Theory of the Poisoning of Oscar J. Dunn," 258–63. The local press covered Dunn's final days, especially the scene in and around the Dunn home, in exhaustive detail.

171–72 "Sudden Illness of Speaker Carter," *New Orleans Times*, November 23, 1871; Perkins, "James Henri Burch and Oscar James Dunn," 327–34; Christian, "Theory of the Poisoning of Oscar J. Dunn," 254, 258–65; Perkins, "Oscar James Dunn," 116–17. The two Perkins articles and the Christian article, all published between 1937 and 1945—within living memory of Dunn's death—assessed the poisoning theory. A combination of factors fanned suspicions: the suddenness of his illness, the symptoms, the degree of rancor between Dunn and his adversaries, the atmosphere of political violence, the lack of consensus among doctors, the refusal of an autopsy by a family spokesperson, and more. "It is extremely difficult to make a judicious appraisal of the poisoning theory which grew out of an atmosphere filled with political rivalry and animosity, clouded with suspicion, and teeming with bald, unsubstantiated rumors," Christian wrote. "Still, even though each clue must be examined with a great degree of caution, a careful weighing of evidence does not negate the Dunn poisoning theory." Perkins interviewed a number of surviving contemporaries of Dunn who even decades later firmly insisted that he had been poisoned. One, Edmund Burke, said: "The conspirators were known. But nobody dared speak out. It would have been unsafe." Perkins interviewed Warmoth many times before the ex-governor's death in 1931 and asked him directly about the poisoning rumors. "Yes," Warmoth responded, "such a rumor was current, but the physicians attending him pronounced his death as due to natural causes." Perkins wrote that Warmoth "did not seem disposed to continue the conversation."

173–74 "Worshippers of the Voodoo," *New York Times*, June 25, 1893; "Blackest Art in Washington," *New York Times*, September 16, 1894. Outrageous popular rumors such as the Voodoo stories may have obscured more credible theories about Dunn's death. Dunn might have taken his life to avoid shaming his family with a scandal—manufactured or not. One report after his death noted that his ascendancy, and the threat it represented to rivals, extended beyond state lines: "Dunn was the acknowledged leader of the Grant wing of the Louisiana Republicans, and was engaged in a movement which, there are reasons to believe, had for its ultimate object the elevation of his name to the place of Vice President upon the Republican ticket next year, or in 1876 at the farthest.... It is believed that the President was willing to take Dunn with him upon the ticket. The object of this movement was the concentration of the African vote of the country in one solid phalanx, with an ulterior view to the triumph of the extreme of the Radical party. The immediate object of the movement in Louisiana was the impeachment of Warmoth and his party." "Lieutenant-Governor Dunn," *Courier-Journal* (Louisville, KY), November 23, 1871.

175–80 "The Funeral of Lieutenant Governor Dunn," *New Orleans Times*, November 24, 1871; "The Late Lieutenant Governor," *New Orleans Republican*, November 24, 1871; "Funeral Obsequies," *New Orleans Republican*, November 26, 1871.

181 WPR, 118–20, 161; Dufour, "The Age of Warmoth," 358–64; Du Bois, *Black Reconstruction*, 479–80; "Louisiana," *New York Daily Tribune*, January 4, 1872.

182 "A Murderous Assault," *Daily Picayune*, January 2, 1872; "The Last Token of Warmoth Reform," *Weekly National Republican* (New Orleans), January 3, 1872. The pro–Customhouse *Weekly National Republican* went further in its accusations, stating that as a bystander named Emma Stackhouse sought to intervene, Pinchback "slapped her violently on the face and pushed her down on the gallery steps" ("Inauguration of the Reign of Terror," *Weekly National Republican*, January 2, 1872). In a different article, the newspaper refers to the new lieutenant governor as "a woman-beater and a thug" ("The Senate," *Weekly National Republican*, January 3, 1872). Pinchback denied that he attacked Chester or the woman, though he admitted being at the scene, attempting to intervene, and walking away when Chester rejected his support ("Malicious Misrepresentation," *Semi-Weekly Louisianian*, January 4, 1872). A man with a lengthy rap sheet named P. Z. Canonge was arrested and briefly jailed, but later that year was honored as a sergeant-in-arms at the Republican State Convention ("Local Intelligence," *New Orleans Republican*, January 12, 1872; "Republican State Convention," *New Orleans Republican*, June 2, 1872). In a letter to his mother in Pennsylvania, Chester wrote: "Persons not connected with Pinchback's crowd, who were present, say that he fired the pistol. Several have so informed me. There seems to be no doubt of that fact in the public mind." "The Chester Outrage," *Weekly National Republican*, January 28, 1872.

183–84 Dufour, "The Age of Warmoth," 358–64; "Yesterday's Important Events," *New Orleans Republican*, December 10, 1872; "Law and Order," *New Orleans Republican*, December 13, 1872; "The New Governor," *New Orleans Republican*, January 14, 1873.

185 Logsdon and Bell, "Americanization of Black New Orleans," 253, 257; WPR, 260.

186–87 Orleans Parish Conveyance Book 100, p. 551, November 5, 1872, NONA; Oscar J. Dunn Succession, Record 35,055, NOCA VSB290; "An Act No. 3," *New Orleans Republican*, March 5, 1872; "Colored Citizens in Council," *Weekly National Republican* (New Orleans), April 14, 1872 and April 16, 1872; "Communication from the Mayor," *New Orleans Republican*, July 24, 1872; "A Noted Colored Lady," *St. Paul Daily Globe*, June 14, 1885; "Deaths," *Cincinnati Enquirer*, September 20, 1885.

188 Act of March 18, 1873, No. 57, 1873 La. Acts 115; *Mardi Gras in New Orleans—Grand Tableau of the "Mistick Krewe," Harper's Weekly*, March 29, 1873, 244. Some historians contend that the gorilla caricature was of recently elected lieutenant governor C. C. Antoine, but no period sources make that connection. The parade mocked the entire Reconstruction era, sending up such long-gone local figures as Benjamin Butler. Comus published a companion booklet that includes an illustration of "the great Gorilla" wearing a crown and holding a guitar—the latter detail possibly referencing Dunn's days playing the instrument (Mistick Krewe of Comus, *Ye Mistick Krewe of Comus 1873*, 31). It wouldn't have been the first time Dunn was insulted in this way. When he was acting governor, a French-language Louisiana paper commented, "Dunn nous fait rebrousser chemin vers l'ére tropicale et bestiale décrite par Darwin," or, "Dunn makes us turn back to the tropical and bestial era described by Darwin." "Correspondance de la Nlle-Orléans," *L'Avant-Coureur* (Lucy, LA), July 15, 1871.

189 Kein, *Colfax Massacre*, xi; "Platform of the White People of Louisiana," *New Orleans Bulletin*, November 2, 1874; H. R. Rep. 43-261, pt. 3, at 18–19 (2d Sess. 1875); Taylor, *Louisiana Reconstructed*, 291–96.

190 "Evacuation Day" and "Now and Then," *New Orleans Weekly Democrat*, April 28, 1877; "Remembered," *Daily Picayune*, September 15, 1891; "Liberty Place Monument Removed on Confederate Memorial Day," *Times-Picayune*, April 25, 2017.

191 "Beauregard Statue Unveiled at City Park by Granddaughter," *Shreveport Times*, November 12, 1915; "The Late Lieut. Governor Dunn," *Weekly National Republican* (New Orleans), March 13, 1872; Du Bois, *Black Reconstruction*, 478–79. "Oscar Dunn died," Du Bois wrote, "and the Louisiana Negroes lost an unselfish, incorruptible leader."

PART EIGHT: MONUMENTS OF MOURNFUL HEARTS

195–97 "Dunn Commemoration Ceremonies," *New Orleans Republican*, December 5, 1871; Chester, "Remember Dunn." Chester's excoriations of Dunn's political rivals this evening may have inspired the attack on him less than a month later.

ABBREVIATIONS

NARA National Archives and Records Administration

NOCA New Orleans City Archives

NONA New Orleans Notarial Archives

ARCHIVAL SOURCES

Burch, J. Henri. Eulogy of Oscar Dunn. In "The Late Lieutenant Governor." *Semi-Weekly Louisianian*, November 26, 1871. https://www.newspapers.com/image/86210515/.

Chester, Maj. T. Morris. "Remember Dunn, and Follow Ingraham!" Speech in New Orleans, December 4, 1871. Minnesota Historical Society Library, St. Paul, Minnesota.

Dryden, James. Reminiscences of Oscar Dunn. In "Death of Oscar J. Dunn." *New Orleans Republican*, November 23, 1871. Microfilm. The Historic New Orleans Collection.

Entry 5514. Muster Rolls, Returns, Regimental Papers. 73rd Infantry, US Colored Troops, Volunteer Organizations Civil War. Adjutant General's Office, 1780s–1917, RG 94. NARA.

New Orleans Office of Policy Planning. *Neighborhood Profiles*. New Orleans, 1978–81. The Historic New Orleans Collection.

NOCA AA430. New Orleans (La.) Mayor's Office. Register of Free Persons of Color Entitled to Remain in the State, 1840–1864.

NOCA VCP91. New Orleans Parish Court Records, 1834–1836.

NOCA VCP320. Louisiana Parish Court. Petitions for the Emancipation of Slaves, 1831–1843.

NOCA VMZ300. Louisiana Criminal Court of the First District (Orleans Parish). Minute Books, 1830–1846.

NOCA VSB290. Louisiana Second District Court (Orleans Parish). Records, 1846–1880.

NONA. Orleans Parish Conveyance Book 7, 1831.

NONA. Orleans Parish Conveyance Book 97, 1869.

NONA. Orleans Parish Conveyance Book 100, 1872.

"A Noted Colored Lady." *St. Paul Daily Globe*, June 14, 1885. https://www.newspapers.com/image/81062291/.

"Oscar James Dunn." Biographical information likely supplied by John Parsons. *Weekly National Republican* (New Orleans), November 22, 1871. The Historic New Orleans Collection.

Proceedings of the Most Worshipful Eureka Grand Lodge of the State of Louisiana from its Organization, January 5, 1863, to January 12, 1869. Iowa Masonic Library, Cedar Rapids, Iowa.

Record 373. Collector of Customs at New Orleans, Microfilm Rolls 1–3 of 25, 1818–1860. Port of New Orleans. US Customs Service, RG 36. NARA.

Thomson, Laura J., and Melissa Smith. "Biographical Note." In Most Worshipful Prince Hall Grand Lodge, Free and Accepted Masons for the State of Louisiana records, 1857–2002. Amistad Research Center, New Orleans.

Zimpel, Charles F., engraver. *Topographical Map of New Orleans and its Vicinity, Embracing a Distance of Twelve Miles up and Eight and Three Quarters Miles down the Mississippi*. 1833. The Historic New Orleans Collection.

PUBLISHED SOURCES

Basler, Roy P., ed. *The Collected Works of Abraham Lincoln*. Vol. 7. New Brunswick, NJ: Rutgers University Press, 1953.

Beale, Howard K. *The Critical Year: A Study of Andrew Johnson and Reconstruction*. New York: Harcourt, Brace, 1930.

Benbow, Mark E. "Birth of a Quotation: Woodrow Wilson and 'Like Writing History with Lightning.'" *Journal of the Gilded Age and Progressive Era* 9, no. 4 (October 2010): 509–33.

Blassingame, John W. *Black New Orleans, 1860–1880*. Chicago: University of Chicago Press, 1973.

Blight, David W. *Race and Reunion: The Civil War in American Memory*. Cambridge, MA: Harvard University Press, 2001.

Bond, James E. *No Easy Walk to Freedom: Reconstruction and the Ratification of the Fourteenth Amendment*. Westport, CT: Praeger, 1997.

Bowers, Claude G. *The Tragic Era: The Revolution after Lincoln*. Cambridge, MA: Houghton Mifflin, 1929.

Brown, William Wells. *The Rising Son; or, The Antecedents and Advancements of the Colored Race*. Boston: A. G. Brown, 1874.

Campanella, Richard. *Cityscapes of New Orleans*. Baton Rouge: Louisiana State University Press, 2017.

Castellanos, Henry C. *New Orleans as It Was: Episodes of Louisiana Life*. Gretna, LA: Pelican Publishing, 1990. First published 1895 by L. Graham and Son (New Orleans).

Central Executive Committee of the Republican Party of Louisiana, The. *Proceedings of the Convention of the Republican Party of Louisiana, Held at Economy Hall, New Orleans, September 25, 1865*. New Orleans: New Orleans Tribune Office, 1865.

Chernow, Ron. *Grant*. New York: Penguin Press, 2017.

Christian, Marcus B. "Men of Worth in Louisiana." *Negro History Bulletin* 5 (March 1942): 137–39.

———. "The Theory of the Poisoning of Oscar J. Dunn." *Phylon* 6, no. 3 (Third Quarter, 1945): 254–66.

Christovich, Mary Louise, Roulhac Toledano, Betsy Swanson, Pat Holden, and Sally Kittredge Evans, eds. *New Orleans Architecture*. Vols 1, 2, 4, and 6. Gretna, LA: Pelican Publishing, 1971–80.

Cimbala, Paul A. *Under the Guardianship of the Nation: The Freedmen's Bureau and the Reconstruction of Georgia, 1865–1870*. Athens: University of Georgia Press, 1997.

Connor, William P. "Reconstruction Rebels: The *New Orleans Tribune* in Post-War Louisiana." *Louisiana History* 21, no. 2 (Spring 1980): 159–81.

Coulter, E. Merton. *The South during Reconstruction, 1865–1877*. Baton Rouge: Louisiana State University Press, 1947.

Cox, LaWanda, and John H. Cox. *Politics, Principle, and Prejudice, 1865–1866: Dilemma of Reconstruction America*. Glencoe, IL: Free Press, 1963.

Current, Richard N. *Those Terrible Carpetbaggers: A Reinterpretation*. New York: Oxford University Press, 1988.

Curry, Leonard P. *The Free Black in Urban America, 1800–1850: The Shadow of the Dream*. Chicago: University of Chicago Press, 1981.

Dauphine, James G. "The Knights of the White Camelia and the Election of 1868: Louisiana's White Terrorists; A Benighting Legacy." *Louisiana History* 30, no. 2 (Spring 1989): 173–90.

Dawson, Joseph G., III. "General Lovell H. Rousseau and Louisiana Reconstruction." *Louisiana History* 20, no. 4 (Autumn 1979): 373–91.

DeLatte, Carolyn E. "The St. Landry Riot: A Forgotten Incident of Reconstruction Violence." *Louisiana History* 17, no. 1 (Winter 1976): 41–49.

DeVore, Donald E., and Joseph Logsdon. *Crescent City Schools: Public Education in New Orleans, 1841–1991*. Lafayette, LA: Center for Louisiana Studies, University of Southwestern Louisiana, 1991.

Dixon, Thomas. *The Clansman: An Historical Romance of the Ku Klux Klan*. Lexington: University Press of Kentucky, 1970.

Dray, Philip. *Capitol Men: The Epic Story of Reconstruction through the Lives of the First Black Congressmen*. Boston: Houghton Mifflin, 2008.

Du Bois, W. E. B. *Black Reconstruction in America, 1860–1880*. New York: Harcourt, Brace, 1935. Reprinted with an introduction by David Levering Lewis. New York: The Free Press, 1992. Page references are to the 1992 edition.

Dufour, Charles L. "The Age of Warmoth." *Louisiana History* 6, no. 4 (Autumn 1965): 335–64.

Dunn, Oscar J. *Lieut. Gov. Dunn to Hon. Horace Greely*. 1871. PDF. https://www.loc.gov/resource/rbpe.02501200/.

Dunning, William Archibald. *Reconstruction, Political and Economic, 1865–1877*. New York: Harper and Bros., 1907.

Dykstra, Robert R. *Bright Radical Star: Black Freedom and White Supremacy on the Hawkeye Frontier*. Cambridge, MA: Harvard University Press, 1993.

English, Linda. "'That is All We Ask For—an Equal Chance': Oscar James Dunn, Louisiana's First Black Lieutenant Governor." In *Before Obama: A Reappraisal of Black Reconstruction Era Politicians*, edited by Matthew Lynch, 63–85. Santa Barbara: Praeger, 2012.

Ficklen, John R. *History of Reconstruction in Louisiana, through 1868*. Baltimore: Johns Hopkins Press, 1910.

Foner, Eric. *Freedom's Lawmakers: A Directory of Black Officeholders during Reconstruction*. New York: Oxford University Press, 1993.

———. *Reconstruction: America's Unfinished Revolution, 1863–1877*. New York: Harper and Row, 1988. Updated edition. New York: Harper Perennial Modern Classics, 2014. Page references are to the 2014 edition.

———. *The Second Founding: How the Civil War and Reconstruction Remade the Constitution*. New York: W. W. Norton, 2019.

———. *Who Owns History?: Rethinking the Past in a Changing World*. New York: Hill and Wang, 2002.

Foner, Eric, and Olivia Mahoney. *America's Reconstruction: People and Politics after the Civil War*. New York: Harper Perennial, 1995.

Franklin, John Hope. "Mirror for Americans: A Century of Reconstruction History." *American Historical Review* 85, no. 1 (February 1980): 1–14.

———. *Reconstruction: After the Civil War*. Chicago: University of Chicago Press, 1961.

Gates, Henry Louis, Jr. *Stony the Road: Reconstruction, White Supremacy, and the Rise of Jim Crow*. New York: Penguin Press, 2019.

Gates, Henry Louis, Jr., Dyllan McGee, Julia Marchesi, Rob Rapley, Stacey Holman, and Cyndee Readdean. *Reconstruction: America after the Civil War*. Aired April 9 and 16, 2019, on PBS. https://www.pbs.org/weta/reconstruction/.

Getz, Trevor R., and Liz Clarke. *Abina and the Important Men: A Graphic History*. New York: Oxford University Press, 2012.

Glatthaar, Joseph T. *Forged in Battle: The Civil War Alliance of Black Soldiers and White Officers*. Baton Rouge: Louisiana State University Press, 2000.

Globus: Illustrierte Zeitschrift für Länder- und Völkerkunde 17, no. 18 (June 1870): 288.

Gordon, Michelle Y. "'Midnight Scenes and Orgies': Public Narratives of Voodoo in New Orleans and Nineteenth-Century Discourses of White Supremacy." *American Quarterly* 64, no. 4 (December 2012): 767–86.

Griffith, D. W., dir. *The Birth of a Nation*. 1915; New York: VCI Home Video, 1998. Videocassette.

Harlan, Louis R. "Desegregation in New Orleans Public Schools during Reconstruction." *American Historical Review* 67, no. 3 (April 1962): 663–75.

Hennessey, Melinda Meek. "Race and Violence in Reconstruction New Orleans: The 1868 Riot." *Louisiana History* 20, no. 1 (Winter 1979): 77–91.

Herbert, Hilary Abner. *Why the Solid South?* Baltimore: R. H. Woodward and Company, 1890.

Historic New Orleans Collection, The, and the Gilder Lehrman Institute of American History. *New Orleans during the Civil War*. 2016. https://www.hnoc.org/sites/default/files/lesson_plans/LessonPlan_CivilWar.pdf.

Hogue, James Keith. *Uncivil War: Five New Orleans Street Battles and the Rise and Fall of Radical Reconstruction*. Baton Rouge: Louisiana State University Press, 2006.

Hollandsworth, James G., Jr. *An Absolute Massacre: The New Orleans Race Riot of July 30, 1866*. Baton Rouge: Louisiana State University Press, 2004.

———. *The Louisiana Native Guards: The Black Military Experience during the Civil War*. Baton Rouge: Louisiana State University Press, 1998.

Holt, Thomas C. *Black Over White: Negro Political Leadership in South Carolina during Reconstruction*. Urbana: University of Illinois Press, 1977.

Houzeau, Jean-Charles. *My Passage at the New Orleans* Tribune: *A Memoir of the Civil War Era*. Edited by David C. Rankin. Baton Rouge: Louisiana State University Press, 1984.

Jones, Howard J. "Images of State Legislative Reconstruction Participants in Fiction." *Journal of Negro History* 67, no. 4 (Winter 1982): 318–27.

Kein, Sybil. *The Colfax Massacre: The Untold Story of Black Power, White Terror, and the Death of Reconstruction*. New York: Oxford University Press, 2008.

———. *Creole: The History and Legacy of Louisiana's Free People of Color*. Baton Rouge: Louisiana State University Press, 2000.

Lachance, Paul. "Index to New Orleans Indentures, 1809–1843." Accessed December 12, 2019. http://nutrias.org/~nopl/inv/indentures/ind-intr.htm#resource.

Landrieu, Mitch. "Truth: Remarks on the Removal of Confederate Monuments in New Orleans." Speech delivered May 19, 2017. http://www.usmayors.org/wp-content/uploads/2017/05/remarks.monumentremoval.051917.pdf.

Langston, John Mercer. *From the Virginia Plantation to the National Capitol: The First and Only Negro Representative in Congress from the Old Dominion*. Hartford, CT: American Publishing Company, 1894.

Lemmon, Alfred E., John T. Magill, and Jason Wiese, eds. *Charting Louisiana: Five Hundred Years of Maps*. New Orleans: The Historic New Orleans Collection, 2003.

Lester, C. Edwards. *Life and Public Services of Charles Sumner*. New York: United States Publishing Company, 1874.

Lewis, John, Nate Powell, and Andrew Aydin. *March*. 3 vols. Marietta, GA: Top Shelf Productions, 2013–16.

Litwack, Leon F. *Been in the Storm So Long: The Aftermath of Slavery*. New York: Alfred A. Knopf, 1979.

———. "The Birth of a Nation." In *Past Imperfect: History According to the Movies*, edited by Mark C. Carnes, 136–41. New York: Henry Holt, 1995.

Logsdon, Joseph, and Caryn Cossé Bell. "The Americanization of Black New Orleans, 1850–1900." In *Creole New Orleans: Race and Americanization*, edited by Arnold R. Hirsch and Joseph Logsdon, 201–61. Baton Rouge: Louisiana State University Press, 1992.

Long, Carolyn Morrow. *A New Orleans Voudou Priestess: The Legend and Reality of Marie Laveau.* Gainesville: University Press of Florida, 2006.

Lonn, Ella. *Reconstruction in Louisiana after 1868*. New York: G. P. Putnam's Sons, 1918.

Louisiana. *Annual Report of the Board of Metropolitan Police to the Governor of Louisiana for the Year Ending September 30*. New Orleans: A. L. Lee, 1869.

———. *Official Journal of the Proceedings of the Convention, for Framing a Constitution for the State of Louisiana*. New Orleans: J. B. Roudanez and Co., 1867–68.

———. *Supplemental Report of Joint Committee of the General Assembly of Louisiana on the Conduct of the Late Elections and the Condition of Peace and Good Order in the State.* New Orleans: A. L. Lee, 1869.

Lynch, John R. *The Facts of Reconstruction*. New York: Neale Publishing, 1913.

———. "Some Historical Errors of James Ford Rhodes." *Journal of Negro History* 2, no. 4 (October 1917): 345–68.

Lynch, Matthew, ed. *Before Obama: A Reappraisal of Black Reconstruction Era Politicians.* Santa Barbara: Praeger, 2012.

McPherson, James M. *Ordeal by Fire: The Civil War and Reconstruction*. New York: Alfred A. Knopf, 1982.

———. *The Struggle for Equality*. Princeton, NJ: Princeton University Press, 1964.

Michel's New Orleans Annual and Commercial Register for 1834. New Orleans: Gaux and Sollee, 1833.

Mistick Krewe of Comus. *Ye Mistick Krewe of Comus 1873*. New Orleans: L. Graham and Co., 1873.

Nystrom, Justin A. *New Orleans after the Civil War: Race, Politics, and a New Birth of Freedom.* Baltimore: Johns Hopkins University Press, 2010.

Palmer, Rev. Benjamin M. "The South, Her Peril, and Her Duty." New Orleans: True Witness and Sentinel, 1860.

Parenti, Michael. *Dirty Truths.* San Francisco: City Lights Books, 1996.

———. *Inventing Reality: The Politics of the Mass Media.* New York: St. Martin's Press, 1986.

Perkins, A. E. "James Henri Burch and Oscar James Dunn in Louisiana." *Journal of Negro History* 22, no. 3 (July 1937): 321–34.

———. "Oscar James Dunn." *Phylon* 4, no. 2 (1943): 105–21.

———. "Some Negro Officers and Legislators in Louisiana." *Journal of Negro History* 14 (October 1929): 523–528.

Perman, Michael, ed. *Major Problems in the Civil War and Reconstruction.* Lexington, MA: D. C. Heath, 1991.

Pitre, Althea D. "The Collapse of the Warmoth Regime, 1870–72." *Louisiana History* 6, no. 2 (Spring 1965): 161–87.

Rankin, David C. "The Origins of Black Leadership in New Orleans during Reconstruction." *Journal of Southern History* 40, no. 3 (August 1974): 417–40.

Reilly, Timothy F. "Benjamin M. Palmer: Secessionist Become Nationalist." *Louisiana History* 18, no. 3 (Summer 1977): 287–301.

Richardson, Heather Cox. *The Death of Reconstruction: Race, Labor, and Politics in the Post–Civil War North, 1865–1901.* Cambridge, MA: Harvard University Press, 2001.

Roark, James L. *Masters without Slaves: Southern Planters in the Civil War and Reconstruction.* New York: W. W. Norton, 1977.

Ross, Michael A. "The Commemoration of Robert E. Lee's Death and the Obstruction of Reconstruction in New Orleans." *Civil War History* 51, no. 2 (June 2005): 135–50.

Saville, Julie. *The Work of Reconstruction: From Slave to Wage Labor in South Carolina, 1860–1870.* Cambridge: Cambridge University Press, 1994.

Schwalm, Leslie A. *A Hard Fight for We: Women's Transition from Slavery to Freedom in South Carolina.* Urbana: University of Illinois Press, 1997.

Sheridan, P. H. *The Personal Memoirs of P. H. Sheridan.* New York: C. L. Webster, 1888. Reprinted with an introduction by Jeffry D. Wert. Boston: Da Capo Press, 1992. Page references are to the 1992 edition.

Simkins, Francis Butler, and Robert Hilliard Woody. *South Carolina during Reconstruction*. Chapel Hill: University of North Carolina Press, 1932.

Simon, John Y., and John F. Marszalek, eds. *The Papers of Ulysses S. Grant*. Digital ed. Charlottesville: University of Virginia Press, Rotunda, 2018.

Soards' New Orleans Directory. New Orleans: L. Soards, 1834.

Stampp, Kenneth M. *The Era of Reconstruction, 1865–1877*. New York: Alfred A. Knopf, 1965.

———. *Reconstruction: An Anthology of Revisionist Writings*. Baton Rouge: Louisiana State University Press, 1976.

Summers, Mark W. "The Moderates' Last Chance: The Louisiana Election of 1865." *Louisiana History* 24, no. 1 (Winter 1983): 49–69.

Sumner, Charles. *Equality Before the Law Protected by National Statute: Speeches of Hon. Chas. Sumner, of Massachusetts, on His Supplementary Civil Rights Bill, as an Amendment to the Civil Rights Bill*. Washington, 1874.

Taylor, Alrutheus Ambush. *The Negro in South Carolina during the Reconstruction*. Washington, DC: The Association for the Study of Negro Life and History, 1924.

Taylor, Joe Gray. "Louisiana: An Impossible Task." In *Reconstruction and Redemption in the South*, edited by Otto H. Olsen, 202–36. Baton Rouge: Louisiana State University Press, 1980.

———. *Louisiana Reconstructed: 1863–1877*. Baton Rouge: Louisiana State University Press, 1974.

Thompson, Shirley Elizabeth. *Exiles at Home: The Struggle to Become American in Creole New Orleans*. Cambridge, MA: Harvard University Press, 2009.

Thornbrough, Emma Lou, ed. *Black Reconstructionists: Great Lives Observed*. Englewood Cliffs, NJ: Prentice-Hall, 1972.

Tourgée, Albion W. *A Fool's Errand: By One of the Fools*. New York: Fords, Howard and Hulbert, 1880.

Tregle, Joseph G., Jr. "Thomas J. Durant, Utopian Socialism, and the Failure of Presidential Reconstruction in Louisiana." *Journal of Southern History* 45, no. 4 (November 1979): 486–512.

Tunnell, Ted. *Crucible of Reconstruction: War, Radicalism, and Race in Louisiana, 1862–1877*. Baton Rouge: Louisiana State University Press, 1984.

Uzee, Philip D. "The Beginnings of the Louisiana Republican Party." *Louisiana History* 12, no. 3 (Summer 1971): 197–211.

Vandal, Gilles. "Black Utopia in Early Reconstruction New Orleans: The People's Bakery as a Case-Study." *Louisiana History* 38, no. 4 (Autumn 1997): 437–52.

Van Zante, Gary A. *New Orleans 1867: Photographs by Theodore Lilienthal.* London: Merrell, 2008.

Vaughn, William Preston. *Schools for All: The Blacks and Public Education in the South, 1865–1877.* Lexington: University Press of Kentucky, 1974.

Vincent, Charles. *Black Legislators in Louisiana during Reconstruction.* Baton Rouge: Louisiana State University Press, 1976.

Warmoth, Henry Clay. *War, Politics and Reconstruction: Stormy Days in Louisiana.* New York: Macmillan, 1930.

Williamson, Joel. *After Slavery: The Negro in South Carolina During Reconstruction, 1861–1877.* Chapel Hill: University of North Carolina Press, 1965.

Wilson, Joseph T. *The Black Phalanx: A History of the Negro Soldiers of the United States in the Wars of 1775–1812, 1861–65.* New York: Amo Press, 1968.

Woodward, C. Vann. "The Political Legacy of Reconstruction." *Journal of Negro Education* 26, no. 3 (Summer 1957): 231–40.

———. *The Strange Career of Jim Crow.* 3rd ed. New York: Oxford University Press, 1974.

INDEX

OLIVE BRANCH
OSCAR JAMES DUNN
1826 — 1871
LT. GOV. LA. 1868 — 1871
GRAND MASTER PRINCE HALL
LA. MASONS 1864 — 67

ABOUT THE CREATORS

BRIAN K. MITCHELL is assistant professor of history at the University of Arkansas, Little Rock, and an associate faculty member at the Anderson Institute on Race and Ethnicity. A New Orleans native, Mitchell relocated to Little Rock as a consequence of Hurricane Katrina and is forever thankful to the state of Arkansas for welcoming him during the chaotic aftermath of the storm. Mitchell received an MA in history, MS in urban studies, and PhD in urban studies with a concentration in public history at the University of New Orleans. Prior to teaching, Mitchell was a senior federal investigator at the Equal Employment Opportunity Commission, where he won a Federal Investigator of the Year award. The author of numerous papers, book chapters, and books, Mitchell's research primarily deals with race, violence, and the Elaine Massacre. Nationally recognized for his public history and digital humanities projects, his work has been covered by CNN, Atlas Obscura, the *New York Post*, the *Guardian*, National Public Radio, and the Associated Press.

BARRINGTON S. EDWARDS, an artist and community activist from Boston, earned a BFA in communication design and an MS in art education at the Massachusetts College of Art. Edwards taught visual arts at the Boston Arts Academy for nineteen years. He is a 2019 Massachusetts State Universities Educator Alumni Award winner, a Surdna and an Expressing Boston fellow, a publisher of comics and graphic media, and works as a freelance artist and consultant. Edwards is a member of the Boston Comics Roundtable, a co-founder of Comics in Color, and is active with the Design Studio for Social Intervention and the Black Speculative Arts Movement. He currently teaches art education at the Massachusetts College of Art and Design. Edwards consistently works to develop his practice as a maker, social interventionist, and teacher.

NICK WELDON is associate editor at The Historic New Orleans Collection, where he edited the exhibition catalog *Enigmatic Stream: Industrial Landscapes of the Lower Mississippi River* by Richard Sexton (2019) and was exhibition editor for *Crescent City Sport: Stories of Courage and Change* and *Art of the City: Postmodern to Post-Katrina*, presented by The Helis Foundation. Originally from Indiana, he is a graduate of Northwestern University's Medill School of Journalism. He was previously senior editor and later writer at large for *Runner's World*, and has written about topics ranging from black bears to basketball to barbecue for *Backpacker*, *Vice*, *SB Nation*, *New Orleans* magazine, *Garden and Gun*, Paper Monuments, *Sports Illustrated*, and ESPN.com.

From left: Edwards, Mitchell, and Weldon at Dunn's tomb in New Orleans.

The Historic New Orleans Collection
MUSEUM • RESEARCH CENTER • PUBLISHER